The Government of
FRANCE

SECOND EDITION

Jean Blondel
UNIVERSITY OF ESSEX

METHUEN & CO LTD
11 NEW FETTER LANE, LONDON EC4

First published in the USA by Thomas Y. Crowell Company
Published in Great Britain by Methuen & Co Ltd
11 New Fetter Lane, London EC4P 4EE
Second Methuen (fourth U.S.) edition 1974
Reprinted 1977

© 1974 by Thomas Y. Crowell Company

Printed in Great Britain by
J. W. Arrowsmith Ltd, Bristol BS3 2NT

ISBN 0 416 83190 7 (hardbound)
ISBN 0 416 82670 9 (paperback)

EDITOR'S FOREWORD

In our time the study of comparative government constitutes one of many fields or specialties in political science. But it is worth recalling that the most distinguished political scientists of the ancient world would have had difficulty recognizing the present-day distinction between the study of comparative government and study in other subject areas of the discipline. Think of Plato, for example, whose works abound in references to the political systems of his own and earlier days. Or consider Aristotle, whose *Politics* and related writings were based on an examination of more than one hundred constitutions. Twenty centuries after Aristotle the comparative emphasis continued to be strong in the work of Montesquieu and Rousseau, among others. In the nineteenth century the comparative tradition entered a period of decline, but there are signs that the merits of comparative political analysis are once again gaining recognition. At many colleges and universities, the introductory course in political science is no longer focused exclusively on American government. The comparative approach—in politics, in law, in administration—is becoming increasingly important in the political science curriculum.

This book, one of a series, is designed to reflect that approach without, however, marking a sharp departure from the substance and method of most comparative government courses. Thus most of the books in the series deal with one national government. Several volumes, however, deal with more than one government, and the approach of the entire series is distinctly comparative in at least two senses. In the first place, almost all of the books include material descriptive of other political systems, especially that of the United States. In addition, the books follow a common outline, so far as possible, that is designed to promote comparative treatment. Of course, there is nothing to keep the instructor or student from treating a particular governmental system in isolation, if he chooses to do so. On the other hand, his approach to political institutions and functions can be as comparative as he wishes.

A further advantage of this series is that each volume has been written by a distinguished scholar and authority in the field; each author is personally and professionally familiar with the political system he treats. Finally, the separate books make it possible for the instructor to design his course in accordance with his own interest or the interests of his students. One book may be substituted for another and any book may be put aside for one semester without affecting the others. The books, in short, unlike most one-volume texts, give the instructor maximum freedom in organizing his course. This freedom will be virtually unlimited as the forthcoming titles in this series complete a survey of representative governments of the world.

But to return to Aristotle once again, it remains true that the best judges of the feast are not the cooks but the guests. I have tried to indicate why, in my view, the recipe for the series is a good one. Let all those who teach comparative government, and all those who take courses in that field, proceed to judge the books for themselves.

ARNOLD A. ROGOW

PREFACE

The Fourth Edition of *The Government of France* is entirely re-structured while also taking into account the changes, indeed the new perspective of politics, which have resulted from the passage of the Fifth Republic into the "normal" period of post-de Gaulle politics. Despite the turmoil of 1968, the Fifth Republic turned out to be even more stable than could be predicted at the time the previous edition was prepared. De Gaulle's influence on the new regime has been more pronounced than anyone suggested when he returned to power in 1958: the institutions have been reshaped—seemingly profoundly; a style of politics has been created, not only and perhaps not so much in relation to foreign affairs. The party system, the relations between government and parliament, the groups and associations now contribute to forming a game of politics which is profoundly different from the game which was played in previous regimes. This is, of course, not just de Gaulle's doing; profound social changes were begun during the Fourth Republic, from which the Fifth Republic, and de Gaulle himself, greatly benefited. It is still too early to know whether the present style of politics will constitute merely an interlude, but it is already clear that the interlude will have a more profound effect on French politics than was seemingly possible given the deep-rooted habits of previous generations. One hopes that this text will therefore give readers a sense of both old and new and of the movements and choices which affect the regime, while still leaving question marks about the future of the institutions and the overall stability of the French Republic.

Although the changes in the new edition are entirely my own, the book continues to owe much to the spirit and vivid style which Dr. Godfrey gave to it in its early editions. I wish to express here my gratitude for the kind manner in which he encouraged me to pursue the enterprise which he started. I wish, too, to record my thanks to Professor M. Kesselman for his most valuable and detailed comments and to the editor of the series, Professor A. A. Rogow, for suggesting aspects of the new framework which help the book to strike a compromise between the obvious needs for history and background and the equally necessary emphasis toward systematic analysis.

JEAN BLONDEL

CONTENTS

PART ONE

FRANCE: ITS HISTORY, PEOPLE, AND SOCIETY

1

History and Society

A perceptive son of France once remarked that throughout history his motherland has been obliged to live dangerously. This observer saw France's perilous history as the consequence of exposed geographic position. Others have claimed that the French people lived dangerously because their Celtic origins compelled them to combativeness; still others have ascribed France's adventurous life history to an inquiring and even aspiring national mentality, which some Frenchmen turned to individual genius in art, literature, and philosophy, while others were building both the most brilliant and the least exalted political traditions. Whatever the true causes, we are here concerned with a people whose relationship to life is as dramatic as their history has been, a people who have employed the same sense of daring in choosing their art forms, their fashions, and their cuisine as they have in building empires, in experimenting with almost every known form of political system, and in fighting innumerable wars and revolutions. It is no paradox, then, that some Frenchmen may have carried their disdain for the norms of middle class life, at any rate in the past, to a point of trembling danger.

France has often been described as a woman. The French people themselves have frequently chosen female figures to symbolize their country, suggesting in so doing the infinite variety they find in their homeland and the range of emotions which it induces in them. Indeed, the Frenchman sees in France all the qualities of femininity—the softness of her countryside, the passion of her people, the pettiness of her national jealousies, the capacity to endure suffering under indignities, even the splendid

3

mixture of beauty and ugliness of her older cities. They may love or scorn France, but because she is a woman they cannot ignore her. In fact, the absorption of the French people with France is the hallmark of their political life.

When a Frenchman speaks passionately of France he may be identifying himself with a moment in her history of which he particularly approves (or which he abhors) or he may be expressing admiration (or despair) at the whole kaleidoscope of French history, accomplishments, and failures. In his mind the motherland has lived not only dangerously but vividly; it has produced heroes and villains, though heroes and villains may not be the same for different men. Napoleon or Robespierre, Riche-lieu or de Gaulle (to speak only of the dead) all belong in some way to the Pantheon of great political Frenchmen; they may at the same time be loved and hated, admired and rejected. Frenchmen never quite relate themselves to one single current of political thought; indeed, they derive considerable satisfaction from sharing in the variety and richness of France's history. For some years, in the early 1960s, it was fashionable to scoff at politics, but, as during previous phases of political "disengage-ment," antipolitical attitudes were a sign of discontent with politics which exploded with a vengeance in the great turmoil of May–June 1968, when for several weeks France came to a standstill, played with, and talked of "Revolution." However, the return to normalcy was surprisingly quick, though politics has once more become important in the 1970s. More profound changes in the relationship between Frenchmen and politics are, perhaps, in process, and much of this book will be about these changes; but in the French political tradition apathy was often a form of protest and a disengaged person one who judged and measured those who were engaged.

Perhaps the cause for the Frenchman's fascination with the game of politics—even though he may be unwilling to cheer any of the players—is that French political history is a continuous current. There are almost no extinct species in French political zoology. Most of the present-day French parties claim multiple connections with the past. The Socialists, for example, claim the Jacobins of 1792 and the Communards of 1870 as their forebears (though the Communists make greater claims to have the latter as their ancestors). It is significant that as recently as the early 1960s, serious political commentators were speculating whether, when de Gaulle would leave the political scene, he would not try to put forward as his successor the Count of Paris, the pretender to the throne which has been empty since 1848. Political traditions and attitudes or beliefs associated with them rarely die in France, though they may be adapted to existing conditions. They may disappear for long periods, but somewhere they are being cherished to reemerge when conditions are again favorable. Even French fascism, which took various forms before World War II (though none of these was really strong), and which certainly seemed to have been obliterated by the national revulsion against the collaborators during and after the German occupation of France between 1940 and 1944, reappeared in the 1950s, and indeed took new roots in Algeria because of the Algerian war in the early 1960s.

For the most part, however, French political movements, although they may cling to the importance of their origins and to a few fundamental points of doctrine, go through a process of evolution as society changes around them, as their electorate shifts away from them, or, in some cases, as the goals which they originally set for themselves are attained. The most celebrated and caricatural example of such a mutation is given by the Radical Socialist party, which began life in the last quarter of the nineteenth century to preserve political and civil liberties as well as lay republicanism when neither was secure in the country. The party scarcely retains anything but its name from its glorious past; far from being radical and socialist, it tends to be conservative, though divisions among its leaders are such that one usually finds its representatives voting in all possible ways. It was, in many ways, the embodiment of prewar French politics: the great ancestors are being praised and honestly admired, but rarely followed; compromises and deals are the daily reality.

THE HISTORICAL PERSPECTIVE OF FRENCH POLITICS

French political history can be seen as a maze of threads beginning in various places, frequently crossing and tangling with one another, with new strands entering from time to time. To unravel this jumble for an understanding of its separate parts, one must begin with the great rent in French history—the Revolution of 1789. With great drama, and eventually with a missionary and military zeal which threatened *anciens régimes* throughout much of the rest of Europe, the French routed the monarchy, the aristocracy, and the privileged Roman Catholic Church in the name of liberty, equality, and the republican form of government. But the old order, though defeated, was not destroyed. Its defenders were able to revive the monarchy in the nineteenth century and to delay for decades any definitive regulation of the Church's powers. Moreover, and more importantly, the antirepublican tradition resisted the passage of time; its supporters were to attempt to undermine all Republics (1792) to the Fifth (1958), and are even today little reconciled to the processes of popular sovereignty.

The defenders of the Revolution and the Republic were not long in dividing over whether they should give priority to equality or liberty. In the early revolutionary period a great effort was made to destroy the unequal political privileges of the titled and aristocratic classes. In keeping with the notion that despotism and oppression were primarily products of the heavy hand of the State, the elimination of privileges was at first undertaken with a minimum use of government machinery, and attempts were made to portray the results as the product of the direct voice of the people manifested through popular meetings. "The Declaration of the Rights of Man and the Citizen," adopted tumultuously in the Revolutionary Assembly of 1789, detailed the expectations of humble Frenchmen to be treated with equal justice before the law and to be regarded as equivalent to all other Frenchmen in the exercise of their rights and in the day-to-day conduct of their lives. The "Rights of Man" was primarily a political document; it represented the momentary ascendancy of the libertarians over the egalitarians; it did not consider the possibility that the economic advantages of a few might, even with a constitutional system, undermine the political liberties of the majority.

There were, however, strong undercurrents in the revolution which were bent on a leveling of all economic and social distinctions between men. The dictatorship of the Jacobins (1793–1794) was a move toward the use of the State as an instrument of vigorous social change. The efforts of the Jacobins did not prevail, and in fact were succeeded by the much more conservative (and stabilizing) regime which Napoleon installed after taking over power in 1799. However, the Jacobins added a new and powerful political strain to the matrix of French political development, which was to assert itself several times in the nineteenth century and most dynamically in the twentieth century.

In the largest part of the nineteenth century the libertarians had only a shaky hold on France. This was a period of adaptation and experiment, as political strands became snarled by borrowing ideas from one another. The antirevolutionaries returned in 1814–1815, though the legitimate monarchy which reappeared with Louis XVIII had to agree to a considerable dose of liberalism: the king proclaimed a charter (though it was significantly dated from the "eighteenth year of his reign"—as if he had come to the throne when the son of the previous king was officially said to have died in prison); he acknowledged civil equality and political liberty. The reactionary attempts of his successor, his brother Charles X, ended in revolution in 1830; the French thought then that they were repeating English seventeenth-century history and put on the throne a cousin of the last king, Louis Philippe d'Orleans, who started as a liberal monarch believing in parliamentary government and ended ignominiously after having made too many efforts at manipulating Parliament instead of concentrating his attention on the new political aspirations of Frenchmen. The Revolution of 1848 (which swept all over Continental Europe as well) put an end in France to the liberal monarchy, and indeed to the monarchy altogether.

THE NAPOLEONIC TRADITION

The most curious intermixture of political strands flowing from the Revolution was the imperial tradition into which Napoleon Bonaparte (1799–1814) stumbled, which his nephew, Louis Napoleon, perfected in the Second Empire (1852–1870) and which some modern commentators felt was reincarnated in the Fifth Republic of General de Gaulle. The Bonapartes cleverly exploited Rousseau's theory of the "general will" which in earlier days had been one of the cries of the revolutionary assemblies. Their apologists insisted that the emperors' mandates to speak and act for France (unfettered by any powerful intermediate body) were legitimate because they served the popular will. To ratify imperial decisions, both Napoleons resorted to the use of the popular referendum (plebiscite was the name in their time, but the word came to have unpleasant connotations precisely because of the Bonapartes' use of the technique). According to their court theorists, the popular will was thereby expressed in the imperial person. Like the Jacobins, the Bonapartes appealed to the masses not only for political approval but for patriotic support (though the second Napoleon had to claim, in order to gain support, that "the Empire meant peace"—which was to be only partly true). The Jacobin "nation in arms" became the Napoleonic conscript army. In fact, however, the imperial tradition was, despite some trappings borrowed from the Revolution, both antiliberal politically, and socially rather conservative (though it was not reactionary, but aimed essentially at maintaining the rights of the newly enfranchised bourgeoisie). The apparatus of the State which Napoleon I devised became a large and often arbitrary instrument, which operated as a force of its own, deriving its powers from the personal strength of the emperor, not from the French people as such. Indeed, in some ways, the Second Empire can be said to have been more progressive than the First; it was the period when France experienced her first and greatest industrial boom and really moved at last from a predominantly agricultural economy to that of a modern and developed society.

The division between the organ of political will—the emperor—

FRENCH REGIMES

To 1789	*Ancien régime:* Louis XIV, 1643–1715 Louis XV, 1715–1774 Louis XVI, 1774–1792
1789–1792	Constitutional monarchy. Constituent Assembly. Constitution of 1791. First legislative Assembly.
1792–1799	First Republic. Convention Constitution of 1793 (not applied). Directory Constitution of 1795.
1799–1804	Consulate. Napoleon, first consul. Constitutions of 1799 and 1802.
1804–1814 and 1815	First Empire. Napoleon I, emperor. Constitutions of 1804, 1814 (not applied), and 1815.
1814–1815 and	Restoration. Louis XVIII, 1814–1824. Charter of 1814.
1815–1830	Charles X, 1824–1830.
1830–1848	Orleans monarchy. Louis-Philippe I, 1830–1848. Charter of 1830.
1848–1851	Second Republic. Constitution of 1848. Napoleon Bonaparte (nephew of Napoleon I) elected president of Republic.
1852–1870	Second Empire. Napoleon III, emperor. Constitutions of 1852 and 1870.
1870–1940	Third Republic. Constitution of 1875.
1940–1944	Vichy Régime. Pétain "Head of State."
1945–1958	Fourth Republic. Constitution of 1946.
1958–	Fifth Republic. Constitution of 1958. Charles de Gaulle, president, 1958–1969. Georges Pompidou, president, 1969– (mandate expires in 1976).

and the organs of State authority—the administration, the military establishment, the judiciary—represented an entirely new and unexpected arrangement after the Revolution had placed the stress on constitutional reform and on the problems of executive-legislative relations. The distinction between government and administration, never very clear until then, was established in part by accident, in part through the maintenance of the well-developed bureaucracy of the monarchy, and in part through the vigorous action of Napoleon I. Through him, France was given a well-functioning administration, codes of law, and a theory of the administrative process which were to be the envy of many countries for several generations. Not only is much of the State machinery created by Napoleon I still in existence in France, but, as under Napoleon himself, much of it remains outside the political arena. Since the last imperial period ended in 1870, many political battles have been fought, but they have largely been fought over governments and their policies, not over the administrative instruments of the governments.

The hardiest political tradition spawned in the Revolution was the republican. In a sense it was the truest revolutionary element; it survived all manner of assaults, distortions, and even the bitter mockery of those who from time to time momentarily eliminated it from the French political scene. As we have already noted, the revolutionaries who rose against the *ancien régime* tended to divide into those who sought political liberty and those who championed equality—although, of course, some pursued both goals. As the nineteenth century wore on and various political forms were tested, the libertarians were to give a meaningful and concrete definition to republicanism, but more and more the image of the Republic was employed by the egalitarians as a necessary beginning for the implantation of their own concepts of society.

REPUBLICANISM AND ITS STRANDS

The republicanism that emerged during the nineteenth century ultimately comprised only a few simple elements: insistence on the expression of the public will through a sovereign; a directly elected assembly; a lay society; and distrust of executive authority as a threat to freedom, against which the people had an obligation to rise when and if tyranny appeared imminent. Several times the people did in fact take to the barricades, though this technique became much less common from the second half of the nineteenth century on, after having been rather successful in overthrowing regimes in the first. Under the Republic, this particular form of civic violence came to have a mythical value: it symbolized the revolt of the people against tyrants (and after having been indeed used rather symbolically against the Germans leaving Paris in 1944, the technique was adopted again by students in the university district of Paris—the Latin Quarter—in May 1968).

The egalitarians, at first socialists and later communists, have always employed the mystique of the barricades and have associated it with their own goals. Indeed, the evolution of French revolutionary regimes made this type of association possible. The Revolution of 1789, as we saw, quickly moved from "bourgeois liberalism" to egalitarian concepts. The Revolution of 1848, ostensibly fought to obtain an extension of the suffrage from the king, led to the end of the monarchy and, in a few months, to the temporary establishment of a semisocialist society (return to normalcy did quickly take place, though, after the more extreme "socialists" were defeated during four days of civil war in Paris in June 1848). The Paris Commune that seized power in the capital following the collapse of the Second Empire in 1870 and the French defeat by the Germans in 1871 included various types of supporters of socialism, anarchism, and extreme forms of republicanism. It was in turn smashed by the more conservative republicans, and ended in one of the bloodiest episodes of repression in French history. Meanwhile, the French people had elected a national assembly composed mainly of monarchists, primarily to negotiate the peace settlement; but the assembly started drafting constitutional laws, hoping that a monarchical restoration could take place when the rival claimants (the "legitimists" and the Orleanists—the supporters of the "branch" of 1815 and those of the "branch" of 1830) would agree. But agreement was so slow to come that the Republic triumphed by default, and almost by accident, in 1875. The Third Republic was born, and the constitution grudgingly put together by an assembly in which a majority of the members were not republican, and many were strongly antirepublican, was to last until 1940. It was destroyed by German arms after corrosive action by a series of attacks coming from both extremes and by the weakness and internal divisions of its supporters, who proved increasingly incapable of solving modern political problems.

THE SECOND WORLD WAR AND ITS CONSEQUENCES:
THE VICHY REGIME AND THE RESISTANCE

Modern French history spans the Third, Fourth (1946–1958), and Fifth Republics (since 1958); it was interrupted between 1940 and 1944 by the corporate state of Pétain, whose authority derived from German victory and not, despite the appearances of a legal transfer, from the will of the French people. In many ways the Vichy regime (so-called because the seat of government was transferred to Vichy, in central France, while northern France was occupied) symbolized all that was antirepublican in French life, while the *Résistance*, which fought it incessantly, has often been described as a pure revival of the republican spirit. Pétain and his followers, composed of old-fashioned conservatives, straight fascists, anti-Semites, disgruntled army officers, and crass opportunists coming from all parties, set about to destroy all vestiges of republican democracy. Political authority was vested in the person of the marshal; he was unencumbered by parliamentary organs, although he created a "national council" in which the interests of vocational and social groups were theoretically to be represented. In practice, employers spoke in the name of the working class, and free trade unions were abolished; special stress was put on the peasantry, which was supposed to embody all the "true" traditions which had made France great; in fact, however, the "return to the land" was simply a means of satisfying the German occupier and of limiting the influence of an industrial working class whose political attitudes were felt to be dangerous. Most telling was the motto adopted by the new regime: "Work, Family, and Fatherland" replaced "Liberty, Equality, and Fraternity." The traditionalist, conservative values of the *ancien régime* were reimposed by fiat on a scornful people who, except for a small minority, quickly came to reject the fumbling and posturing of a government which retained power at the point of Nazi bayonets.

The *Résistance* that began organizing about a year after the French defeat contained elements from all shades of French republicanism, ranging from conservative nationalists (such as de Gaulle) who despised the ignominy of German occupation and the pandering of the Pétainists to tough communist leaders who had been forced underground during the war and who turned ultra-patriotic after the German attack on Russia in 1941. Several distinct *Résistance* networks existed in metropolitan France; many retained particular political colorations, others were heterogeneous. As Allied victory became imminent, the *Résistance* organizations expanded operations, and adopted military as well as political characteristics. Eventually, they came to dominate much of French life; in many parts of the country (and particularly in the mountains) *Résistance* elements were in control well before the arrival of Allied troops. When liberation was finally achieved, the *Résistance* was the main political force which counted in the country, though de Gaulle had created a government in exile long before, first in London, and later in Algiers. No wonder, then, that the new constitution which emerged in 1946 from the ruins of postwar France was a reaffirmation of republican principles with strong left-wing overtones adapted from the teachings of underground *maquisards*.

THE FOURTH AND FIFTH REPUBLICS

However, the strength of the Left was not sufficient to overcome some of the most awkward historical legacies of French political institutions. In fact the Fourth Republic was in many ways a streamlined version of the Third, emphasizing the purest republican traditions of a powerful, sovereign, popular assembly, a weak executive, and an administrative apparatus which floated in an ambiguous limbo below the government. Remote from democratic responsibility, the bureaucratic administration did not only have permanency, however; it was to be the most powerful machine of change in modern French society; as we shall see, it was to use all the techniques at its disposal to give strength and energy to the new forces, gradually diminish the opposition of the traditional groups, and give to France, after little more than a decade, one of the most flourishing economic systems of the world. While the premiers and their cabinets were becoming targets of widespread criticism by the French public, and while criticism turned to disgust, the administration saw its influence increase. The end of the Fourth Republic coincided with the coming of age of a curious mixture of technocracy and democracy within the bureaucratic machinery itself.

The governments of the Fourth Republic were so weak and so transient, however, that they were unable to solve the major political problem which faced France at the time, decolonization. Indochina undermined the political system markedly, though after eight years of war, in 1954, a strong and determined prime minister, Pierre Mendès-France, produced a settlement which effectively disengaged France; but he remained in power for only six months afterward. Meanwhile, the war had begun in Algeria; by 1958, it had created such divisions between the supporters of the status quo, backed by a million French settlers in Algeria, and those who, in one form or another, wanted to introduce reforms, that successive government became impotent. Yet this government sent a million French conscripts to the other side of the Mediterranean, thus increasing antiwar feelings among much of the youth and many other groups. By May 1958, the army high command had come to question the legitimacy of the regime: pushed by civilian extremists, commanders in Algiers ceased to recognize the authority of the Paris government; a small force landed in Corsica; and rumors of an impending army landing spread throughout France, which, true or false, created a climate of tension, plots, and counterplots. De Gaulle was called by a large majority of the Assembly, some hoping he could keep Algeria French, while others thought that only he had the power to "solve the problem." The Fifth Republic was born.

Created in these dramatic circumstances, the new regime was soon to have a distinctive mark. In a sense it does borrow from innumerable political strands in French history. Conceived in adventure, it is in the best tradition of all those which came before it. But it has already fashioned a mystique of its own, and a style of politics to which many do object—in the usual French way—but has survived its founder more smoothly than had been predicted. It is thus becoming embedded in the continuous flow of French political life.

THE BACKGROUND OF THE SOCIAL ORDER

In the 1950s and 1960s, France moved fast socially and economically; indeed, for many, the tragedy of modern France has been that politics did not keep pace with socioeconomic change or has been very slow to respond to it. But, while the transformations of French society gradually seem to bring about attitudes which were almost totally unknown to the French of previous generations or were only shared by a small minority, the traditional background remains strong and visible in many parts of the country and in many groups of the population. Among the long-standing characteristics of this social order, four, perhaps, have special prominence. First, the French population, long static at forty million, now over fifty million, has peasant origins, and the peasantry has been for centuries (we saw that Pétain tried to revive the "old spirit") the backbone of society and the basis of the political system. Second, and allied to it, France was a very divided nation, composed of several ethnic groups, with very different feelings, attitudes, and behavior, and often with little in common (not even, for a long time, the language). Third, the class system and particularly the division between "bourgeois" and "worker" (*ouvrier*) was of great importance; it was a question of status, of style of life, as well as of income. Fourth, France has always been, at least nominally, a Catholic nation; she was the "Eldest daughter of the Church," according to the traditional saying, and this led to religious wars and to the persecution of Protestants (mainly Calvinists) in the sixteenth, seventeenth, and eighteenth centuries, as well as to fierce political battles over the "lay" character of the State in the nineteenth and twentieth. It was on such a social landscape that the kings first and Napoleon later built a centralized administrative machine and that the Republic imposed a centralized political culture, both these characteristics being as important to the understanding of the strains and stresses of the traditional social order as the other long-standing forces in the community.

PEASANT ORIGINS
France was for a long time a peasant nation—indeed perhaps the only peasant nation in the world. This is not only because as

many as 50 percent of French men were engaged in agriculture in the middle part of the nineteenth century, and as many as a third before World War II. It is also because the vast majority of the persons occupied on the land were owners of small plots, inherited from their parents, to which they were passionately attached. The Revolution of 1789 did not wholly, nor indeed even wholly deliberately, create the peasantry, which became attached to the Revolution inasmuch as it had given them the land (Napoleon stabilized the situation and made any return to the previous state of affairs impossible). But the peasantry was also, in a very modest way, part of the "capitalist" or "bourgeois" society, as the ownership of land created attitudes of individualism, of respect for property, and of fear of any social system which might lead to dispossession; these were to weigh strongly against any attempts made by various revolutionary movements to take over the government of the country.

OCCUPATIONAL BACKGROUND OF THE FRENCH POPULATION

	Percent of the Active Population		
	1954	1962	1967
Farmers and farm laborers	26.5	24.0	16.0
Owners of businesses	12.0	10.0	9.0
Higher management and professions	3.0	4.0	5.0
Middle management	6.0	7.5	10.0
White-collar workers	11.0	12.0	14.0
Manual workers	33.5	35.0	37.0
Service workers	5.0	5.0	5.5
Other (army, police, etc.)	3.0	2.5	3.5
	100.0	100.0	100.0
TOTAL (millions)	19.3	20.1	20.7

The traditional life of the peasant was difficult and even harsh. Plots of land were small; the problem of smallness became compounded by the division of farmlands. Many peasants owned farms fragmented into odd-shaped and even noncontiguous parcels that resulted from generations of dividing and subdividing the family heritage, as the civil code of Napoleon decided that estates were to be divided equally among all the children. Fragmentation of land came to reach such proportions that productivity, even in rich areas, tended to be smaller in France than in neighboring countries; incomes did not increase—and to counteract the fall in their living standards, French peasants took to limiting sharply the number of children (though many also left the country for the towns) with the result that the birthrate became lower in France than in all other developed nations. Psychologically, the effect was catastrophic; the toughness of rural life came to be associated with a generally pessimistic view about the future. Preserving what one had became a primary goal; change contained potentially terrifying dangers. The outside world, whether the city, the government, or the weather, came to be considered the source of the gravest threats to the minimal stability of the present. Though peasants never ceased to respond when called to defend their country (in the European wars and in the colonies), their general relationship with the State was peculiarly unfriendly. They were organized democratically in their own communities (the *communes*), but they had few feelings of brotherhood and democratic association with the rest of the nation (and indeed with their fellow peasants).

As we said, the flight from the land was one of the means by which the lot of the remaining children of the family could be in part alleviated (though in practice only in part, as the children who stayed on the land had to repay in cash, over a number of years, the estate of those who had left). Movements from village to city were, all through the nineteenth century, characteristic of Western Europe; they had in France less influence on the new city-dweller than in other countries, however. Frenchmen who had left the land kept the mark of their peasant origins for long periods and often during the whole first generation. They had become urbanized, insofar as they had no desire to return to farming, but they did not shed their psychological heritage. Indeed, the reverse was even true; under the influence of the newly arrived peasants, residents of cities tended to take on attitudes more characteristic of the land than of urban communities. Preconceptions, fears, worries, and a rather negative and anarchistic individualism came to dominate much of the middle-class and lower middle-class levels of French society—the shop-keepers, artisans, mechanics, workers in commerce and even in industry, as well as the large numbers of French civil servants. While by tradition and love of independence many arrivals wanted to set themselves up in business, however small, unlucra-tive, and tiring, others longed for security and looked for State posts, complete with holidays and pensions, to be protected against the future. The peasant roots of so many Frenchmen (often refurbished and revamped by yearly returns to the family house for holidays, births, marriages, or funerals) tended to stamp indelibly some leaders, members, or sympathizers in all the political groups. They accounted for a strange understanding between people who found themselves otherwise on different sides of the ideological (or indeed even physical) barricade. They led to the development of a skeptical mind, suspicious of those in high places; they explain the love for the "small," "honest" man, who is nonetheless prepared to bend the rules, and the dislike for large combinations where vast sums are at stake and which Paris and Paris alone could be wicked enough to generate.

The peasant complex, as this orientation might be called, is thus a strong element in that much-discussed French characteris-tic, individualism. But it is also combined, in a strange associa-tion, with other elements, and this quickly shows its limits. It appears in the negative way in which Frenchmen react (or reacted, traditionally at least) to voluntary groupings; they did not believe in them, scarcely supported them, and thus could demonstrate, as through a self-fulfilling prophecy, that they received few benefits from them. But the respect for negative criticism, the fear of appearing "naïve," the suspicion of all men and institutions were all forms of conformity, and indeed of conformism. These characteristics had considerable drawbacks for the French economy, made experiments an object of ridicule, and were indeed the very cause of the outside imposition of rules which the peasant community could not and would not establish. Society is always an equilibrium between various forces; in the French traditional social order, peasants and bureaucracy came to be opposites, the equilibrium being maintained by the contrasted action of both forces. But the society lost much strength by this perpetual warfare; curiously enough, the social democracy of the peasants was perhaps one of the main factors which slowed the development toward political democracy.

In the postwar period, however, these characteristics have come to change. The flight from the land has taken such proportions in the late 1950s and in the 1960s that new horizons are being perceived and hopes for a better future have come within the village. The action of the government and of the administration, as we shall see in Chapter Eight, transformed the economic conditions, and slowly the social conditions, in which peasants had to live. With less than one person in six employed in agriculture, France has ceased to have, distinct from the rest of the nation, a body of citizens who alone can tilt the scales of the political system by strongly infiltrating all political parties. But political mores die hard; while social transformations affect the countryside and mold the attitudes of the coming generation, the present generation of politicians still thinks and acts in part like their older constituents. The political order on the land remains a product of the past, and the peasant origins of Frenchmen account, as we shall see later, for much of the behavior of the political parties.

REGIONAL SECTIONALISM AND THE INFLUENCE OF PARIS
The second characteristic of the traditional French social structure is its sectionalism. This was maintained partly by the size of the peasantry, but more general historical and geographical characteristics are also involved. Mountains or plateaus separate the country into natural regions and isolate certain areas from the main communication axes. Brittany in the West, the Southwest (sometimes known as Aquitaine), the Massif Central (a plateau which is in parts very rugged and desertlike), the Alpine area, Provence (named from the Latin *Provincia*—the southeastern tip along the Mediterranean has a very hilly interior though tourists tend mainly to think in terms of the *Côte d'Azur*), constitute sharply differentiated regions which remained, until fairly recently, culturally isolated from each other. They were isolated and

different from the more accessible northern and northeastern parts of the country, which have more plains, and thus an easier agriculture, more industry, and more natural lines of communication. History molded itself on these geographical constraints, and added a further dimension to them; local particularism was very widespread throughout the whole of the *ancien régime*, and many parts of the country, acquired as a result of marriages in the royal family or of wars between the king and the nobles who established their authority over whole provinces in the Middle Ages, still kept many of their traditions and their legal customs, despite the centralizing efforts of the monarchy. The Revolution abolished provinces, created a uniform local government system, and began the process of unifying the law. But these efforts at centralization were the consequence of the weight of regional sectionalism, not a natural growth of the social system.

It is difficult to describe adequately the contours of French sectionalism. It manifests itself, as everywhere, through differences in accent, in turn often the product of the survival of local dialects, some of which, as in the South, have a Latin origin and are related to Italian (Provençal) or Spanish (Catalan), while others (Alsatian, Flemish) have Germanic roots and yet others (Breton or Basque) have little or nothing in common with the main European languages. But different forms of living are often also the consequences of the different climates, and these vary sharply if one moves from the humid but temperate Brittany to the cold Massif Central or Alsace and to the pleasant, almost Californian Mediterranean coast; the shape of traditional houses gives such a characteristic outlook to towns and villages in Alsace, Provence, or the Paris area that they seem to belong, in reality, to different countries. But these variations are the symbols of other and more profound variations in modes of living; the outdoor life in the clement South and Southeast contrasts with the indoor life of the much tougher North and East.

These differences have naturally led men to be very attached to their *petite patrie*, to their home area, and prevented them from feeling at ease when they move to another region. Conversely, the "stranger" who establishes himself in a new area finds real human relationships slow to develop, partly because he is not himself

HISTORY AND SOCIETY   21

aware of traditions and customs. This, as we shall see, has important consequences, as it effectively prevented for a long time candidates from running for office in areas where they had no local roots. The effect is cumulatively increased in rural areas, admittedly; the general fear and dislike of strangers is simply accentuated (and rationalized) if the immigrant comes from far away. Doctors or lawyers have often found it difficult to establish practice in a small town or village if they did not come from the neighboring district and did not have a feel for the local customs. Though recent changes, and in particular the spread of the car and of television, have increased mobility and interpenetration, the sense of identity of the various regions, perceived in the wide sense, is far from dead. It may even be argued that present trends toward administrative regionalism will have the effect of maintaining some of the differences and, occasionally, of reviving them.

The peculiar position of Paris has to be considered in connection with the sectionalism of the "provinces." The political, social, economic, and cultural preeminence of Paris is beyond doubt, but it does generate resentment. Paris is much larger than any other French city or metropolitan area: while eight million people live in the Paris area (administratively the city proper is only about two million), the next three metropolitan areas, Marseilles, Lyons, and Lille, barely reach a million. None of the provincial capitals can even remotely be considered as alternatives or challenges to the metropolis; they are further down in an urban hierarchy in which the holder of the top position is undisputed. Unfortunately for the general health of the country, a kind of social hierarchy parallels this population hierarchy. Important things happen in Paris, whether in the theater or in the government, in university research or in business; things which happen in the large provincial towns are often derived from Parisian decisions, or are experiments conducted or controlled by men in the capital. Ambitious people, in all walks of life, either have always lived in Paris or aspire to live there; they may be sent to the provinces by the government or their firm, but such a posting in the field is not meant to last (people often keep their flats in Paris, or even continue to reside in Paris in order not to be out of touch).

Anyone who has "arrived" has to be in Paris—and anyone who is not in Paris will sooner or later, in many subtle ways, feel that he has not arrived.

The rule, of course, is not universal. Some Frenchmen are deeply attached to their provincial town; there are exceptions to the social law according to which people will eventually finish their working life in Paris if they are really good. But such exceptions tend to be noted, and they have to be explained. Most of those who stay in medium-sized or even large cities unquestionably feel the weight of the capital in many aspects of their daily life, and have some sense of deprivation which comes from not belonging to it. There is a general inferiority complex in French urban life which explains many political reactions from provincial representatives, anxious to assert the individual character of their towns. In recent years, problems in the social services, particularly in transport and housing have become so aggravated by the size of the metropolis that, under government influence, firms were urged to "decentralize" and to expand their business outside Paris. The move has not met with considerable success as the cost, economic and psychological, is often heavy. But some rejuvenation of provincial life is at present taking place, particularly as the factors which work against sectionalism, the car and television, also bring Paris nearer to an increasingly large number of Frenchmen. The move will probably gradually bear fruit; French participation in the wider economic context of the Common Market tends also to decrease the social and cultural preeminence of Paris. But for perhaps another generation, Paris will remain an extraordinary pole of attraction to Frenchmen, as well as a drain on the better resources of the provinces, to an extent which is not comparable in any other European country. The pull London exercises and the resentment it causes in Britain, or New York City in the United States, are small, less dramatic, and much less prejudicial to these countries.

SOCIAL CLASS

The third influence affecting most Frenchmen, class consciousness, is a function of the cleavages which have torn the fabric of modern society. To a certain extent it is an outgrowth of the industrial revolution which started hitting France in the late eighteenth century but only acquired its full momentum at the end of the nineteenth. Social distinctions run sharp and deep, particularly in the large cities. Although they began to diminish during the mid-1950s, they are still very noticeable and sometimes come to take a tone of profound bitterness, which accounts in part for the permanence of a very large communist section of the electorate. Class is mentioned less commonly in France than in England; it is not an object of constant conversation; it is even less the subject of jokes. This is probably because, in the last resort, it is more profoundly felt as an unjust barrier. Though Frenchmen rarely recognize it, class is as easily manifest as in Britain, through accents, gestures, sometimes even dress; it is, of course, linked to sectional characteristics and to the peasant origins of the French, for someone who comes from the peasantry or lives in a small provincial town experiences greater difficulties in moving up the social ladder than someone who comes from fairly humble origins but lives in Paris. But class is in itself a means of distinguishing between Frenchmen irrespective of geography, and Frenchmen, in the depths of their hearts, know that the distinction exists.

To talk about class is not to deny social mobility. Indeed, movement from class to class takes place at about the same rate in France as in other developed societies. These do not constitute new developments, moreover; through education in particular, large numbers of sons of peasants, of lower middle-class employees, and even of manual workers have entered the middle class. Some educational channels have indeed always been known to make social promotion possible: a number of prestigious graduate schools, in particular the *École Polytechnique* and the *École Normale Supérieure*, have been powerful instruments of social mobility open to the very talented. At lower levels, numerous other schools or examinations, particularly those leading to the middle ranks of the civil service, the armed forces, or the railways, enabled the brighter sons and daughters of poorer families to enter the rather large French lower middle class. Finally, thrifty working-class children often set up small businesses which they hoped slowly to expand—the owners of the business thereby acquiring a status (and a freedom) which their original jobs did not give them.

More perhaps than in other countries, social class is based primarily on occupation, partly on education, and only marginally on income. Though there is in France a tradition of respect for craftsmanship (governments often extol the skills of French craftsmen), the esteem for industrial manual work has always been very low, and this has an effect on the workers themselves; there is more pride among British workers, for instance, than there is among French *ouvriers*. This was perhaps because France only partially achieved its industrial revolution before the 1950s and did so mainly in the northern and eastern part of the country. This was perhaps also because the traditions of independence and individualism of the peasantry created a climate in which it was felt that those who worked for others, particularly if they sold only manual labor, were degrading themselves by showing themselves incapable of mastering their own fate; they were giving up and allowing their destiny to be controlled by someone else. Thus there arose both contempt for the worker and hatred for the man who was wicked enough to employ (and in some sense degrade) fellow human beings. Meanwhile, social tensions were relaxed by large-scale immigration of workers from parts of southern and eastern Europe where wages were lower. The mines, the building trades, certain sections of the engineering industry were (and still are) manned by men coming from Poland, Italy, or Spain and, since the 1950s, North Africa, Portugal, and even Turkey. A subtle form of discrimination usually enabled the French to move up rather more quickly to supervisory functions, while the immigrant population, more transient, sometimes illiterate, generally incapable of organizing itself in associations or trade unions, tended to contribute in large numbers to the supply of unskilled labor.

As in other aspects of the social order, considerable changes took place in the characteristics of class consciousness in the 1950s and 1960s. It has been argued that France now has a new working class, much more integrated in the fabric of society, much less prepared to reject the whole of the social system and anxious to share more widely in the affluence of the new capitalism. This is undoubtedly true. Wages have increased substantially in the postwar period (despite an earlier Communist claim that the proletariat was becoming poorer), and industrial organizations are now bargaining with employers, as we shall see in Chapter Four, much more pragmatically and much more successfully than they did in the past. As everywhere in the Western world, differences between manual and white-collar workers have decreased; as in the United States, class distinctions tend gradually to be based more on incomes than on occupation. As the peasant mystique becomes less widespread, as middle-class gadgets and a middle-class style of life (from the car to holidays abroad) are increasingly spreading and are spreading on the basis not of what people do, but of what they earn, traditional class cleavages cease to be so sharp. Vast new high-rise projects, financed largely from public funds, house together people who work in widely different types of jobs; they contribute to a social melting pot which contrasts with the kind of separation, and almost of segregation, which used to characterize working-class districts. By the 1980s, the characteristics of French social life will probably have been transformed to such an extent that most traditional differences will cease to be appreciated, at least by the younger generations. The break with the past will obviously take place more quickly in Paris and the large cities than in the more community-minded small towns, but the majority of the working class also lives in the large urban centers. Old French values may suffer from the change, but a happier social order will emerge.

Here too, however, a cultural and political lag may outlive the social transformation. As we shall note later, the rejuvenation of the French economy since the late 1940s had little or no visible effect on the behavior of most leaders of the French working class. These attitudes have been shaped by generations of workers and have been reinforced by the stagnant character of the economy in the interwar period. More perhaps than in many industrial countries manual workers are angry about their fate, but their pessimism is eroded only in a limited and gradual fashion, as witnessed by the sporadic strikes of semiskilled workers angry about the routine character of their work. An operation of psychological conversion is in progress, which takes place perhaps more slowly in the more collectively organized working class than among the more individualistic peasants. The break is unlikely to manifest itself in the form of dramatic changes on the political front, but the behavior of individuals will change, however permanent some trade union attitudes may be. This gradual movement is perhaps one of the most fascinating movements to follow in contemporary France.

THE CHURCH

France is essentially a Catholic nation; one million Protestants (Calvinists in the South, Lutherans in Alsace) and less than half a million Jews are the only other sizable religious groups. But this Catholic nation is profoundly anticlerical, in parts wholly de-Christianized, and still very affected by the great political battles which led to the separation of Church and State in 1905. For the majority of Frenchmen, Roman Catholic practice is limited to baptism, marriage, and funeral. Weekly attendance at mass and general observance of religious prescriptions is limited to a minority, averaging about a third, but it is not uniformly spread throughout the nation. Brittany and Alsace are areas of strong Catholic practice; the western part of the Massif Central and the Southeast are antireligious, or at best areligious. The historical origins of these variations are complex. Much seems to be due not to the priest but to the local gentry: where, as in Brittany, the mass of the peasants were kept deferent, the authority of the gentry managed to buttress that of the Church. Where, as in the Center-West, the local gentry was discredited and had to leave during the Revolution, the Church suffered irreparable damage.

Hence there is a traditional association, in France as in most predominantly Roman Catholic countries of Western Europe, between Church and social order, between religious practice and political conservatism. Throughout the nineteenth century, the Church hierarchy maintained close contacts with the leaders of the Right and this had considerable influence on the increasingly bitter attacks made by the Left, including the moderate Left, against the Church. In the last decades of the nineteenth century, the situation gradually became tense, as the Third Republic ceased to be led by conservative monarchists hoping for a restoration and came into the hands of the Republicans. In the 1890s, the climax was reached with the Dreyfus case, in which a Jewish officer was accused and condemned for having betrayed secrets but, despite numerous signs that a judicial error had been committed, the military refused for a long time to reopen it.

On the whole, the military, the conservatives, and the Church appeared united in their opposition to the principles of the modern liberal state. Though separation between Church and State would probably have eventually taken place, "the Affair," as the Dreyfus case came to be known, precipitated the divorce. In 1905, by an act of Parliament, the privileges which the Church had enjoyed were abolished, priests lost their status of civil servants and were no longer paid (with the side effect that Protestant ministers and rabbis also lost their State salary), and various religious orders were disbanded or had to leave the country (among them the Jesuits who were not to be "tolerated" again before 1918 and not formally allowed in the country before World War II). The "Elder Daughter of the Church" had completely broken with her past.

Most Roman Catholics became profoundly bitter against the Republic. However, some started to realize that no amelioration could take place until and unless the Church ceased to be associated with the "reaction" (to take the common political phrase used by the Left against the Right). In the eyes of the progressive Catholic minority, what was needed was an effort of adaptation based first on the acceptance of the Republic and of its liberal principles (which many Catholics were still not prepared to tolerate), second on missionary work among the workers (who were quickly becoming wholly unchristian) and the peasants (many of whom lived in de-Christianized areas), and third, on the development of a new social policy, based more on charity and compassion than on respect for authority. The changes had been helped in the 1890s by the pronouncements of Pope Leo XIII, though his successor, Pius X, seemed to return to more traditional views of the role of the Church in society (indeed, the first progressive Catholic movement, created in 1894 by Marc Sangnier, *le Sillon*, was condemned by the Pope). But a new spirit had come and at least a fraction of the Church was henceforth to work for the reconciliation between Catholicism and the "living forces" of the nation.

Progress was slow in the interwar period, however, the main breakthrough occurring only in the 1940s and 1950s. The Christian Democratic party was formed and, as we shall see in Chapter Five, it was for a while to be one of the largest parties of postwar France. Workers and peasant organizations grew in strength, in particular among the young. The role of the workers' priests (condemned and disbanded in 1953 after the movement had appeared to the hierarchy of the Church to be dangerously secular in character) has been often mentioned, but, though less spectacular, the part played by the Catholic youth movements has been more profound and has contributed to alter significantly the image of French Roman Catholicism; indeed, these movements can even claim to have been instrumental in the general transformation of French society and to have quickened the pace of social modernization in many sections of the community.

Some antipathy against the Roman Catholic Church still exists, however; moreover, while the status of the Catholics and of the Church increased—enabling Church schools to obtain State subsidies, first in a limited way in 1951 and on a much broader scale from 1959—the main object of the change, the re-Christianization of France, has probably not even begun to be achieved. Religious practice has not increased; indifference is probably as widespread; the weight of religion in the cultural life of the society is probably lower than at the turn of the century. It is, of course, impossible to know whether, had progressive Roman Catholics not taken a new line, the fate of the Church would not have been worse. But the social consciousness of the Church has enabled Catholics to have a higher status in society, though it has not enabled the Church as such to play a greater part. The political influence of the Church as an organization was probably more effectively destroyed by the 1905 separation than had been assumed at the time.

THE ADMINISTRATIVE AND CULTURAL CENTRALIZATION OF MODERN FRANCE

Divisions run deep in France. Not all are due to the Revolution, as we saw; many date back from an earlier period. They cut across each other and lead to a fragmentation of the basic social attitudes which accounts for much of the ideological and political sectionalism of the country. There are oppositions between town and country, employer and worker, the provinces and Paris, Church and anti-Church. Admittedly, under the impact of modernization, many differences have become blurred; France is gradually becoming easier to understand and, as a result, simpler to govern. But the changes are slow and some political moves seem to reawaken oppositions which commentators had perhaps too quickly declared dead. On the surface, anticlericalism does not appear to stir the population, for instance, yet, in 1959, State subsidies to Church schools roused more opposition than any other issue, and millions of Frenchmen signed a petition against the bill which Parliament was discussing. For a while, it seemed that the question of Church schools would outstrip, in the minds of Frenchmen, the Algerian problem, unquestionably the most important issue of the day, particularly in view of the consequences it had on the morale of the army. Admittedly, the opposition to subsidies to private schools had more general political aims; opponents of the new Gaullist regime thought of rallying support by creating a major conflict over a traditionally contentious issue. But they did, significantly enough, rally massive support, and for a while France seemed more politically militant than she had been for years. The contrast between the total apathy at the death of the Fourth Republic and the interest shown over the Church schools issue seemed to demonstrate how deep traditional oppositions ran and how slowly the modernization process was taking place in contemporary French politics.

The very number and complexity of the social divisions account for State centralization, both administrative and cultural. If the French kings, and later the Empire, had not given the country a strong and unified administrative system, it would probably not have survived. If the Republic had not attempted to give the country a uniform political culture running across geographical and social barriers, the Republic would probably not have survived. Administrative centralization was practiced by all regimes; it led, as we shall see in Chapter Eight, to the setting up of an impressive network of State agencies throughout the whole country. The Republic inherited these agencies from the monarchy and Napoleon; it never really attempted to dismantle them (an early endeavor between 1789 and 1792 was soon to prove, or at least to appear to the government, very damaging to the unity of the nation). The changes which took place when the Republic became more accepted at the end of the nineteenth century were piecemeal, remained somewhat limited, and still left the government with the right to intervene in the last resort if it so desired. Paradoxically enough, administrative centralization did not come seriously under attack before the second half of the twentieth century, precisely at the time when Western European countries were all becoming gradually as centralized as France under the impact of economic intervention and of social welfare legislation. In the nineteenth and even in the first half of the twentieth centuries centralization, however strong, was tacitly recognized by all as necessary for the State's survival; as a result, and almost by accident (though "enlightened despotism" characterized the French State for centuries), France came to have one of the best and most modern forms of State planning and one of the most enlightened civil service structures in the world. This may not have been in the past the main aim of centralization, but governments had quickly realized that a strong hand could be accepted only if it had a visible effect on the landscape, the cities, and the social benefits.

The real contribution of the Republic, mostly since the 1880s, was the new political culture; this spread almost uniformly, through the centralized educational system which was a by-product of the more general centralized structure of the State. For Republican leaders of the late nineteenth century, the state education system was to give Frenchmen a political culture. This was to be liberal, lay, egalitarian; it was not to be imparted in a totalitarian fashion; it was to aim at developing the critical faculties of children. But it was, nonetheless, a culture imparted to all, primarily at the primary school level. It was based on the spirit and frame of mind which characterized the writers of the eighteenth century French Enlightenment, particularly Voltaire, who had waged for about half a century a war against the power of the Church and of the State; these, in his view, not only robbed men of their liberty and reason, they deliberately opposed rational thinking in order to reduce criticisms of the social order. From Voltaire comes the open mind, the persistent inquisitiveness, the rejection of authority which were to be (or are said to be) the characteristics of Frenchmen. The tradition was kept alive during the Republic by men such as Emile Chartier (1868–1951)—known under the pen name of Alain—a professor of philosophy in one of the best known state secondary schools (the Lycée Henri-IV in Paris) whose influence on many generations of intellectuals was considerable. Alain preached an unflagging resistance to authority in all its forms. Indeed, his teachings, though based on suspicion and defiance of tyranny of the highest order, clearly fostered the French negative attitudes toward government which were to prove damaging for the morale of the country at the time of World War II.

This critical frame of mind was probably instilled too quickly to too many, through the village schoolteacher, the *instituteur*, who was to become the "priest" of the Republic and whose opposition to the *curé* became the classic joke of French parochial politics before the two groups settled down in the second half of the twentieth century to a more stable and easy-going relationship. The republican ideology undermined the tradition of authority on which all states, even republican ones, have to be based; only the centralized administration could enable the State to maintain itself. But France probably needed to go through a period in which an ideology of criticism was paramount. At a time when most European countries were still governed by authoritarian governments and after the nation had gone through various regimes in the nineteenth century, authoritarianism seemed a permanent threat and the republican regime felt that it needed to instill in the masses a profound aversion to the "powers"; France might have been able to move gradually toward a liberal form of democracy even if the government had not tried to spread such an ideology, yet it is understandable that politicians of the time should have thought it necessary to defend the regime in which they believed by extolling republican virtues and decrying nonrepublican ones. By emphasizing the right to criticize, by teaching others to use and to abuse their critical minds, they created problems for their successors; the political system has been bedeviled in the twentieth century by the very success of the Republicans of the 1880s and 1890s who bequeathed their political culture to masses of their fellow citizens. But had the Republicans not been so successful, France might not have been a Republic for long. By and large, the mass of the population generally agrees, after over a century of fighting and opposition, to the tenets of republicanism. Many historical and geographical divisions of French society have thus been overcome, and the achievements of centralization, both administrative and cultural, surely constitute an interesting and, in the last analysis, tolerably successful experiment in social engineering.

2

The Three Basic Roots of French Politics

Cleavages are deep in French society. For generations, France remained torn by conflicts between rural and urban life, between Catholics and non-Catholics, between government officials and grass-roots politicians, between supporters of the many brands of liberalism and upholders of a variety of authoritarian creeds. Not surprisingly, no French regime has remained unchallenged; few functioned effectively; and only one lasted for more than two decades. France seems to have accumulated conflicts to an extent that most Western countries have not. In Britain and Scandinavia, the development toward liberal democracy was gradual and linear. In France, a stalemate occurred between opposing forces. This, admittedly, prevented France from suffering from the worst excesses which characterized some of her Continental neighbors. Liberalism has been relatively strong in France for almost two hundred years; the country was after all the first on the Continent to undergo a revolution which, at the beginning at least, took place in the name of liberty. But this liberal movement remained in competition with other forces working in almost wholly opposite directions. Hence the view of some observers that France is, to use the expression of the American political scientist, Stanley Hoffman and the French sociologist Michel Crozier, a "stalemate society." Hence the need to analyze the French political system not just as a "liberal democratic" system, but more as an "imperfect" liberal democratic system in which other tendencies are as strong as the liberal democratic trends.

To understand the French political system, we should therefore view it as a combination of contradictory elements. Juridically, and to a large extent also in practice, France is a liberal democracy. But it is also, and has been for centuries, a "developing country" or a "modernizing state"; indeed it was perhaps the first developing state, "enlightened despotism" having started in France long before it became widespread throughout Europe in the eighteenth century. The philosophy of development also lasted longer in France than elsewhere, being rejuvenated and refurbished at almost every generation. It is precisely because the ideology and reality of enlightenment and of development policies lasted for so long that they became intertwined with—indeed, inseparable from—the liberal democratic framework. The French political system has thus some characteristics of a Western liberal democracy as well as those of a developing society.

But developing countries are also always in part traditional societies. Leaders of the modernizing states of the Third World wish to modernize their polities precisely because they feel them to be unduly subjected to traditional forces which prevented progress. A developing country is thus always a hybrid of old and new structures and patterns of behavior; in France, too, a similar mix of traditional and modernizing elements prevails, though the proportions may not be the same as in other countries. The changes which we began to describe in the previous chapter have unquestionably reduced the weight of tradition, particularly among the peasantry and in the provinces. But tradition is still sufficiently strong in post-de Gaulle France to play a substantial part in the institutions of politics, in administrative structures, and in the society as a whole. Combined with liberal democratic traits and modernizing tendencies, traditional forces contribute to give the French political system a complexity which accounts for much of the erratic movements and the many sudden outbursts in the society.

FRANCE AS A REAL BUT IMPERFECT LIBERAL DEMOCRACY

Constitutional structures are only a part—if an important part—of the machinery of liberal democratic polities. Indeed, judged by constitutions alone, the large majority of countries of the world would rank as liberal democracies. To be implemented in practice, a liberal democratic system needs of course to be based on a network of groups and bodies which give an *open* character to the society. To use a more technical language, the system must be such that demands can be formulated freely, pressed on the decision makers, and converted into outputs by the governmental machine. This implies elaborate mechanisms of articulation and aggregation of demands; this implies a communication system by which ideas, suggestions, pressures, are able to move freely between the leaders and the led and vice versa. Only when this happens are political institutions able to fulfill their functions in a liberal democratic manner. Thus no country has ever been and no country will ever be a perfect liberal democracy; some countries are more liberally democratic than others, and France is less so than other countries in Europe and elsewhere.

Of course, France is in many ways, and has been for a long period, a real liberal democracy. Much has been written about the authoritarianism of de Gaulle, which was undeniable. But, even under de Gaulle, the main features of the liberal democratic system were in existence. The provisions of the Constitution of 1958 have given the president and the whole executive very strong powers. But these are not without checks and the people have had a say in the life of politics. Broadly, the regime has been based on consent—and it was in some ways based more on consent under de Gaulle than it had been previously. Since 1965, the president of the Republic has been elected by universal suffrage, and the election was truly competitive: de Gaulle won because, after a free and clean contest, he obtained more votes than his opponents. Since 1958, referendums have been called on a number of occasions; some have smacked of "plebiscites," as de Gaulle always put his authority in the balance in the referendums which he proposed. But the contests were open; only once, on the vote to ratify Algerian independence, was the majority overwhelming —over 90 percent—and de Gaulle did suffer defeat in 1969. In 1972, Pompidou's referendum to approve British entry in the Common Market was not a great success. It is at best highly exaggerated to equate French referendums with the plebiscites in which majorities typically reach 99 percent.

Parliament saw its status and influence markedly reduced by the Constitution of 1958; but it is not as impotent as is sometimes suggested. Before 1958, the French Parliament was more powerful than others; the political process was often blocked as a result. Since 1958, the pendulum has swung too far in the other direction, that of parliamentary impotence, but it has not swung as far as is often alleged, and it has not swung very much further than in many other European countries. Of course, the French Parliament now faithfully supports the government, but so do the parliaments of many European states; of course, it approves the bulk of the government's legislative proposals, but so do the parliaments of many European countries. Various procedures restrict the rights of legislators over amendments or the budget, as we shall see, but the rights of British MPs are also severely curtailed. It is true that the Constitution of 1958 limits sittings of Parliament to six months, instead of nine or ten elsewhere, but this is surely different from the fate of African parliaments which sit only for a few weeks, let alone of Communist parliaments, which meet only for a few days. Furthermore, debate over many issues takes place regularly.

Indeed, below the institutions, the climate of French politics has been for generations—except during the German occupation —one of freedom or tolerance of opposition. Elections are free. Parties develop freely, including a large Communist party ostensibly adamant to destroy the fabric of the liberal society. The press is as free as in other Western countries, and it includes periodicals ranging from the extreme (almost fascist) Right to Maoists, Trotskyites, and anarchists. While the State radio and television network has long been criticized for being too closely in the government's hands, various peripheral stations (in Luxemburg, the Saar, Monte Carlo, Andorra) are manned by French journalists and give to French listeners the same pluralism of views as in other Western countries; even the State corporation has become more open since the late 1960s. Few limitations prevent associations from being created. The right to demonstrate is only interfered with to a small extent and this interference takes place in the context of the disorderly behavior of many groups, such as shopkeepers, farmers, students, who seem anxious to attack the police and provoke occasional riots. True, the police, principally in Paris, have often overreacted, but this is not unknown in other liberal countries and protest is not always in France a wholly peaceful affair, even though the ugliest forms of shooting and bombing tend rarely to occur. Beyond the trimmings of liberal democracy, France has a widespread acceptance in political life of the consequences of popular sovereignty.

What are, then, the limitations of liberal democracy in France? They stem from an apparently deep-rooted distrust of the value of associations and of the spirit of compromise which these need to develop. The Revolution of 1789 was fought in part against groups, which were held to have been previously instruments of "selfish" sectionalism against the general will; individualism prevailed as an ideology. In the 1830s, Tocqueville contrasted the basic tendency of Americans to form associations to the opposition which groups encountered in French society; he was one of the first to note that democracy in America was in large part sustained by the natural American propensity to congregate. Since the 1830s, numerous associations were formed in France, ranging from political parties and trade unions to a host of pressure groups. Yet objections against these bodies remained strong in many quarters: part of de Gaulle's appeal was due to his promise to make the State more independent of the activities of interest groups and lobbies. He did not succeed, quite the contrary, as we shall see in Chapter Four. But it is characteristic of the French political system that groups are viewed to some extent with disfavor and that the population prefers to remain on the sidelines rather than to join existing groups or form new associations.

The most important groups—and trade unions in particular—are therefore appreciably weaker in France than in other Western countries. Political parties have also been, for the same reason, smaller, less well organized, and less effective. Most members of associations and parties are passive in liberal democracies; in France even the passive members are proportionately less numerous. The membership of parties and trade unions is not just a minority of the electorate, it is a very small minority. Thus parties in particular remain so to speak above the "man in the street"; they do not provide strong links between people and government. The population lacks therefore the channels—almost deliberately cuts itself off from the channels—through which demands could be made on the decision makers. Though appreciable changes have taken place during the postwar period, in particular among some unions and with respect to some consumer groups, the society is not yet fully pluralistic since groups are viewed as inevitable evils rather than natural instruments for the transmission of demands.

The relatively limited role of groups and parties in French society parallels the low esteem in which the idea of compromise is held in the political system. Compromise is not viewed as the necessary and universal mechanism by which policies can be ironed out within the context of conflicting groups. Many compromises have of course to be made, in France as elsewhere; one of the oldest parties, the Radical party, flourished on compromise. But the prevailing climate is intellectually and ideologically opposed to such a pragmatic approach to decisions. Compromise is viewed with disfavor; it smacks of deals made under cover. It is not seen as the essence of politics, and thus extolled as a virtue, but as an evil which should be eradicated. Liberal democracy is thus to some extent on sufferance: politicians may know that they have to engineer compromises, but they are subjected to attacks for this very reason, from both the Right and the Left. If groups had been recognized as *the* means by which decisions have to be taken, compromises would be seen as the means by which the decision-making process necessarily takes place. As groups are not truly "recognized," compromises between groups can be dismissed as undermining the polity. But the unrealistic character of the attack is never brought to light.

Thus the sociopsychological bases for liberal democracy are

partly lacking in France. Admittedly, many hold an alternative view of democracy, nearer to Rousseau's conception of the "general will" and based on the merging of individual differences in the common goals of the community. This ideal is shared by many while politicians of both Right and Left play on the ideal somewhat demagogically; this contributes to undermining the support for governments and regimes, as these in practice have to compromise between conflicting views. This notion of democracy, which Rousseau himself felt impractical, at least in a large state, helps thus to emphasize a negative approach toward the polity. This is possibly why so many French liberals have tended to be negative ("the citizen *against* the powers") rather than positive, anarchistic rather than constructive, intellectual rather than concrete. As long as these views prevail and as long as groups and parties are not recognized by all in a pluralistic framework, the support for liberal democracy is likely to remain insufficient, though real enough to prevent the system from being overthrown despite its common—or at least periodic—political ineffectiveness.

FRANCE AS A TRADITIONAL POLITY

It may seem exaggerated to view the French political system as being, even if only in part, "traditional." The French Revolution was fought, nearly two hundred years ago, against a society already more "developing" than traditional, though it was not liberal. Since 1789, industrialization and its concomitant social transformations, such as urbanization and educational advance, have moved France even further away from the type of traditional society which one finds primarily, in the contemporary world, in parts of the Middle East, Southeast Asia, and Black Africa, and which, even there, is gradually eroded by social and economic change.

Two important elements of a traditional political system are indeed absent in France. There is no legitimate monarch whose authority is unquestioned or little questioned; France has been a republic continuously for over a hundred years, and the legitimacy of the monarch was in doubt long before. Yet, in a traditional system, the authority of the king is critical in holding the country together. It is particularly critical because traditional polities are organized on the basis of many social groupings such as tribes, whose members tend to believe without question in past traditions and have little interest in what happens outside the group. The monarchy provides unity where divisions among groups would otherwise prevail. In France, as we just noted, these groups were shattered along with the monarchy in 1789.

Yet, paradoxically, while monarchy and traditional groups were destroyed, the limited opportunity of the peasantry helped to maintain patterns of political authority which were very similar to those of traditional societies. First, the revolution left a legacy of scars. Furthermore, because the influence of the aristocracy was not undermined everywhere to the same extent geographical divisions were reinforced. Besides, the vanishing aristocracy was rarely superseded by a successful and modern industrial elite: the independent peasantry was the Revolution's great achievement. Village leaders were naturally found among peasants, shopkeepers, lawyers, all wishing to maintain their local traditions and apt to resist change, especially if imposed from outside. This gave the *real* political life in much of the country characteristics of a traditional society, even if these were often hidden under a liberal democratic surface.

The existence of stable human relationships in villages and small towns led to closed, almost unchallengeable values prevailing in each community; hence the limited support for pluralism at the grass roots level. Political relationships were also more often personal than ideological: a family (doctor, lawyer, farmer) could be prominent for generations, irrespective of the views which these men might hold or irrespective of the goals of the organization which these men might be leading. The structure of the rural society was static for so long (up to the 1950s) that both value patterns and human relationships often became ossified. This is why French political life in the countryside typically had the characteristics of tribal or semitribal societies more than those of modern communities. True, the *origin* of these relationships was not tribal; in most cases it was not even strictly "traditional," because it was rarely the result of the long-standing predominance of a landowning class. But the effect was the same; the local elites of *notables,* drawn from the professions and occasionally from among shopkeepers or medium-sized farmers, enjoys the allegiance of the rest of the population on the basis of a mixture of intellectual superiority, family influence, and limited patronage. These relationships exist within the context of a divided country where sectionalism is powerful. The allegiance to local *notables* contributes to reinforce this sectionalism; these are the spokesmen for the village or area, not part of a national group linked together for a common cause.

Thus the existence of a personal type of allegiance, in many parts of rural and semirural France, down at least to the late 1950s and early 1960s, has contributed to give a social basis to the traditional elements of the political system. This has been buttressed by a psychological resistance to change often surprising on the part of segments of the population which do not benefit from the *status quo.* Perhaps the two world wars, with their dramatic toll in lives, the general setback to the economy which they provoked, and the decline in France's status in the world which followed them were in part responsible for the maintenance of the belief that "things were better before," just at a time when economic progress might have led to a transformation of social and political attitudes. Thus only when the economy again began flourishing in the early 1960s was it possible for the first time in two generations to look for a future better than the past and present. While economic change in rural France led to improved conditions for some, it brought about the abandonment of a former life-style. The bulk of the French population may become in the long run less pessimistic about its future and less cynical about economic progress and social reforms, but traditional values will remain for many decades one of the elements of the French political system: they may no longer account for political institutions (in contrast with the Third and Fourth Republics), but they are likely to slow down the development of groups and to reduce the parties' appeal for many years to come. They account for a political climate in which changes and reforms are received with cynicism or anger; they explain in part the outbursts and anomic reactions which periodically occur, while contributing to the need for institutions designed precisely to combat tradition and to give a "modernizing" or "developing" character to the society.

FRANCE AS A MODERNIZING SOCIETY

Besides being traditional, the French political system is "modernizing," in that efforts have been made by the government and the bureaucracy to modify the social and economic structures and patterns of behavior. These efforts were most visible during parts of the seventeenth century, under the two Napoleons, and in the postwar period. Thus France possibly deserves the title of the oldest and most persistent modernizing polity.

A modernizing society is necessarily authoritarian and centralizing, at least to a degree. Since the aim is to destroy the structures of the past, clashes with those who benefit from or are simply accustomed to these structures are thus unavoidable. There are also limits to the extent and speed of change, as there are limits to what leaders can impose. Authoritarian regimes cannot always find the men who will implement decisions. If the gap between traditions and the aims of the modernizing leaders is very large, or if these leaders wish to bring about change abruptly, conflicts may increase to the point that the regime is toppled, with a passive population simply not participating in the efforts required to change the social structure. If the regime is to implement its aims, on the other hand, it needs to benefit fully from two advantages. It needs men with technical skills—"technocrats," who have the ability and the will to move society away from tradition and in the direction of a modern State. But to buttress "technocrats" the regime also needs a modern political elite which can help to mobilize at least large sections of the population toward the new goals. The single political party is the common instrument in many developing countries; but this is often replaced, or in other cases helped, by a popular leader who embodies the "new polity" in the eyes of the common man.

France has had a modernizing ideology intermittently for centuries. It has the reservoir of technical skills to achieve the goal, but it had only infrequently the requisite political superstructure; much regime instability is due to this failing. Many French governments, from the kings to the Fifth Republic, have felt the need to improve the economy, often for prestige reasons. While commerce and industry developed naturally in England and the Low Countries, in France, trade was the driving force behind industrial progress, government help was needed; the government was never prepared to let the country decay, as the Spanish Empire or the Italian cities. State industries were created, fostered, and protected. The postwar planning program of the Fourth and Fifth Republics thus continued a form of traditional *dirigisme* aimed mainly at economic improvement and to some extent at social reform. Social and economic "engineering" is thus second nature, while being reinforced by the static character of the traditional rural and small town society.

This urge for development led to the creation of the civil service, which in turn came to be a powerful supporter of the "modernizing" ideology. This ideology was of course not shared by the political leaders who were the representatives of the villages and small towns and who wished primarily to keep their traditions. Nor was the modernizing ideology shared by liberals or socialists whose main goal was more democracy or more equality. Yet neither traditional leaders nor liberals and socialists ever were strong enough to uproot the civil service. Liberal democracy thus coexisted with the modernizing goals of the bureaucracy. At times during the Third Republic, and especially during the 1930s, the ideology of modernization receded, but the role of the civil service was never wholly brushed aside. When, after World War II, rapid socioeconomic change became once more the main goal, the liberal leaders often clashed with "technocrats" and came occasionally to ally with those who supported the more traditional life which was being threatened by modernization. This naturally raised questions of political leadership; de Gaulle's "charismatic" rule is thus not merely a consequence of the Algerian war. Like Napoleon III a century before, de Gaulle managed to contain both the traditionalists and the modernizers and owed much of his power to having been able to retain the loyalty of much of provincial France while giving a free run to many "technocrats." Meanwhile, traditional structures became weaker; the pluralistic elements became stronger, and the need for development became more widely accepted. But conflicts between these forces simmer below the surface: they might be strong enough to undermine once more the stability of the political system.

It could almost be said that France combines three different and juxtaposed political systems—a traditional system, a modernizing system, and a liberal democratic system. Traditionalism is rampant, not in the British sense in which symbols are maintained, even long after the reality has ceased to justify them: tradition is perpetuated by the somewhat limited horizons of many of the "small men." But tradition bred among other men the urge to modernize; an instrument was found with the civil service. Some authoritarianism ensued: this reinforced supporters of liberal democracy in their belief that only constant vigilance can stop the excesses of the bureaucracy. One has to be "irresponsible" in the defense of liberty if one is to avoid a massive extension of the bureaucratic state. Hence a vicious circle: more bureaucratic measures have to be taken if society is to function, let alone develop. The society reaches a stalemate— or is engaged in a pernicious form of dialectic between the various models of the political system. But the stalemate remains, as each of the three strands of the political system can be found embedded in each institution and indeed in the minds of every

3

The French Political System: An Overview

The three different roots of the political system naturally came to produce a chaotic regime; the surprise is that it functioned for almost ninety years, from 1870 to 1958, with only one break, due to occupation, between 1940 and 1944. Since 1958, the changes which took place seem to have altered markedly the conditions of the game. While the divisions between liberal democratic tendencies, traditional forces, and modernizing trends still lie close to the surface, there is more convergence than in the past. Temporarily perhaps, a new—and possibly a viable—equilibrium has seemingly emerged. The constitutional structures have given greater strength to political leaders; these have been more anxious to link to the "technocrats," who in turn are more aware of popular demands, though charges of "bureaucracy" have repeatedly been made. Meanwhile, the traditional characteristics of French society became less prominent; despite—and even to some extent against—de Gaulle, groups became more influential and the party system became more streamlined. Recurrent conflicts have not been avoided, rather, they have resulted in turmoil, as in 1968. But there is at least a chance that the system might produce, if technocrats and liberals come closer together and if traditionalists continue to lose strength, a more integrated political system.

45

THE CONSTITUTION

THE FREQUENT CONSTITUTIONAL CHANGES SINCE 1789

As in most countries, a constitution is in France a means of legitimizing a new social or political situation which is sufficiently different from past conditions to necessitate a redefinition of the political-legal base on which the authority of the government and the rights of the people are anchored. Implicit in this definition is the existence of dissatisfaction with previous arrangements—dissatisfaction often strong enough to justify defiance of the most basic legal contours of the State. In France, this defiance has often been expressed first by violence, with adjustment of constitutions following shortly afterward. This is by no means a uniquely French phenomenon, but it has happened more often in France than in other Western nations. From 1791 to 1958, France has known sixteen constitutions, most of which were admittedly short-lived, and two of which (those of 1793 and 1814) were not applied at all. Eight of the sixteen were born and died in the quarter of the century which elapsed between 1789 and 1814; but, even if one considers the period after 1814, constitutional change has tended to take place every fifteen years or even sometimes less. The Revolution of 1830 brought about a new charter for the monarchy. The Revolution of 1848 led to the Constitution of the Second Republic. The *coup d'état* of Louis-Napoleon, who was to become emperor under the title of Napoleon III (and not Napoleon II, because the son of the great Napoleon was deemed by the Bonapartists to have reigned, though he spent almost all of his short life in exile) brought about the Constitution of 1852. This authoritarian document was liberalized by stages in the 1860s and replaced by an altogether parliamentary text by the emperor himself in 1870. The war, defeat, and Revolution of 1870 led in 1875 to the Constitution of the Third Republic, the only French constitution to date to have lasted over twenty years. It achieved a kind of political equilibrium seemingly satisfactory to most Frenchmen. But the regime collapsed in the defeat of 1940, the last Parliament of the Third Republic having voted full powers to Pétain. After the Liberation, de Gaulle pressed for a new constitution, but the one which was passed by popular referendum in October 1946 (after a previous draft had been rejected by the people in May of the same year) was much too similar to that of the Third Republic to be of de Gaulle's liking. The Fourth Republic was indeed to be short-lived, having collapsed in May 1958 over the Algerian problem, almost in the same infamous way as the Third, this time by handing over near-full powers to de Gaulle, who submitted a new constitution to the people in September 1958. This was approved by 80 percent of the voters in a record turnout of 85 percent. The Fifth Republic was born.

It may seem legitimate to ask what a constitution means in the minds of the citizens of a country which has known so many. But, in fact, the answer is simpler than it would seem at first sight, at least for the French of the present generation. Since 1875, except for the Vichy regime, France has had three republics, but has remained "the Republic." With the expression of "the Republic" a number of concepts, of myths, even of emotions are profoundly associated. What the Third, Fourth, and Fifth Republics have in common is a certain vision of the character of politics, based as we saw earlier on liberal, lay, democratic, and unitary principles. Differences among the three constitutions are, in the main, at the level of institutional arrangements; they are concerned with the types of changes which may be, could have been, and indeed sometimes are dealt with by amendments. In fact, perhaps the most momentous change which occurred since 1875 took place not through a wholesale constitutional upheaval, but through an amendment approved, admittedly, by referendum: the 1962 reform which led to the election of the president of the Republic by universal suffrage.

Yet if "the Republic" and its principles are generally approved of, Frenchmen are well aware of the impermanence of constitutions. This does to some extent affect their behavior. The long spell of constitutional stability in the Third Republic has been superseded once more, since World War II, by a period in which French politicians are very unlikely to consider the constitutional document under which they live as "sacred" or even very significant. It does not follow that they are markedly more cynical about their constitution than the citizens of other democratic countries, but more politicians in France than elsewhere are simply inclined to think of overall constitutional change as more than a remote possibility and to play down "mere" amendments when they can revamp the general frame. The events of 1958 clearly reinforced these feelings, as the constitution changed once more; for a few days, the turmoil of 1968 seemed to justify similar hopes. As a result, many have "waited for Godot" ever since the beginning of the Fifth Republic and remained on the sidelines with a new constitution in mind, though the number seems to have decreased in the early 1970s.

THE CONSTITUTION OF 1958

It was a commonly held view that the Constitution of 1958 was tailor-made for General de Gaulle, who was to become, in December 1958, the first president of the Republic under the new regime. This is, in fact, only partly true; it would be truer to say that the constitution *became* more and more tailor-made for de Gaulle, partly as a result of constitutional amendment, partly as a result of customary change. The 1958 document emerged as a compromise between Gaullist and other political forces which were deemed to be electorally strong at the time. Many political leaders agreed on the desirability of more effective governments, and suggestions had been made for some time which devised various procedures by which this aim could be achieved. Meanwhile, however, de Gaulle wanted an entirely different type of executive, in which the president would have a much loftier position and would be concerned with the "permanent" interests of the nation.

The compromise was difficult to achieve because the French "republican" tradition is suspicious of strong presidential government. As a popularly elected Bonaparte overthrew the Second Republic, the supporters of liberal government subsequently backed the view that France needed a parliamentary system, with a weak president, and indeed a relatively weak prime minister responsible to a chamber highly suspicious of executive initiatives and always ready to censure them. Admittedly, as the experience of the Third and Fourth Republics was to show that a weak government and a weak prime minister led to almost complete ineffectiveness—*immobilisme* was the expression—it had been argued by many since 1940 and increasingly in the early 1950s that various devices should be introduced to strengthen the prime minister *vis-à-vis* the Assembly. These devices would in particular prevent members of the chamber from slowly eroding the legislative program of the government by a variety of dilatory and other tactics designed ultimately to make the prime minister give in or give up. A few timid moves in this direction had even been inserted in the Constitution of 1946 which established the Fourth Republic; they proved to be so timid, while the mores of parliamentarians remained the same, that no change seemed to ensue. In particular, the most obvious, and best-known characteristic of the French parliamentary system, governmental instability, continued to prevail as before. On the average, governments fell every six to seven months in the Fourth Republic as in the last years of the Third.

Such was the basis for the reforms demanded by many politicians. But de Gaulle's conception of the role of the executive was a much more exalted one. His views were partly molded by his own past, which was that of a nationalist member of the military in the 1930s, but they were reinforced by the events of 1940, when the last president of the Third Republic, Albert Lebrun, gave in to the defeatist policies of Pétain and agreed to the combined demise of the Republic and of independent France. De Gaulle was determined to modify the institutions in such a way as to make the repetition of such events impossible. Back from Algiers in 1944, he hoped that the newly elected constituent Assembly would strengthen the executive, and in particular turn the president into a "guide" or "steward" of the nation. He failed then and resigned in January 1946; he was determined not to fail again in 1958.

Yet, despite de Gaulle's wishes, the Constitution of 1958 was born as a compromise between the "republicans," who belonged to the political parties of the Fourth Republic and were generally in agreement about the need for some increase in the stability and effectiveness of the *executive,* and de Gaulle and his followers, who wanted primarily to enhance the role of the president. From the day de Gaulle came to power and committed Michel Debré to draft the new constitution, the constraints stemming from tradition and the need for compromise were evident. In delegating its constituent powers to de Gaulle on June 3, 1958, the National Assembly refused to let the new head of the government establish a presidency on American lines. It was stated that the president had to be a different person from the prime minister (a key distinction of the "parliamentary" or "cabinet" system of government, as it makes it possible to have both a government which determines the policy, and a president—or king in monarchies—who "reigns but does not govern," thus ensuring the continuity of the state); it was also stated that the government was to be "responsible" politically to Parliament and that it should remain in office only as long as it had the confidence of the majority of the National Assembly (this, too, being one of the key distinctions between the parliamentary and presidential systems of government). Perhaps somewhat surprisingly, de Gaulle accepted these limitations to his freedom to shape the constitution; indeed, when presenting the new document later in the summer, Michel Debré argued very forcibly that the new system was parliamentary *not* presidential. As a result, de Gaulle was not at liberty to implement to the full his conception of the presidency. Debré held the president to be an "arbiter," not a "leader" or "guide." Admittedly, arbitration is an ambiguous concept; one could vary the interpretation from the idea of a more positive role (clearly de Gaulle's view) to that of a more neutral function (clearly the "correct" interpretation of the constitution).

THE MOVE TOWARD "PRESIDENTIAL" GOVERNMENT SINCE 1958. THE ROLE OF REFERENDA

Being unable—and probably unwilling—to turn the constitution into a fully "presidential" document in the legal sense, de Gaulle did succeed in introducing two provisions which sought to give the president an important say in the affairs of the country. One has not proved to be of much practical value. This is the right to claim special powers in an emergency through the celebrated Article 16 of the constitution which caused more controversy in 1958 than any other clause. The other power remained almost unnoticed at the time the constitution was discussed but was to have a much greater—indeed perhaps a decisive—impact; this was the extended use of the referendum which was used by de Gaulle and later by Pompidou as an *alternative* to the normal passage of laws by the legislature. The referendum had not been unknown previously, but it had typically been associated with Bonapartism. It was not allowed by the Constitution of 1875, and the Constitution of 1946 had only provided for it in constitutional matters and under some conditions; in fact, no referendum took place between the adoption of the Constitution of 1946 and the adoption of the Constitution of 1958.

Clearly de Gaulle liked referenda, from both a theoretical and tactical standpoint. Referenda gave him the opportunity to have a direct link with the people; they were to give him in practice means to bypass Parliament and to establish the bases of a semipresidential regime. Indeed, only thanks to the referendum could he introduce a major constitutional amendment—that of 1962, by which the president became popularly elected. Between 1958 and 1962, the French people were asked for their opinion in no less than four cases (two of which concerned Algeria). While the procedure was not used in the following six years, de Gaulle tried to reestablish his authority after the turmoil of 1968 by using the same device, failing this time in April 1969 over a deliberately ambiguous question which linked a mild reform of regional government to the decrease of the powers of the Senate. De Gaulle had made it clear at previous referenda as well as in 1969 that he would consider the result as a vote of confidence in himself; the referendum was almost the equivalent, between president and people, of the vote of censure which enables the National Assembly to dismiss the prime minister and government. Having failed to have his way in the 1969 referendum, de Gaulle duly resigned. But the practice was sufficiently established for de Gaulle's successor to use the procedure to assert his power over and alongside Parliament. In 1972, Pompidou appealed to the people on the seemingly uncontroversial question of British entry in the Common Market. He was mildly rebuked by the electorate, a decisive majority being in favor, but with abstentions reaching the record level of 45 percent; this may have undermined the value of this presidential weapon for future occasions!

A marked form of "presidentialism" did therefore prevail in the implementation of the constitution, though perhaps not quite in the way de Gaulle himself would have predicted before 1958. But the cunning use of constitutional powers—indeed sometimes stretched beyond a strictly "correct" interpretation—enabled the president to establish himself well above not only the Assembly but the rest of the executive. Yet, because the constitution was a compromise, other devices had also been introduced to strengthen the power of the executive in general *vis-à-vis* the legislature and to prevent the return to what had been previously known as a *régime d'assemblée*. These devices amount to a very complicated and at times bizarre set of procedural arrangements, from the restriction of the duration of parliamentary sessions, limitations on the right of the opposition to censure the government, and the clipping of powers of committees, to the strengthening of the second chamber—the Senate (though this body proved in fact less "Gaullist" than had been anticipated). Power was also given to a Constitutional Council designed to adjudicate between government and Parliament; the Constitutional Council had often been called the executive's poodle because of its very narrow interpretation of the powers of Parliament by contrast with those of the government. Altogether, taken with the presidential powers, these devices have markedly contributed to giving to the Fifth Republic an air of authoritarianism. It is as if France could only oscillate between the extremes of sovereign assemblies anxious to demote the executive, as before 1958, and that of weak parliaments whose wings are so clipped that they cannot have more than a marginal influence on the life of the country and governmental policies.

Yet it is not only because of the constitution that such changes occurred. It was de Gaulle's "charisma" which helped the constitution to be adopted, made possible the president's election by popular suffrage, and twisted the constitution toward "presidentialism." It was also because social changes occurred coincidentally that a large Gaullist party emerged at the 1962 election. The Fifth Republic has been the product of this accidental meeting between a powerful leader and profound changes in the society.

THE NEW "NATIONAL" CHARACTER OF GROUP AND PARTY POLITICS

The constitutional changes implied a direct relationship between president and people: de Gaulle distrusted the "intermediaries" who, in his opinion, had been responsible for the apparent decay manifested by the defeat of 1940. Yet, though the great shadow of de Gaulle was critical in maintaining for ten years the new regime and leaving the next president with very different institutions from those of previous decades, these developments were only possible because, at the same time, French politics and society had become more pluralistic and more uniform—or "national." De Gaulle began his term of office with thundering remarks about the dangers due to groups; he had attacked for the previous ten years the "régime of the parties." Groups and a new refurbished party system were nonetheless the instruments of his political system; without them he would not have left the presidency with institutions which, even though challenged, appear at least viable.

THE CHANGES IN THE GROUP STRUCTURE

Traditionally groups were weak, divided, and unrepresentative. Unions grew slowly in an atmosphere of opposition; they were intensely ideological. Since World War II, they had been sharply divided on party lines and, except for short periods, as in 1946, their membership was small, hence seemingly justified criticisms against their irresponsible character. Other groups, business groups in particular, seemed to be small coteries of self-seeking men, more anxious to obtain personal favors or advantages than to represent a profession. They were not pressure groups in the modern sense. Newspapers would typically "reveal" shady activities or scandals of a lobby, whether that of the wine growers or that of the beetroot growers. The Left regularly attacked the "two hundred families" which, in particular in banking and in iron and steel, were alleged to control France by the backdoor through the manipulation of civil servants and politicians. Naturally enough, for the majority of Frenchmen and for de Gaulle himself, groups *as such* were therefore viewed as objects of scandal and corruption, not as potential channels of representation or as means to iron out compromise policies.

This picture became altered only slowly in the postwar period. Even in the more "modern" conditions under which groups operate in the 1970s, beliefs about them are not wholly positive; business scandals still occur, especially in housing and the building sector, and these reinforce built-in prejudices against interest groups. But a host of more representative groups of business and the professions have now emerged; the agricultural organizations have been transformed beyond recognition, and, despite continued internal divisions among unions, these have, by and large, become more responsible and more accepted. Besides, cultural and social groups have come to exert pressure for large numbers of causes. Interest organizations have become part of what might be termed a new landscape of politics. The mass media, Parliament, the executive and the bureaucracy are now accustomed to treating groups as potential and actual intermediaries in clear and paradoxical contradiction with the "direct" link between president and people which de Gaulle sought to foster but which even the founder of the Fifth Republic chose to accept rather than combat.

A Changing Party System

Groups play a large part in French politics. As a result, the country has become closer to the "associational" model of liberal democracy; it has become more unified, more "nationalized," since types of arrangements based on the sectional leadership of "notables" are being superseded by deals between representative bodies. Similarly, the party system has become, during the same period, more national and more associational. Largely because of the changes in the society, but in part also because de Gaulle had to foster the growth of a large disciplined party if he was to control Parliament, the French party system has become altered beyond recognition. The 1962 general election was to be the turning point; this was to be the first time in modern French history that a political party gained a majority of seats in Parliament and that an election gave a clear "mandate" to a government.

In order to understand this change we need to return briefly to the situation which prevailed for the best part of a century and had characterized the Fourth Republic until its end in 1958. Contrary to what is often thought, France was not unique in having a large number of parties: various continental European countries, and Scandinavian countries as well, have many parties. She was not unique in having loosely organized parties: American parties are also loose federations. France was already somewhat original in having a combination of both. But the French party system had two other characteristics which made it really unique: first, there were both ill-disciplined parties, eager to compromise, and rigid, almost totalitarian organizations; second, many parties were not only decentralized, they were volatile and split with great frequency. It was thus more an "anarchic" party system than a multiparty system. The Italian system, for instance, is complex and riddled with factions, but it displays great cohesion and more eagerness to carry on with the job of government.

THE COMPLEX HISTORY AND GEOGRAPHY OF FRENCH POLITICAL PARTIES

History and geography, sociology and psychology have all to be called for help if one is to attempt to explain this strange development. The complex political history of France may explain why up to recently a section of the population did not accept the Revolution, while others were extreme revolutionaries. But history and geography have to be linked if one is to account for the permanence of traditions in some areas more than in others. Right and left, the antirevolutionary Right and the revolutionary Left as well as other forms of right, center, and left have traditionally been written in the countryside, so to speak, as are geographically circumscribed the areas of deep religious practice and the areas of "de-Christianization." In the main, the northern half of the country has always been more right wing than the southern half, the West and East are Christian, traditional, and inclined to vote conservatively, while the Center and Southeast are both "progressive" and de-Christianized.

This first sketch needs to be complicated by various lines which gradually emerged in the course of French history. As the

Revolution had two stages, a liberal and an egalitarian, one finds, through the nineteenth century, "moderates" and "progressives" among the "republicans." These often changed names, almost at every generation: when, in the 1880s, a moderate was labeled "republican," the progressives called themselves "radical"; but "radicals" grew in numbers and expanded into the Center, and progressives, dissatisfied with the more timid of the "radicals" moved toward "radical-socialism" and indeed socialism. For many progressives inside the Socialist party, at the end of World War I, a socialism which had condemned the war in principle but joined it in practice seemed a weak form of "progressivism": communism came into being, under the impact of the Russian Revolution, of course, but naturally embedded in what appeared to be the perpetual leftward movement of the current of French politics. Indeed, though the movement seems to have stopped for a generation, developments since the late 1960s and which followed from the student revolt and general strike of 1968 begin to suggest that the Communist party may be in part overtaken on its left.

We thus encountered three parties on the Left—Radicals, Socialists, Communists—emerging from the prorevolutionary currents. But two other forces were born from the Revolution. They stemmed from the royalists and the "Bonapartists," but were soon to be modified as no king was to return and as Napoleons ceased to be in sight. They created two trends in politics. Royalists turned "traditional conservative," and were anxious to maintain the status of those who had status, the "notables," the Church, the army. Bonapartists were more progressive in their outlook and more aggressive in their nationalism; they were "fascist" before the day, though with a stress on authoritarian rather than dictatorial government. They provided those Frenchmen who were both disgruntled and petty bourgeois with an outlet and an example. All, or nearly all, authoritarian or semiauthoritarian movements of modern France come from them, whether directly, as with General Boulanger in the 1880s, the "leagues" in the 1930s, or less directly, as with "Poujadism"— the radical Right of the small shopkeepers of the 1950s—and indeed Gaullism in the 1950s and 1960s.

If we now add two further ingredients, the religious question and the role of the peasantry, we can see the degree of complexity of the party system in its traditional form. Basically, the Church has been associated with the Right ever since the Revolution of 1789, which was at times strongly anti-Catholic; a syndrome was thus created which associated Church with Right and "republicanism" with anti-Church attitudes. Some efforts were made early in the twentieth century to break this association, but only in the 1940s, and indeed for little over a decade, did Catholicism emerge as a political force both distinct from the traditional Right and anxious to be recognized as "republican" and socially progressive. Thus three forces on the Right—traditional conservatives, Catholics, and the authoritarian Right—came to constitute the counterparts of the three forces on the Left. But both Right and Left, Communists as well as radicals and conservatives, were affected to a varying degree by the highly sectional character of politics: the "notables" were important in the major parties. Political allegiance was based to a large extent on traditional geographical lines, and indeed to a large extent still is, even after the changes in party allegiance stemming from the Fifth Republic. There are thus sharp "borders" between types of political attitudes. One such border exists in the center of France, along a North-East–South-West axis and divides the *Départements* of Creuse, Corrèze, and Lot, which are left-wing, from those of Puy-de-Dôme, Cantal, and Aveyron, which are right-wing. The role of the village and small town has been such that the "locality" rule remained strong in many areas and that, on balance, voters did not support candidates because they had received a party label, but because they were local. Once elected, the local man was in a position to negotiate with party headquarters. Hence the lack of party discipline of many parliamentarians; hence the not surprising fact that many, particularly on the Right, called themselves "independent," to the extent that the traditional conservatives came to be known officially as the "Center of Independents and Peasants." If cross-pressured between party and local demands, these traditional conservatives and many others used to opt for local demands without reservation; if their position was secure locally, no amount of party pressure could influence them.

NEW PARTY CLEAVAGES

These modes of behavior have not altogether disappeared, and we shall indeed see in Chapter Five that some ill-defined groups, such as the "independent conservatives" still exist. But the strength and weight of these practices has become more marginal to the political system. The turning point was the second, rather than the first general election of the Fifth Republic, that of 1962, though the results of the 1958 election had already pointed toward the new trend. While, at the 1956 election—the last of the Fourth Republic—the Gaullist party had seemed on the verge of disappearing, the 1958 election gave to the newly constituted Union for the New Republic 26 percent of the votes and over a third of the seats, thanks in large part to the reintroduction of the two-ballot single member majority system instead of the proportional representation system which had prevailed during the Fourth Republic. But the real import of the result was missed by politicians and observers. Most had indeed felt that, after the new constitution had been approved by 80 percent of the electors, a gain of 26 percent of the votes and of one third of the parliamentary seats was not a real victory for the Gaullist party. During the following four years, speculation was rife about the extent to which the new party would split; some Gaullist parliamentarians did indeed leave the party, largely because they felt de Gaulle's policy on Algeria to be too liberal. By 1962 Algeria had become independent; a coalition was formed in Parliament, comprising politicians who disapproved on Algerian independence as well as politicians who approved of it. The coalition succeeded in defeating the government in Parliament on the point that de Gaulle's proposed referendum on the election of the president by universal suffrage technically should be first submitted to the National Assembly. But de Gaulle won the referendum; he then proceeded to win the election one month later, while members of the coalition were sorely defeated. The Gaullist party won over 40 percent of the votes and a near majority of seats, in part, to be sure, because of de Gaulle's appeal, but in part also because the changes in the social structure which France had undergone in the previous decade had helped to reduce the role of local men and to bring about a new sense of national politics. The electorate rejected the "notables" to elect, in many cases, unknown candidates often without local roots. From this point, party cleavages moved in the two-party direction, the Gaullists and their allies on the Right, intermittent coalitions of Socialists, Communists, and some Radicals (Liberals) on the Left, while a small Center uneasily survived between the two blocs.

The general election of 1962 is thus a watershed in French politics; it was crucial for de Gaulle because, had he not won that election and had he been forced to agree to a compromise with the "traditional" politicians, the presidential character of the new regime would have been seriously impaired. He might have been forced to resign before the new institutions had been fully tried out and the party system restructured. He would thus have been unable to hand on to a successor an enhanced presidency. But the election was also crucial for the whole pattern of French political life: from 1962 on, old local cleavages, the old instability, and the old individualism disappeared probably forever from French party politics.

THE KEY ROLE OF THE CENTRALIZED STATE

THE TRADITIONAL INFLUENCE OF FRENCH ADMINISTRATION
The administrative structures are an important counterweight to the "plebiscitary" character of the new French regime. But they were already previously an important source of power. While the country changed its constitution on average every fifteen years, and perhaps because of this, the underlying organization of the "State" (a juridical expression which in France embraces all public bodies, whether in Paris or in the provinces, whether local or central, and whether created by the government or elected autonomously) did not vary very much. The territorial units of the State—the *département* (county), the *canton* (rural district), and the *commune* (the basic local unit, whether town or village) were scarcely affected by any boundary change once the Revolution had created them and broken the traditional provinces which

were alleged to embody the reactionary tradition of the past. Nor did many variations affect the principles of organization of government departments, whether in Paris or in the provinces, though new ministries were created and existing ones expanded. But the hierarchical arrangements remained the same. Above all, the system has been continuously crowned by a higher civil service drawn from a number of prestigious training schools which open to their most successful students entry into a number of elite *corps,* known as *grands corps.* Both the training schools and the *grands corps* contribute to giving French administration and even the whole political system as a whole a markedly "technocratic" outlook which contrasts vividly with the character of Anglo-Saxon and Scandinavian democracies. The schools have their entry restricted by highly competitive examinations which students prepare for several years after the end of their secondary schooling. The best known, and one of the oldest, among the technical schools is the *École Polytechnique* whose top students provide a large number of applied—and even pure—scientists in many walks of life, as well as engineers in the government and in the private sector. Created in 1795, it had been imitated in France in other fields and in many countries abroad. On the administrative side, the National School of Administration (ENA), with virtually the same characteristics, was created in 1945 and its products, known colloquially as *enarques*—with their mixture of arrogance and paternalism, their sense of the duty owed to the State coupled with their belief in their unquestioned right to preside over the destinies of the country—have been particularly influential in molding the characteristic style of the Fifth Republic.

The French "administrative State" is thus based in part on the skills of a civil service which not only trains its own staff, but contributes to the training of a large segment of the private sector, as well. But it is of course also buttressed by administrative structures which, ever since Napoleon, have placed civil servants in a strong position in relation to politicians at the national and local levels. Legalism and bureaucratic practices are used effectively to prevent private business from being as "private" as it is in Anglo-Saxon countries. This proved to be of value (although it also reinforced a perennial tendency toward bureaucracy) when, after the stagnation of the 1930s and economic destruction of the country after World War II, strong central direction was needed if France was to give its citizens a high standard of living and to remain a world power. Administrators planned the reconstruction, not only—and indeed not primarily—of the houses, plants, roads, and bridges destroyed by the war, but of the whole fabric of the French economy. The political collapse of big business, the almost total disruption of the capital market, indeed the demands for nationalization of major undertakings, all helped to enhance the influence of public officials; it enabled them to control the level and direction of investment more than in any other Western country (except perhaps Italy). Somewhat paradoxically (as many American businessmen were to notice), the program of American aid, channeled through the government, was to be a major determinant of this successful takeover, as only large sources of capital, which the United States did provide, could finance reconstruction. Inflation, too, was used for the same purpose by the new economists. Since social demands were large and governments of the early postwar period were willing or obliged to meet them, inflation was to play the role of deterrent which could not be obtained from a self-imposed discipline or from an authoritarian government. From 1945 to 1949, a repeatedly devalued franc lost 85 percent of its value, and only since 1958 has the currency become strong (except for a year or so after the 1968 turmoil) and even used by de Gaulle's nationalistically inclined government as an instrument in a tug-of-war with the United States.

FRENCH PLANNING
This was the philosophy which led to the first French Plan, which started modestly, almost under cover, in 1946. It was then intended to help "reconstruction and equipment." In the course of the following twenty-five years, the plan has broadened its objectives, becoming concerned with general economic development first, and with economic and social development later. From relating primarily to the basic economic infrastructure of the country (coal and steel, railways, electricity, etc.), it became

increasingly involved in the overall program of industrial development, in exports and in social investment—in housing and
education for instance. Admittedly, planning remained in France
indicative: unlike in the Soviet Union, planners never had power
to coerce either other administrators, central or local, or private
businessmen. But investment was always much controlled by the
government; foreign exchange controls remained very severe for a
very long period, and indeed up to the present, first because the
franc was weak, later because it was strong. From various forms
of financial inducements, from the general outline of the plan,
from the status of the civil service, and from the general tendency
of the French to rely on civil service leadership emerged a *de facto*
administrative rule, scarcely challenged in fact, if grumbled about
in theory, which is unparalleled in the Western world.

It may not seem natural to mention the social and economic
plan as one of the important elements of the French *political*
system. Yet, particularly in the seventies, the plan is perhaps more
a political machine than an economic organ. The "technocrats"
most helped by the plan are probably not—or are no longer—
those of the plan itself. Administrators in the technical ministries
and in the ministry of finance are, however, more clearly helped;
they can invoke the plan to guide economic and social managers
in the private and public sectors. Thus, like the referendum, the
plan is a political procedure with symbolic importance. As the
civil servants can use this instrument—even against ministers—
they hold political power through their use of the plan.

CIVIL SERVANTS AND POLITICS IN THE
FIFTH REPUBLIC

The plan is not their only instrument. Other ties link civil servants
to the politicians, in the Fifth Republic as in previous regimes.
The training schools are means of entering the elite and are thus
comparable to Harvard or Yale in the United States, and to
Oxford or Cambridge in Britain. Civil servants become politicians; ambitious young men enter a *grande école* and become civil
servants in order to become politicians, while other politicians use
younger civil servants on their staff to help prepare documents

and even suggest policy. They give ministers the legal or technical advice which these ministers need. Thus a symbiosis brings many civil servants in the political world.

The Fifth Republic continued a practice of the Third and Fourth Republics, one which had first come to prevail in the two bureaucratic empires of Napoleon I and Napoleon III. But the expansion was such after 1958 that, for a while at least, the whole political class seemed to be submerged. Civil servants entered the government, while old-style politicians were being set aside. A new class of "technocrats" seemed to take over, with only one "politician," de Gaulle, left to act as a link between State and people. Thus France seemed around 1960 to come close to the model of the modernizing country, as a charismatic leader was surrounded by civil servants highly dependent on him to maintain their influence. But this "technocratic" period became superseded when the Gaullist party came to acquire more reality. The civil servants who had entered the government became members of the party and were elected to Parliament. The civil service turned once more to be, though somewhat more than before, an *avenue* to politics, not the nucleus of the new political class.

The role of the *enarques* and other technocrats came also to be challenged; the events of 1968 were the culmination of a general, though diffuse, discontent. The State was run from above, even if with modernizing aims. Associations became more assertive in their criticisms; even some civil servants began to question their role. Attacks were made commonly against the centralization of the State and the weakness of local government; regionalism became a major issue. This did not mean a clear and direct demise of the "technocratic State" as dissensions among opponents of the centralized State have prevented a real challenge to age-old traditions. Not much regionalism has been implemented; the local government structure remained broadly unchanged. But the challenge exists. The clash between the traditional, the modernizing, and the liberal democratic "models" comes once more to be seen, as the civil service faces greater problems of "legitimacy." Its underlying power, however, if somewhat undermined, will remain a feature of the French political system for many years to come.

The French political system thus remains a complex picture of elements, old and new, liberal and authoritarian, modernizing and associational, despite the unquestionable streamlining of the party system and the development of interest groups. Alongside this development, we should neither underestimate nor overestimate the role of the constitutional changes of 1958. The existence of a new constitution after 1958 made it possible for de Gaulle first, and for others after him, to alter the political relationships. The existence of a new constitution enabled de Gaulle to practice a brand of "half-presidentialism" which may please neither constitutional lawyers who object to such a hybrid system nor the liberal observers who wish France to adopt a less authoritarian—or paternalistic—system. Yet this constitution has come to fit French reality rather better than had been anticipated, though the outcome is also different from that which de Gaulle had envisaged. Safeguards do exist and, whatever has repeatedly been said, the referendum is one of them, as the rebuke of 1969 and the half-rebuke of 1972 have shown. The party system is more streamlined. Parliament may have lost much of its power, but elections have become more meaningful, precisely because it is no longer up to members of Parliament to make and unmake governments without any control. The bureaucracy is so powerful that it seems at times politically responsible to no one, not perhaps even to the president, let alone the people; but the challenge it faced in the late 1960s suggests that its accountability may have to increase, though the pace may be slow. The Fifth Republic is neither a true liberal democracy nor an authoritarian "administrative State." It is evolving, if at all, toward a form of responsibility which did not exist in previous republics which legalized *immobilisme* and indecisiveness in the name of liberty. But it is still challenged; the extent of future change is difficult to forecast with so much uncertainty in the transformations which the various structures, to which we are coming, are now undergoing.

PART TWO

THE REPRESENTATIVE ORGANIZATIONS

4

Groups in the Political Process

Groups now play a large part in the political process; as we saw, the advent of the Fifth Republic coincided with the strengthening of a variety of interest organizations ranging from trade unions to consumer bodies. Almost two hundred years of antagonism have thus been profoundly undermined. This had started with the Revolution of 1789 which was fought in large part against the "Corporate State" of the *ancien régime*, in which each trade was organized in closed associations to be entered only after long periods of apprenticeship, though they provided their members with monopoly privileges. In the name of liberty, the Revolution abolished corporations; it forbade individuals to coalesce to limit production or regulate the entry of others into a profession (with several important exceptions). This philosophy was to die hard: trade unions were only tolerated legally three quarters of a century later; they waited a further twenty-five years before being officially recognized. Other groups suffered even more from the general opprobrium. Indeed, antigroup attitudes were once more reinforced because the Vichy regime used the German occupation to try to reintroduce a corporate state, modeled on fascism; this alienated workers because it denied them means of expressing their grievances, businessmen because it limited free enterprise, and all Frenchmen simply because production was insufficient. But the movement toward interest groups developing in an associational society was not long stopped, for groups became influential and numerous by the end of the 1950s.

One should not overestimate the extent of modern pluralism, however. Alongside modern interest groups, traditional bodies with a local basis continue to play a part in the society. The policies of many groups, and of trade unions in particular, are often characterized by a kind of systematic opposition which is at substantial variance with an associational model where the goal is to reconcile differences. First, they aim at extracting concessions, by force if necessary, from a State authority which they deem to be hostile; the approach to negotiations is rarely based on respect of the stand which the "opposite number" takes. Second, it is mainly the State which is the object of attack launched by groups. Collective bargaining between firms and unions is recent and still viewed with suspicion, and the typical approach is still to ask the State to make the provisions or to force (for instance, by law) the private employers to make the provisions. The weakness of unions accounts in large part for such an attitude. But the strength of the State has been traditionally such that legal arrangements have always been held superior to private negotiations. The idea of "partnership" between economic actors is only slowly gaining ground in this prevailing climate of mutual hostility.

TRADE UNIONS

WORKERS' UNIONS
The French trade union movement is very divided, largely for political reasons. It is also weak; only a small minority of workers belong to trade unions, though many more vote for union candidates at works councils organized by law in firms beyond a certain size. This ineffectiveness stems from many factors, the two main ones being the late development of an organized working-class movement and the tendency of French trade unionists to divide between rival, if not warring, ideological camps. French trade unionism had a difficult early history; the law giving it full recognition was passed as late as 1884. It was virtually wrenched into full life by the aggressive efforts of the anarchosyndicalists, who believed in direct action and managed to displace from the

leadership by the turn of the century the more reformist or even Marxist elements who could have gradually turned the organization into a powerful force directed against the employers. Syndicalists (who were by no means prominent only in France at the time, but who succeeded in having more strength in France than in other Western countries) believed in an uncompromising attitude toward the politicians and they were not prepared to enter into any agreements with the Socialist party, which was expanding rapidly at the time. Indeed, the basic charter of the *Confédération Générale du Travail* (the CGT), created in 1895 as a federation of all major trade unions, was modified at Amiens in 1906 in order to prevent any long-standing arrangement with the Socialist party. The official policy was based on the belief that working-class victories would not be won piecemeal through parliamentary means, but in one major push, through the general strike. But the union was never powerful enough to launch any such action, and indeed, when war broke out in 1914, trade unionists, whether syndicalist or not, defended the "bourgeois" state.

After World War I, the majority of labor leaders adopted a more reformist attitude, but the appearance of communism brought about a split and introduced politics into the trade union movement. The CGT followed more closely the Socialist party, under the leadership of Léon Jouhaux, while the more extreme elements entered the Communist-led *Confédération Générale du Travail Unitaire* (CGTU). This was not very successful, however, and was disbanded in 1936 when a "popular front" alliance came into being, its members rejoining the CGT. Communist trade unionists gradually acquired more influence in the newly reunited body and, by 1945, thanks to the *Résistance*, the CGT had come under their overall domination. Socialist trade unionists tried unsuccessfully to recover some of the lost ground, but, in 1947, when the unions came to be openly used for political reasons in a wave of strikes launched by the Communists, they broke from the CGT and created a new CGT-*Force Ouvrière* (the name of the newspaper of those who held these views).

Meanwhile, Catholic trade unions had gained considerable ground. Created in 1918, the *Confédération Française des Travail-*

leurs Chrétiens (CFTC) gradually increased its following among the white-collar employees and in the strongly Christian parts of France (Alsace in particular) to manual workers and the whole of the country. By the 1950s, it had become the second trade union, easily beating *Force Ouvrière* and producing a strong challenge to the CGT in many areas. In order to widen its appeal, it decided in 1964 to drop the word *Christian* from its title and to rename itself *Confédération Française Démocratique du Travail* (CFDT); a small segment of the trade union refused to follow and continued under the old name of CFTC.

There are thus three main trade union organizations catering to manual and white-collar workers, plus at least one smaller one, despite the fact that the following of each of them is relatively small: though French unions are rather secretive about their (limited) membership achievements, it seems clear that *Force Ouvrière* does not reach half a million members, that the CFDT has perhaps three quarters of a million and the CGT between two and three times as many. In all, about three million workers are unionized—20 to 25 percent of the total work force with considerable variations between occupational groups. The typical French worker still does not seem committed to a union which, in turn, is normally unable to help him with strike funds and other facilities.

This division has been detrimental to the working class, as it enabled governments to pay less attention to workers' demands by playing one union against the other, at times led unions to get involved in demagogic proposals in order not to be overtaken, and convinced many French workers that unionization was not necessary. Admittedly, the division is not everywhere as clear-cut as it might appear on paper. In some cases (as in printing) all the members of an occupational group belong to the same union; in many firms and offices, one or at best two unions tend to predominate. The CGT is strong mostly in the coal mines, on the docks, and in mechanical engineering (particularly around Paris); the CFDT's strength tends to be in light industry and among white-collar workers; *Force Ouvrière* leads among textile workers in the North and among civil servants everywhere. But competition between two unions is common and, at the national level, all three major unions take stands and are involved in consultations between themselves, with the government and with the employers.

The combination of this traditional weakness of unions and of legislative efforts to integrate the working-class representatives into the society led to a characteristic though paradoxical mixture of compulsory cooperation at the top and of semianarchistic and often ineffective outbursts at the bottom; these show at least one limit of the associational model of group involvement in the political system. Laws, particularly since 1945, have introduced working-class representation in a large number of bodies. The social security system is largely run by the trade unions; firms have a factory committee (*comité d'entreprise*) in charge of large sums devoted to leisure and cultural activities; boards of national-ized industries have union representatives. Many advisory com-mittees of the government, both in Paris and in the provinces, include union men; thus the committees of the planning and the regional economic development committees have trade unionists. This has sometimes led to difficulties with the CGT, as this organization tends to follow a Communist party line of noncol-laboration with the government and capitalist enterprises and boycotts many discussions, though more recently, it has partici-pated somewhat more. Overall, greater formal State-union collab-oration is achieved in France than in most Western countries.

Thus the *de facto* position of unions is typically weaker in France than elsewhere. Unions are indeed often unable to press seriously their demands at the level of the firm, factory, or office. The various unions often do not agree on a common stand. They cannot promise members any financial help in case of strike; workers thus often continue to work when a strike is called hoping to reap the benefits whatever the outcome. This divorce between workers and leaders is often in turn exploited by the government and private employers; it contributes as a result to a general feeling of bitterness. Traditionally, strikes have been of two types. Either unions resort to one-day stoppages or to slowdowns, as these imply less involvement of the rank-and-file though they are also less effective; there is usually talk of further action, but little is done in practice. Or strikes come from the bottom, almost unorganized, sometimes on a vast scale. It seems more than a coincidence that such "anomic" movements of protest should have recurred with regularity every fifteen to twenty years since the beginning of the century, as in 1905, 1919, 1936, 1953, and 1968; the widespread strikes of 1968 should therefore be seen as part of a general context of disgruntlement and not as the sign of a new alienation in a consumer society. It is a phenomenon that might recur unless conditions change markedly. These movements are indeed typically followed by a rapid return to normalcy, as was the case in 1968—to the surprise of all concerned. Unions do not control these vast periodic outbursts; the CGT leaders wanting to stop strikes in June 1968, after an agreement had been secured with the government and employers, were hissed and shouted down. Yet, a few days later, the movement was exhausted, as if it had to follow a natural cycle. Such strikes do not strengthen the trade union movement, however; they do not lead to an increased integration of the worker into society, though they can win them substantial benefits, as in 1936 and 1968, particularly if they are followed by rapid economic growth.

This traditional picture may be changing under the leadership of Christian unions. In the 1950s, the CFTC (now CFDT) campaigned for a new approach to the question of the relationship between worker and society. Typically, the weakness of French unions was held by union leaders, and in particular by the CGT, as proof of the domination of capitalism; the only hope was therefore held to be the overthrow of the system. Little analysis was done of the intrinsic defects of the working-class organizations; little blame was placed on the workers for their apparent unwillingness to become members, as the model put forward by the CGT did not suggest that workers would be able to extract concessions from the employers if they were to bargain more realistically. The CGT (and the Communist party) put forward a "cataclysmic" model; they preached both that the revolution through which everything was to change was around the corner and that by definition workers could make no gains in the capitalist system. Following this line to the end, they even claimed that the proletariat was actually becoming poorer as time went by, an obvious untruth which had little impact on French social and economic elites and probably did not even appeal to the workers themselves. As long as the revolution had not come, however, the CGT could be merely a vast bureaucracy; little needed to be done to make workers participate more in union life, or in that of the firm. An attitude of noncollaboration was preferred as collaboration meant accepting norms of reformism.

The CFDT's outlook has been different. Rather than placing their hopes in a long term which was never coming, and while they did show their preference for a humane form of socialism different from that experienced in Russia or other Communist states, leaders of Christian unions wished to embark in the process of educating workers toward new attitudes in the factory and society at large. Instead of emphasizing the need for workers' organizations to prepare for an eventual onslaught on the State, as the CGT traditionally tended to do, the CFDT aimed at developing cooperation. Instead of basing its statements on ideology and slogans, it produced an economic analysis of society and of the firms and confronted employers with realistic requests, gradually going beyond wage demands and extending into the general environment and life of the worker. It saw trade unions as one of the instruments of gradual change in society.

The CFDT is therefore prepared to make more short-term deals with employers than the CGT; but it is also more radical than the CGT in attempting to change workers' attitudes as well as those of other economic and social "partners." The CFDT's realism was shown by its willingness to use and extend collective bargaining, which had come very late, in large part because neither the employers nor the CGT, given its attitudes, believed in this method. Though legalized in 1936, collective bargaining was stopped by the war and was only finally reintroduced in the legal machinery in 1950. Yet only by the end of the 1950s did it become fashionable when, through the efforts of the CFDT, a collective agreement was signed in 1958 in the Renault works; this was later followed by other agreements (on the basis of the type of tactics used by the American UAW to extract concessions from successive employers). The success was such that even the CGT had grudgingly to admit that the agreement was more than a mere "capitalist plot." Meanwhile, the CFDT laid much emphasis on the need to improve job conditions, and in particular to reduce boredom and repetitiveness. This found a large echo among younger workers, but led to the accusation from the CGT that the Christian Union was being "irresponsible" and "anarchistic." In 1968, as well as before and since, especially in connection with strikes of the semiskilled, of women, of the lower paid, the CFDT's support often forced the CGT to follow suit.

Indeed, even though the 1968 strikes showed the continued strength of anomic movements in the working class, attitudes have begun to change. Many strikes of the 1960s have been tougher and prolonged, as with miners in the winter of 1963, seamen in 1966, semiskilled Renault workers in Le Mans in 1971. The distinction between attitudes of an "old" and a "new" working class is an oversimplification, admittedly. Each French worker carries within him attitudes of protest and disgruntlement which stem in large part from long-standing grievances. But many now realize the opportunities which are given to change society in a gradual fashion. The CFDT itself reflects this ambiguity. It is both more realistic than the CGT and more prepared to protest about general conditions. But even the CGT is slowly affected, and simple "anticapitalist" stands are no longer professed with the same assurance. Yet much has still to be done for unions to be strong, followed by a mass rank-and-file, and truly prepared to use this power with cunning and realism.

OTHER UNIONS

The three major trade union organizations cover, in theory at least, all types of employees. But many white-collar workers, the bulk of lower and middle management (*cadres* is the French expression), the professions, and students have typically been organized in different unions (even if a minority belong to the three major organizations). These often have a different ideology; together with the CFDT, some have emphasized "participation." They sometimes play a part in society not commensurate with their numbers, through the status of their members, the dynamism of their leaders, as well as because of the division of working class unions.

While workers' unions are in principle "general," sectional

organizations exist commonly among professional men—among doctors, dentists, lawyers, for instance. These categories are typically self-employed and come close to the small businessmen whose organizations will be examined in the coming section. Sectional unions, however, also exist for other groups, as for school and university teachers. The primary school teachers' organization, the *Fédération de l'Education Nationale*, is a large trade union which covers teachers of all ideological creeds and is indeed run almost on party lines, with Communists constituting about half the total. Other teachers' organizations outside the three main unions are basically conservative: the *Société des Agrégés*, which groups the best paid and most successful secondary school teachers, has continuously and systematically opposed reforms designed to bring about a democratization and modernization of school teaching and greater equality among teachers.

For a while, in the 1950s and early 1960s, students succeeded in creating one of the best and most active French trade unions, the *Union Nationale des Étudiants de France*; it had a large membership and combined care for the welfare of individual students (organization of holidays or provision of hostels) with an interest in the broader aspects of the life of the country, thus constituting a model and even leading other unions. However, first under the impact of the Algerian war, and later out of the momentum of the student revolt, it became increasingly involved in radical politics and antagonized a large fraction of the student body; it also became a field for the personal antagonism of various student leaders who conceived of their role as being that of a vanguard of the "revolutionary movement." Its very hour of triumph—the beginning of the open revolt in 1968—coincided with its disintegration; the activist protest of Daniel Cohn-Bendit and his colleagues (together with those of some junior teachers' leaders) created such opposition, after a period of initial success, among politicians, trade unionists, and the population at large, that the whole student movement lost its credibility. The subsequent splits led to the greater influence of Communists in a much reduced organization, as Communists appeared more respectable than the Maoist and other leftists (*gauchistes* is the French expression) who tried to perpetuate some agitation in the following two years. By the early 1970s, the leaders of 1968 were seemingly absorbed by the society and the students' organization had lost its liveliness.

Most of the employed middle class—the various levels of management in commerce and industry—are organized in a general union, the *Confédération Générale des Cadres* (CGC), which is basically conservative and aims at maintaining the differentials which the *cadres* have acquired in the growing French economy. Together with the three major workers' unions, it participates in general government-union discussions, while, in common with the CFDT and *Force Ouvrière*, it is anxious to increase the scope of collective bargaining and the amount of participation of its members in the life of firms. But clashes between the CGC and workers' unions are unavoidable, in view of the profoundly antiegalitarian tendencies of the former and of its belief in the virtues of free enterprise. Thus the government finds yet another means of dividing the various "partners" in the game of social relations. Associationalism and interest group behavior have markedly increased, but there is still a long way to go before workers and employers or workers and government recognize each other as full and equal components of the social fabric.

BUSINESS ORGANIZATIONS

The configuration of business organizations is somewhat simpler than that of manual and white-collar workers. But, even there, some divisions exist, due both to the traditional influence of small business and to the economic changes which have benefited large firms. Yet a new climate of business-government relations developed since 1945 whereas earlier, while industrial pressure on government was common, it tended to occur in secret and outside the framework of organizations: it was the pressure of industrialists more than that of industry. The turning point occurred when the first French Socialist government elected in 1936 initiated general negotiations between government, unions, and business. This led to an agreement (the *Accords Matignon*) which stressed for the first time the importance of the CGPF, the *Confédération Générale de la Production Française*. This body was succeeded in 1945 by the *Conseil National du Patronat Français* (CNPF) which started to operate in an unfriendly environment. Although it elected as its president a man who had suffered in deportation, Georges Villiers (he was to remain at the head of the organization for twenty years), the stigma of collaboration with German occupiers, both political and economic, was attached to French employers as a class. Nineteen forty-six was a year when Communists were in the government, when nationalizations were taking place, when workers' councils were created. Employers seemed divided among themselves. Though the council was a federation covering all types of firms, small and medium-sized enterprises were organized, under Léon Gingembre, into a semiindependent confederation, the *Confédération Générale des Petites et Moyennes Entreprises* (CGPME) which, because of the larger number and the smaller incomes of its members and the cult of the *"petit"* which prevails in France, could afford to be more militant. Employers of large firms were uncertain about their rights; a section of the *patronat* organized into a *Centre des Jeunes Patrons* displayed more progressive attitudes and criticized their colleagues for their conservatism.

The return to normalcy which characterized the early 1950s benefited the employers; big business leaders appeared indeed more politically reliable than many other sections of the middle class, which took to voting for various parties of the extreme Right—first the Gaullists (who attacked vociferously the Fourth Republic when de Gaulle left office for the first time in 1946, as we shall see in the next chapter) and later the Poujadists (who tried to organize shopkeepers toward direct action). On the whole, the CNPF and the men in charge of large-scale industry behaved "responsibly." They accepted the plan, possibly first out of opportunism, since they quickly realized that, in view of the dearth of capital for investment, only State-supported schemes would be likely to expand. They renewed the links which they had with officials in the economic departments of the bureaucracy; the comradeship of the members of the *grands corps*, which we mentioned in the previous chapter, came to be reestablished. But, perhaps more importantly, they soon realized that State-led developments would produce direct benefits. They would increase their profits through the expansion of their activities. If they could have a say in the investment and fiscal policies of the government, they could participate in a continuous boom. They came to discover that planners and the State needed the collaboration of business if the plan was to succeed and, in the Fifth Republic, if France was to be in front in the competitive enterprise of the Common Market.

Not unnaturally, small business was in a different position. These firms came to be viewed increasingly with suspicion by civil servants anxious to rationalize the economy and by the public who found cheaper goods in supermarkets and discount stores. They lost some of the tax advantages which had been granted to them earlier, when the cult of the small man made good political capital. Discontent was first channeled through the CGPME, which organized token strikes of shopkeepers but remained broadly within the bounds of legality. As anger mounted among small businessmen, particularly in the Center and South, which were both economically poorer and less law-abiding, calls for direct action were made more frequently. In the early fifties, a small shopkeeper in a village in central France, Pierre Poujade, achieved quick national fame with a program of refusal to pay taxes and attacks against tax offices. The success was such among shopkeepers and small artisans that, in the middle of the general climate of instability of the last few years of the Fourth Republic, Poujade turned his movement, the *Union de Défense des Commerçants et Artisans*, into a political party and gave it a general program, which had a nationalistic and indeed fascist flavor; the defense of the French in Algeria became one of the main themes of the new party which obtained 10 percent of the votes at the 1956 general election.

The party, the movement, and the *Union* itself disappeared in the political upheavals which led to the creation of the Fifth Republic. Discontent became subdued, and the problem appeared solved. Links between big business and the government increased; the CNPF appeared as one of the instruments of French industrial development, especially when, for a period, the government wished to promote financial orthodoxy to give the franc the strength which de Gaulle needed to launch his campaign against the dollar. But the general discontent of the late 1960s which led to the 1968 explosion also affected business, and once more shopkeepers and heads of other small businesses came to raise their voices and provoked a second wave of Poujadism. Under the leadership of Léon Nicoud, the CID-UNATI (*Comité d'Information et de Défense-Union Nationale des Artisans et des Travailleurs Indépendants*) had largely the same aims and employed the same direct action methods as the UDCA; Nicoud himself has been jailed several times for being involved in direct action operations against government buildings, though damage always remained slight and the overall level of tension has been fairly low.

The Fifth Republic thus did not prevent the recurrence of outbursts of the "underdogs" of French business, despite economic growth and despite the more streamlined political institutions of the new regime. Admittedly, the CID-UNATI has not embarked on a political campaign; it did not field candidates at the 1973 general election. The party system of the Fifth Republic has been better able to contain the extremists of the Right than was the previous regime. But the problem remains. The contrast between the well-organized and "civilized" forms of pressure group activity of large businesses and the somewhat anomic and more violent actions of the small men is a further indication of the mixture of associationalism and traditionalism which continues to characterize contemporary France. For Poujadists or the followers of Nicoud, the "past" was better and their views find echoes among wide segments of the population who, objectively, *are* better off now than they would have been thirty years earlier, but who feel sympathetic to attacks made against "State inquisition," "big business profits," and "bureaucratic laziness" by the more extreme representatives of the small men. On the outcome of the battle between the two groups depends much of the political and social development of France and the stability of the regime in future decades.

FARMERS' ORGANIZATIONS

The evolution of agriculture has been more rapid than that of any other section of French society. The flight from the land and the development of mechanization have altered the conditions of the peasants in every part of the country by giving to those who stayed more elbow room and some scope for expansion, though they have also been confronted with acute problems of capital and investment. Admittedly, the demands of the farming community differ widely. In the North and in the Paris area, the wheat and beetroot growers had for a long time constituted an aristocracy. Plots were larger, mechanization was widespread, and incomes were rather high; many agricultural workers were employed in what were often industrial firms dealing with production on the land in a capitalist fashion. Most of the rest of French agriculture, however, was run by small farms, sometimes efficient (particularly where they grew fruit, grapes, or vegetables, as especially in the valleys), but often quite inadequate in size and producing small incomes for large amounts of human work seldom relieved by machinery. This inefficiency was increased because many peasants worked on very small strips, sometimes separated by long distances, and, though legislation had for a long time attempted to cover the problem, it had not succeeded in bringing about before the late 1950s a rearrangement (*remembrement*) of the parcels which had come to each family through accidents of inheritance.

As a result of this diversity, the individualism of the peasantry was rather reinforced; the main pressure group of the farmers, the *Fédération Nationale des Syndicats d'Exploitants Agricoles* (FNSEA) often found itself landed with suddenly-expressed demands from the rank-and-file which it had great difficulty in channeling and turning into a coherent program. Even the creation of this body, in 1947, was progress, however. Before World War II, the farming community had known a number of attempts at organization, often of a political origin, from both Right and Left, but these never had much impact on the bulk of the peasants and had usually floundered after a few years. Some semiofficial channeling of demands did take place through the *Chambres d'Agriculture*, created in 1924, but these were consultative bodies operating within an administrative framework, rather than interest groups in the normal sense.

The FNSEA was thus the first true pressure group of the

farmers. It emerged out of a governmental attempt at organizing in 1945 an all-embracing *Confédération Générale de l'Agriculture* (CGA) which was to include cooperative as well as agricultural workers alongside farmers. It quickly proved unable to solve the conflicts among its various components. Only one of these, which represented the farmers proper (the *exploitants agricoles*) did survive; it even succeeded in enlisting the membership of about a third of all Frenchmen working on the land. For most of the 1950s, the organization came to be led by the representatives of the larger northern farmers; though this gave an air of respectability to the agricultural interest group, the danger of a break, leading to similar developments to those occurring among businesses was a clear possibility.

The challenge did indeed increase as rapid change was taking place in the structure of agriculture and in its relation with the rest of the community. For a period, anomic protests of small farmers began to resemble those of shopkeepers. Roadblocks and the dumping of unsold vegetables, in the West, Center, and South, became fairly common, as means of demonstrating anger against middlemen and against the government, accused of fixing at too low a level the price of the products which it controlled (such as wheat and milk) or of not achieving parity between industrial and agricultural prices. Though the government had made funds available through credit institutions (the *Caisses Nationales de Crédit Agricole*) to enable farmers to improve and modernize their plants, to buy tractors, and to increase the amount of fertilizers used in agriculture (in most cases French farmers used three or four times fewer fertilizers than Belgian, Dutch, and German farmers), discontent seemed to be rising as mechanization was spreading.

Yet the eventual attitude toward mechanization and modernization became gradually less negative as a result of the part played by groups of progressive younger farmers, in particular Roman Catholics. These accepted the long-term benefits of the "industrialization" of farms, which was to give them greater leisure and higher incomes. They endeavored to educate the farming community to participate in the modernization process and to promote the spread of cooperative ideas in a section of the population hitherto highly individualistic. They pressed first for more concerted action with respect to the leasing and buying of equipment, and increasingly with respect to various aspects of marketing in order to bypass middlemen. These views were channeled first through the *Jeunesse Agricole Chrétienne,* which had been created before World War II by the Church in order to stop the de-Christianization of the countryside but which gradually became independent from the hierarchy to be concerned with the problems of the farming community in general. Many farmers acquired as a result an awareness of social and political problems; this led them to create the *Centre National des Jeunes Agriculteurs* which became in the early 1960s a powerful challenging force to the more traditional FNSEA. As the CFDT among workers, the CNJA had helped to introduce both more competence of a technical character in the debates over the future of agriculture, as well as a humane and pluralistic approach to the role of farmers in the nation. Indeed, as CNJA leaders were not averse to State intervention, but looked on the contrary for a collaboration between the government and the farming community, they often allied with the civil servants in a common stand for modernization.

Not surprisingly, CNJA leaders came to clash increasingly with leaders of the FNSEA on the future of the farming community in a modernized economy. They challenged the traditional leadership at elections within the agricultural pressure group and were even successful for a period in the mid-1960s. The representatives of the larger farms succeeded in regaining control at subsequent elections, but the atmosphere had changed. Divisions between larger mechanized and smaller backward farms ceased to constitute the main cleavage; the only body which represented the older individualistic and antigovernment approach was the Communist-supported *Mouvement de Défense des Exploitations Familiales* (MODEF), which had some following in the central part of the country but had not succeeded in making a real breakthrough. In the middle of the flight from the land which characterized the 1960s, the condition of the remaining farmers could improve; technological change was assimilated. Slowly, personality clashes declined in importance; Michel Debatisse, the best known leader of the CNJA became president of the FNSEA without much opposition at the turn of the 1970s. Agriculture is the sector of French social life where the move away from tradition has been the largest, through a combination of internal education, government help, and expanding horizons. There is probably more genuine internal democracy than elsewhere, as well as more realism. Even if French agriculture has been markedly helped by the Common Market, the opportunity was seized, largely because the Christian youth movement was able, at the right moment, to channel discontent toward a more modern vision of the role of the farmer in the nation.

OTHER GROUPS

In particular since the mid-1960s, groups have come to play a regular part in the panorama of French political life. The development is still patchy and limited, admittedly, and the main associations remain those of anglers and hunters. Much of the expansion has also been due to imitation of groups in the U.S. and other European countries (indeed the expansion of many groups in Europe can probably be ascribed to the imitation of the U.S.). Moreover, some of the larger associations which defend sections of the community are constituted on political or semipolitical lines. Veterans' and pensioners' associations, for instance, were created by the Communist party after World War II and compete against noncommunist organizations. There are organizations which support private schools (mainly Church schools) and organizations which defend State schools; as we saw in Chapter One, the conflict between these groups led to very active demonstrations in the late 1950s, and the lull in their activities in the 1960s should not be interpreted as a sign of total discomfiture, let alone a proof of the end of the influence of party political divisions on group activity.

Yet a marked development of associationalism manifests itself through newly created consumer and environmental groups, particularly at the local level. In the early years of the Fifth Republic, France still differed markedly from her neighbors by the small part played by "interest groups," possibly because the campaign against the Algerian war mobilized the energies of potential protesters. While the nuclear disarmament campaign, for instance, reached its climax in Britain in the late 1950s and early 1960s, there was almost no equivalent in France, though the subject could have been alive, since de Gaulle had embarked on a worldwide nuclear strategy which was opposed by the Left. Thus the main upsurge of group activity at the turn of the 1960s was concentrated on Algeria and on the question of the institutions. Nineteen fifty-nine and 1960 saw the development of a variety of "clubs," primarily political in outlook, in some ways the heirs of the "salons" of the eighteenth century. These clubs (the most famous being the *Club Jean-Moulin*) sprang up in order to foster political discussion at a time when the institutions seemed to become increasingly authoritarian, though the collapse of the previous regime had shown that a major reform of attitudes and political structures had to be undertaken. Documents and even books were published as a result of club discussions, and they made some impact on the political process. One should not exaggerate their role; admittedly they were essentially Parisian affairs and grouped exclusively members of the upper middle class. But they probably had more influence on politics than they were given credit for by the "regular" politicians. They accustomed French leaders or would-be leaders, as well as the members of the bureaucracy, to view pragmatically all aspects of social and political problems and slowly induced the government to engage in discussions with the various "social partners" and thus to accept the inevitability of interest groups in the society.

But it was the Algerian problem which led to the creation of organizations of protesters. Some were underground, though others remained tolerated; some were more militant than others: the more extreme helped Algerians to flee from the police or young Frenchmen to desert from the army and live abroad. As none of the political parties was prepared to take an unambiguous line on Algeria, not even the Communist party, which was anxious to retain the support of rank-and-file workers often markedly opposed to Algerian fellow-workers, the antiwar organizations sprang up and developed in a much more independent fashion than the more classic defense groups. They received some support from some segments of the Catholic Church and of Christian organizations, but the hierarchy itself remained aloof. The strength of the protest movement on Algeria should not be exaggerated; there is no evidence that de Gaulle's policy was altered as a result of antiwar feeling. Yet a climate of greater pluralism was created; this was indicative of the changes in French society.

The end of the Algerian war in 1962 made antiwar groups obsolete. The gradual reassertion of the leadership of the opposition by the parties of the Left, both Socialist and Communist, made clubs less important, though some of their leaders were absorbed in the process of party realignments, as we shall see in the next chapter. But new groups were created. Consumer associations began to inquire into the quality of products, forms of marketing, and relative costs. Preservation societies started making a strong impact in the late 1960s, with some apparent success: they campaigned against the pollution of the seaside or the development of private beaches; they attacked the takeover of vast areas for army camps; they opposed plans for highways over good agricultural land or in residential areas. Some groups are purely local and are exclusively concerned with one issue, others have a national character and foster general aims. As in the United States and elsewhere, women's groups have been particularly active and have ceased to be mere appendages of the political parties (though the Communist *Union des Femmes Françaises* still exists) or of the Church; in 1971, a convention, known as the *Estates General of Women* took place, rather symbolically, at Versailles (where the 1789 Estates General had taken place) and showed that women's organizations were to be counted as a force in French political life.

Finally, perhaps the most active—or vocal—interest groups are those which promote various forms of regionalism. Long limited to the Bretons and (though less so) to the Basques, regionalist ideas have now extended to large parts of the country, particularly in the southern half, in which the militants of the *Mouvement Occitan* claim that an end must be put to the "colonization" of the country by the North and by Paris. The specific demands are somewhat vague; few suggest full independence and much remains at a purely cultural level. It is still sometimes difficult to distinguish romantic desires from really developed proposals. Yet these groups, as the environmental and preservation associations, suggest that the French have become increasingly association-conscious and are eager to take a greater share of the responsibility of conducting their own affairs. In a country where the bureaucracy has been overwhelmingly strong for decades and even centuries, the appearance of these groups constitutes a sign of profound change in the attitudes of citizens which State authorities can no longer dismiss.

GROUPS AND THE POLITICAL SYSTEM

The Fifth Republic began with an antigroup bias. De Gaulle was adamant to tame the lobbies, yet he was immediately confronted with protest on two traditional lines—the rights of veterans and the position of State schools. The government took little notice of the huge demonstrations which took place, and it won. Groups had showed their liveliness, but de Gaulle did seem to have proved his point: when the "State" is "strong," it can withstand the demands of groups. Gradually, however, trade unions, farmers' organizations, and shopkeepers' associations began to increase their pressure on the new regime, and it became slowly more difficult for the leaders of the Fifth Republic to ignore the demands, though the shadow of de Gaulle and the more executive-centered political system made it somewhat easier, for a period at least, to play down protest movements. But this "benign neglect" also led to an accumulation of grievances among all sections of society. It was clearly in part responsible for the scale of the explosion of May–June 1968, though the immediate causes of the turmoil were student demands (not all of which were unreasonable and most of which were due to the marked increase in the amount of higher education in the 1960s). Since 1968, leaders of the Fifth Republic have become more cautious. Attitudes of politicians and members of the bureaucracy have not wholly changed (and some changes had already occurred before —as between civil servants and leaders of farmers' unions), but the fear that a similar explosion might recur unquestionably played a part in the proposals for a new social policy, for a new "social contract" almost, which de Gaulle's successor, Georges Pompidou, and his first prime minister, Jacques Chaban-Delmas, tried to "sell" to the country and to the groups themselves.

Consultation is not an entirely new development in the French administrative process, admittedly. Its origins can be traced to the old monarchy and to the Napoleonic system. For the emperor, consultation was indeed a substitute for representation. The reduced status of the legislature was compensated for by the creation of a number of consultative councils, typically one or more in each ministry, but these were mostly staffed by civil servants. In the course of the nineteenth and twentieth centuries, consultative bodies became more representative; new ones were created, which included spokesmen for the various sections of the population who were concerned by the problem. When trade unions themselves were more inclined to collaborate with the government, after World War I, an economic council was instituted; it was to be given constitutional status in 1946 and in 1958. Composed of representatives of all sections of the nation (including consumers and "intellectuals"), it gives advice on bills and on the more important government regulations; it debates the Five Year Plans, and has done so increasingly seriously. Together with the many representative bodies on which trade unionists are present (boards of nationalized industries, social security boards) or to which farmers (*Chambres d'Agriculture*) or businessmen (*Chambres de Commerce*) are associated, the Economic and Social Council helps to give a large formal basis to the consultative process.

What had been lacking until very recently was therefore not a formal machinery for consultation, but a will to discuss or a climate in which projects and proposals were looked at by all concerned before they were made law. There was neither an automatic tendency to press for demands on the part of aggrieved persons, nor any real responsiveness on the part of the civil service, particularly at the regional and local levels. Consultation was viewed merely as the examination of drafts presented by the government. There was little or no "partnership" leading to the general discussion of problems before a solution was reached;

those who were consulted had therefore little or no opportunity to change policy. Only with one privileged sector, that of big business, did such a partnership exist; the personal ties between leaders of industry and higher civil servants made informal discussions possible and indeed frequent. For small business, agriculture, employees, and consumers, no similar relations existed. Admittedly, the uncooperative and unrealistic attitudes of many trade unions and of many other groups can be blamed, but these uncooperative attitudes were of course in part the product of an earlier lack of partnership.

The aim of the "new society" proposed by Chaban-Delmas in 1969 was in part to break the deadlock. It has been only partly achieved. The purpose was to generalize and improve on the consultative machinery which had been devised in relation with the plan, particularly at the local level, whereby social and economic leaders at the regional level were asked to make alternative suggestions to those proposed by the planners. This had been dismissed in some quarters as being a sham, the representatives of workers being always in a small minority. Thus, following the demands for greater participation at all levels which had been aired during the 1968 "Revolution," the government suggested a policy of "concertation" through which all, and workers in particular, were to benefit directly from the growth of the economy. "Contracts of progress" were to be negotiated within each branch of industry; bargaining was to become the norm, thus making it difficult for trade unions to maintain the spirit of aggressiveness against the State which had characterized them mostly in the past.

Because old attitudes are entrenched, a "new society" such as that outlined by Chaban-Delmas cannot be brought about in a short time. The policy did seem to have some impact, as the number of strikes was reduced in particular in the public sector. But the resentment against the government and the State is still common. By the time Chaban-Delmas left office in the summer of 1972, there was seemingly as much opposition to his policy (though some recognition of the honesty with which he held his views) as there was in the past to the policy of previous governments. The main difference was perhaps the extent to which the civil service seemed prepared to entertain opposition and to allow groups to participate in decisions relating to the environment. The characteristic speed with which the administration could decide on projects (the third Paris airport, for instance) seems to have given way to a recognition of the need for more consultation. Indeed, the change in attitudes seemed at times surprisingly rapid and appeared to affect the form, more than the content of decisions. But the need for "concertation" is at least recognized, and even repeated rebuffs by unions or other groups are unlikely to alter the course of a government which has been traumatized by the 1968 events.

The role of modern interest groups in the French political process is therefore increasing. Only in remote areas, now mostly depopulated, does the classic individualism of Frenchmen still fully prevail; even there, the old isolation from the main currents of society is fast diminishing. Representation takes place through national groups or through local groups (if grievances are local) with a potentially national structure. The role of the "notables" is no longer large; leaders do not emerge because they belong to a traditional elite, but because they succeed in mobilizing interests in a forceful, and at times extreme fashion (as with shopkeepers' organizations), or when they make a determined effort to educate members and to bring about greater cooperation (as with farmers' unions). Yet much has still to be done to reconcile Frenchmen with the basic need for and the real value of associations. As long as workers do not belong to unions, unions remain weak; as long as they are weak, their leaders feel ostracized and many resort to blanket opposition. Much has still to be done also, despite recent changes, to bring government and civil service nearer to the nation; a centralizing spirit, and centralized structures, form major handicaps to a real "partnership" between groups and the State. There, perhaps more than anywhere else, lies the major problem of French society.

5

The Party System

In the course of the 1960s, France moved from a loose and indeed almost indescribable configuration of parties to a streamlined system, simple to understand and fairly predictable in its developments. It is a multiparty system with a dominant party. It resembles the party systems of several European countries in the relative strength of its various components; it bears some relationship with the Italian party system, though it is less complex; it bears also some relationship with the multiparty systems with a dominant party which exist in most of Scandinavia, though the dominant party is in France on the Right, while it is on the Left in Scandinavia. Basically, France has a large, near-majority, conservative party, the "Gaullist" party, which has had various names since its creation in 1947 and has adopted the title of *Union des Démocrates pour la République* (UDR) since the late 1960s. Allied with the Gaullist party are a number of small groups of prominent individuals, usually fighting under the "Independent" label; these have been associated with Gaullism since the beginning of the Fifth Republic and constitute somewhat difficult satellites of the major party. On the other side of the political spectrum, two medium-sized parties share the electorate of the Left somewhat unequally: the Communist party and the Socialist party, the Communist party being rather larger. The Left also includes some tiny groupings and one small party, the United Socialist party. A variety of attempts have been, and continue to be made, to tie Socialists and Communists more closely together. Between Right and Left, two parties (in essence only the remnants of a more brilliant past) at times work together and at times pull in opposite directions: the Radical party, somewhat comparable to Liberal parties elsewhere in Europe, usually leans toward the Left; the "Center party" (*Progrès et Démocratie Moderne* or PDM) leans toward the Right, being composed of men who were originally either conservatives or Christian Democrats mildly opposed to Gaullism but often prepared to work with and support the majority party.

The Gaullists and their independent allies mustered regularly since 1962 about 45 percent of the electorate. The two parties of the Left jointly receive between 33 percent and 40 percent of the vote. The two groups of the Center can count on only about 15 percent of the vote; they are thus in a weak position which contrasts with their key position before 1958, when they belonged to almost every government. Divisions between Communists and Socialists continue indirectly to help parties of the Center; yet a tendency toward the polarization of politics developed as a result of the dominance of the Gaullists. If the UDR remains a broadly based conservative party throughout the 1970s, further steps toward the streamlining of the system are likely to be taken.

THE UDR AND ITS ALLIES

The UDR. The Build-up of the Gaullist Majority in the Fifth Republic

On December 2, 1958, the French woke up to find to their surprise that the newly created *Union pour la Nouvelle République* could muster, together with deputies elected by Algeria who were deemed at the time to support de Gaulle's policies, a majority in the first Parliament of the Fifth Republic. But the result was soon interpreted as exceptional. Admittedly, the Gaullist party had jumped from 18 to 26 percent of the votes from the first to the second ballot of the single-majority system which had been reintroduced for the first time since World War II, as we shall see in Chapter Seven. Yet, although this electoral system had been adopted as a compromise deemed to favor traditional parties and parties of the Center in particular, the outcome had been the rallying of many electors to often unknown candidates of the Gaullist party. But France had already known a "Gaullist wave"

ELECTIONS TO THE NATIONAL ASSEMBLY SINCE WORLD WAR II

A. *Percentage of votes cast for each party (metropolitan France only)*

	Total Votes (millions)	Comm.	Soc.	Rad. & Ass.	MRP	Ind. Cons.	Gaull.	Other
1945	19.2	26.5	24	11	25	13	—	0.5
1946 June	19.9	26	21	11.5	28	13	—	0.5
1946 November	19.2	28	18	11	26	16	—	1
1951	18.9	26	14.5	10.5	13	12	22.5	1.5
1956	21.5	26	15	15.5	11	15	4	13.5 (mainly Poujadists)
1958 1st ballot	20.5	19	15.5	11.5	11.5	23	17.5	2
1958 2nd ballot	18.0	20.5	14	8	7.5	23.5	26.5	—
1962 1st ballot	18.3	22	15	8	9	15	32	—
1962 2nd ballot	15.2	21.5	16.5	7	5	9.5	40.5	—

	Total Votes (millions)	Comm.	Federation and Other Left	Democratic Center	Gaullists & Independent Gaullists	Other
1967 1st ballot	22.9	22.4	21.0	12.8	37.8	6.0
1967 2nd ballot	18.8	21.4	25.0	7.1	42.6	3.9
1968 1st ballot	22.5	20.0	21.2	10.3	43.6	4.9
1968 2nd ballot	14.6	20.1	22.3	7.8	46.4	3.4
1973 1st ballot	24.3	21.2	23.6	12.4	38.4	4.1
1973 2nd ballot	21.3	20.6	26.4	6.1	46.3	0.6

B. Seats (France and overseas)

	Total Seats	Comm.	Soc.	Rad. & Ass.	MRP	Ind. Cons.	Gaull.	Other
1945	586	161	150	57	150	64	—	4
1946 June	586	153	129	53	169	67	—	15
1946 November	618	183	105	70	167	71	—	22
1951	627	101	107	95	96	98	120	10
1956	596	150	99	94	84	97	22	50 (mainly Poujadists)
1958	578	10	47	40	64	129	206	81 (mainly from Algeria)
1962	480	41	67	45	38	51	234	4

	Total Seats	Comm.	Federation and Other Left	Democratic Center	Gaullists & Independent Gaullists	Other
1967	486	73	121	30	244	18
1968	487	34	57	27	296	9
1973	490	73	104	32	262	19

in 1951; the 1958 election was therefore seen by some as a repetition of a previous Gaullist success which had proved short-lasting. The fear of the unknown—indeed of a military coup—if de Gaulle were to retire could explain why many electors had plumped for the UNR. In somewhat similar circumstances, the earlier Gaullist party, the *Rassemblement du Peuple Français*, had obtained great successes at the municipal election of 1947; it gained 22 percent of the votes at the 1951 general election, only to collapse to less than 4 percent in 1956.

Four years later, it was difficult to interpret the result as a mere "Gaullist wave." At the first ballot of the 1962 election, the UNR had obtained 32 percent of the votes; this was a breakthrough and indeed an entirely new departure in French electoral history, as no party had previously obtained even as many as 30 percent of the votes. Yet the results of the second ballot, a week later, were even more astounding; the UNR received 40 percent of the votes and elected 229 members of Parliament for metropolitan France (almost exactly half). Many had been elected in direct competition with supporters of "French Algeria," now bitterly opposed to de Gaulle. Overall, the UNR needed 242 members to muster an absolute majority; with some overseas supporters it could muster 234. It could count on about two dozen faithful supporters who had been elected with the Gaullist label, mostly from among the "Independents," though a few had also been originally Christian Democrats. France had come near to majority government in 1958, almost without noticing it; the voters repeated, and indeed confirmed the trend at the subsequent election.

The Gaullist party thus became recognized as the largest French party, though the true extent of the transformation of French electoral habits was underestimated or simply not noticed. Thus, though the result of the 1967 election was a mild setback for the Gaullists and their allies (a few seats were lost and the majority became paper thin), the underlying long-term trend was confirmed. There was no return to the pre-1958 situation where a number of small and medium-sized parties could enter a variety of complex governmental combinations. In fact, the 1967 election more than consolidated the new party system and the strength of the Gaullist party. It was followed, little more than a year later, by the dissolution of Parliament in the wake of the 1968 "Revolution"; the elections brought back—again largely to the surprise of observers—an unprecedented Gaullist majority, with UDR candidates obtaining 44 percent of the votes at the first ballot and over 45 percent at the second and gaining 360 seats out of 487. The fear of the Left and the multiplying effect of the majority system had produced this exceptional result. But the 1973 election continued to surprise observers by merely reducing the Gaullist majority; helped by the still prevailing fear of the Communists, the Gaullists sustained the attack of the Left remarkably well at the first ballot and rallied most electors of the Center at the second, thus ending with over 270 seats out of 490 in the National Assembly.

Ups and Downs of Gaullism in the Fourth Republic

The temporary ups and downs of the Gaullist party are therefore less important for French politics than the seemingly permanent feature of a majority party. Yet, as observers often noted, the UDR is scarcely a mass party in the normal European sense. In this it differs markedly from the RPF of the late forties. When de Gaulle retired for the first time early in 1946, he spent some months in total silence in his retreat of Colombey in eastern France and came out in the open only after the French people had rejected the first draft of the constitution which had been presented to them. At first, he simply let a *"Union Gaulliste"* emerge in Parliament, spoke his mind about the role of the president in a speech at Bayeux which was to remain famous, and saw with pleasure a third of the electorate abstain on the second draft of the constitution (which was adopted only with a slim majority). In the middle of 1947, he launched a new movement, which was pointedly called a "Rally" (*Rassemblement*); this was in part because de Gaulle wanted to indicate that what he was creating was different from all the other movements (he excluded only Communists whom he called "separatists" at the time and attacked violently); this was also because he was cunningly hoping to attract to the Rally politicians who would still remain in their party. He did indeed succeed in creating much havoc among some parties, to the eventual detriment of the RPF, as we shall see. The Rally was an immediate success and seemed to pose a direct threat to the Fourth Republic, which had scarcely begun its existence; at a time when the Communists were thrown into opposition and started a series of massive strikes, the RPF fought ruthlessly against the institutions of the regime and seemed to find a profound echo in the population. At its first electoral contest, the municipal elections of 1947, the Gaullists swept in most large towns, obtaining as many as 40 percent of the votes. De Gaulle started a campaign for the dissolution of Parliament and organized his Rally to fight the election which he assumed would soon come.

The opposition to the Gaullist party was bitter among supporters of the Fourth Republic because, much more than the UNR at any time since the beginning of the Fifth Republic, "the Rally of the French People" smacked dangerously of fascism both in its organization and in its ideology. Authority and power were concentrated at the top and subordinate organizations of the party were asked only to show discipline. Admittedly, some "notables," whether Conservatives (mainly from the West), Radicals, or Christian Democrats, joined the new movement. But the structure was one of hierarchical leadership flowing through a network of professional cadres enlisting thousands of rank-and-file members. At one time, the Rally did even claim to have a million members, more than any French political movement ever had before or afterward. But these members were viewed as an army of followers of the leader who, alone or nearly alone, took the decisions and who had little patience, indeed only disgust, for committees and "conventions": these were known as *Assises Nationales* and organized to present to the outside world the disciplined enthusiasm of followers, not to debate matters of policy.

The policies were, on the whole, those of an authoritarian Right. Admittedly, de Gaulle was to believe consistently in the idea of collaboration between capital and labor. A profit-sharing scheme was put forward, with which the name of Louis Vallon, a progressive Gaullist, was associated, but the details of which were scarcely worked out in practice. The bulk of the thinking was nationalistic, strongly anti-Communist (support came to the Rally mainly for this reason), and somewhat reactionary on colonial matters (particularly on Indochina), though the position of the leader on this question was kept ambiguous. What was more apparent than ideology was the physical presence of the movement. French political life, normally complex, individualistic, and tiresome, is not usually ugly, but, with the appearance of the RPF, fighting started to break out, local Communist party headquarters were burnt, even thugs appeared. Later the Poujadists and even later the supporters of French Algeria were to do rather worse, though they did not quite reach the level of German pre-1933 politics, but it could be said that the Gaullists had shown the way. Some Communist retaliation took place and a repetition of the last years of the Weimar Republic or of pre-Mussolini Italy seemed in process.

This explains largely the opposition which the RPF met in many quarters—an opposition which lasted into the Fifth Republic, made the call for de Gaulle difficult in 1958, and probably accounts for the underlying feelings against de Gaulle and Gaullism in a large section of the political class even in the 1970s. But this sense of disgust was long to be associated with a sense of failure, as de Gaulle and the other RPF leaders clearly underestimated the stubbornness of the politicians of the Fourth Republic. Far from giving in to de Gaulle's demand for elections, leaders of the Center parties engaged in a process of containment and slow attrition of the Gaullist party. First through skillful maneuvers, and second with the help of the apparent good sense of the French people, the tide receded. When elections took place at their normal time, in 1951, the Gaullists, somewhat handicapped by a new electoral law, succeeded only in obtaining little over 20 percent of the votes and in electing 120 members of Parliament (less than a fifth of the assembly of the Fourth Republic, which was larger than that of the Fifth); many of these RPF members were old parliamentarians simply hanging on to Gaullist coattails. This enabled Fourth Republic leaders to give the last blow. The Gaullists had hoped to break the coalition of the parties of the Center by bringing up the question of State aid to Church schools, which sharply divided clericals from anticlericals in the ruling coalition. The ruling parties retaliated by splitting the Gaullist party instead. A Conservative, Antoine Pinay, was chosen prime minister; he presented a program which appealed to the conservative-minded Gaullists who voted for Pinay and left the RPF. The rest of the Rally was badly shaken; in the country, members ceased to pay their dues, failed to turn up at meetings, and finally left. De Gaulle, sorely shaken in his pride (for the second time he had been unable to impose his views), disbanded the movement in 1953. The few Gaullists who remained entered governmental coalitions and behaved like other politicians: in the 1956 election they were mostly defeated. Only twenty-two returned, electors of the extreme Right having found Poujadists more to their liking.

THE STRUCTURE OF THE UDR

Thus, in 1958, the record of de Gaulle in the minds of many liberals, politicians and observers alike, was both one of failure and one of having posed a serious threat to democratic institutions. Thus, not surprisingly, few were profoundly impressed by the 1958 result; not surprisingly either, many predicted the break-up of the newly formed UNR, which seemed torn between sympathies for French Algeria and the tortuous policy of decolonization of the leader. But de Gaulle had learned his lesson; he no longer had trust in large mass movements, nor was he to allow politicians of the old guard to enter the new organization which he was creating, since the RPF had been lost in 1952 through these politicians. The UNR was formed from above; it was to enlist only truly faithful supporters of de Gaulle, those who had been with him consistently since the war years. Its first secretary-general was to be a businessman entirely new to politics, Albin Chalandon, who owed to de Gaulle his newly acquired position. The UNR was also to be somewhat less rigid than the RPF. More importantly perhaps, the party was to be much smaller; no effort was made to attract a mass rank-and-file, as this could not be trusted at a time when passions were running high on the Algerian problem. De Gaulle could hope, through various forms of patronage, to manipulate members of Parliament or an executive committee, but hundreds of thousands of members would have been dominated by factions and would have constituted the basis of a powerful machine against de Gaulle himself. Indeed, almost immediately, at one of the first UNR congresses, an attempt was made to take over the party. This might have been successful had the membership been larger and Albin Chalandon's men less skillful, in particular in preventing Jacques Soustelle's pro-French Algeria supporters from infiltrating the party in large numbers.

The UNR thus never was a movement in the sense that the RPF had been. It started primarily as a parliamentary party plus committees at the national level and in the provinces. These were held together by bonds of loyalty. Of course, the leadership included some well-known personalities; indeed a number of these had had to be accepted as candidates to Parliament because of their record of help to de Gaulle in the last few weeks which had preceded his return to power. These were the ones who were to prove unreliable almost immediately, but they constituted only a very small part of the 1958 party. The open rebellion of men such as Soustelle was therefore to have scarcely any impact on the parliamentary rank-and-file. A few left, at different times during the early years; they went out of politics, their names being almost forgotten a decade or so later. Those who remained loyal were to be recompensed by being returned to Parliament in 1962 and in subsequent elections. By having chosen mostly unknown men to form the bulk of the parliamentary party of 1958, de Gaulle avoided repeating the mistake of 1951 while giving France for the first time a disciplined conservative party.

In the course of the following years—where any danger of split in the party had wholly receded—the organization was somewhat expanded, but never to reach the proportions of the old RPF, nor indeed of a truly organized party elsewhere in the West. The major reorganization took place in 1967, when the UNR became the UDR. The structure of the secretariat was changed, as well as much of its personnel; regional bodies were better staffed and made more alive, while the basic unit became the parliamentary constituency, the function of this unit being mainly to select the parliamentary candidate and help him during his election campaign. Despite efforts made at local elections in the early 1970s, the UDR is still primarily a party at the national parliamentary level as well as in a number of large and medium-sized towns; it is not truly implanted locally. Some effort has been made to compete with the traditional elites, but this has had only moderate success, possibly because the position of Gaullists at the national level remains better assured if support at the national level can be traded against neutrality locally.

Efforts have also been made to expand the membership somewhat, but this has remained small. While the party had probably around 50,000 members in the early 1960s, it had somewhat over three times that figure in the early 1970s. Membership drives occur from time to time; they seem neither to be pushed hard nor to be really successful. More efforts are made to integrate substantial numbers of supporters (though not the "masses" in the true sense of the word) through a number of ancillary or satellite organizations, of women or young people, for instance; there are also bodies emphasizing their personal allegiance to de Gaulle, some of which sprang up, seemingly suddenly and almost from nowhere, after the turmoil of 1968. Various "clubs" or "institutes" of an apparently semiacademic character have the public relations function of producing a flow of pamphlets and press statements and thus of giving an impression of intellectual liveliness to the Gaullist movement.

Not much changed in the structure of the UDR after de Gaulle's disappearance. The president of the Republic, Georges Pompidou, who was chosen as the party's presidential candidate without opposition almost immediately after de Gaulle resigned, is the real head of the party. The secretary-general never achieved, nor indeed aimed at achieving, true political influence; he is, as Chalandon was at the start, the key "manipulator" on behalf of the leader. His role is to run the party efficiently, to dampen internal opposition, and to generate enthusiasm. He does contribute from time to time to political debates (as René Tomasini did in the early 1970s over vexed questions of "toughness" against students and other "agitators"), but this seemed primarily to be for internal party consumption; it seemed necessary to reassure supporters distressed at seeing the government becoming "soft" (as the reform of university structures seemed to suggest). Neither under de Gaulle—except in the troubled period of 1958–1960—nor under Pompidou—perhaps more surprisingly—has the leadership of the president of the Republic been seriously challenged by members of the UDR, whether in Parliament or outside.

The UDR is thus in no way the fascist party which the RPF seemed to have been earlier. It is not fascist in its organization. It is not fascist in its ideology and program, indeed it has often been criticized for having no program. The only point on which it seemed the whole party had a clearly expressed view in 1958 was Algeria, which it wanted to see remain French, and after less than four years, it agreed to a settlement which meant complete separation. Hence the sneer that the UDR has been de Gaulle's poodle and has had to accept from above, without discussion or participation, all of its policies. This is exaggerated, first because Gaullist parliamentarians and the rank-and-file at large trusted de Gaulle to find a solution—a solution which the politicians of the Fourth Republic had proved unable to find, and indeed entrusted de Gaulle to find—and second because on other matters a "community of feeling" or a common approach has existed between de Gaulle and his supporters in Parliament and else-where. Of course, many would have disagreed about tactics whether in foreign affairs or home affairs, but both in foreign affairs and in home affairs, most Gaullists agreed on the basic aims. The idea of French independence vis-à-vis the United States (and the Communist World), the desire to enhance France's prestige through aid to the Third World, and other somewhat dubious symbolic manifestations of "greatness" were shared between de Gaulle and his followers, as was shared a certain view of the relationship between employer and employee which was epitomized by the idea of profit-sharing between capital and labor. Gaullism always had a "populist" streak which distin-guished it somewhat from conservatism and which nearly all supporters, and in particular the "unknown" faithful, approved and indeed enthusiastically underwrote.

Yet it would be wrong to view the party as monolithic. Discipline is strong in the Gaullist parliamentary party, but it is accepted and "whips" have never been imposed in a ruthless fashion. In parliamentary debates, criticisms may not have been voiced on major matters, but they are often expressed on less important questions. This is because of the agreement on aims which we just described; this is also because internal committees of the party allow a more open and freer discussion than is usually assumed, in a way which is broadly similar to the style of the British Conservative party to which the UDR can be compared in many ways. De Gaulle thus succeeded in creating a party where the broad mass of members of Parliament have a sense of loyalty to the leadership and recognize that governments have, in general, to be followed. But the corollary has also been, on the part of the government, both under de Gaulle and under his successor, that attention is paid, more than is usually given credit for, to the feelings and basic sentiments of the rank-and-file. Georges Pompidou was hailed as a successful prime minister between 1962 and 1968 precisely because he paid attention to members of Parliament. Conversely, prime ministers have been dismissed in part because they lost touch with or failed to lead the parliamentarians. There has always been a substantial rotation of the various office-holders, in part to ensure a circulation of "elites," in part to help new policies to be started. There is clearly a need for greater influence for the rank-and-file, as well as for greater attention to be given to the party program. Yet it is a substantial achievement that, in a country which has almost constantly oscillated between uncontrolled individualism and ruthless authoritarianism, the Gaullist party should have kept together men holding very different views as well as a large electorate, while remaining at least tolerably liberal in its methods of government and pluralistic in its relationship with groups in society.

THE ALLIES OF THE GAULLIST PARTY

In 1958, the first government of the Fifth Republic included Socialists, Radicals, Christian Democrats, Independent Conservatives as well as Gaullists. Gradually, however, most of these parties withdrew their support, the only element which remained faithful during the whole period being a fraction of the Conservatives led by one of the most brilliant ministers of finance that France had had for generations, Valéry Giscard d'Estaing. Since the late 1960s, some individuals, ex-Radicals or ex-Christian

Democrats, came to join the government, as efforts were made to broaden the base of the administration and to project a "consensual" image. Thus the allies (some might say satellites) of the Gaullist party tend to include personalities of various origins, mostly without party following though usually endowed with personal support in their constituency, such as Edgar Faure in his district near the Swiss border. The satellite group which can be described as a party is thus constituted by the "Giscardiens" conservatives, though even they should primarily be seen as the network of the "friends" of their leader, while some elements of the Center have also gradually come into the orbit of the majority. These are also almost all that remains of the Independent Conservative party which, during the Fourth Republic and in the early years of the Fifth, seemed promised to the destiny of ruling the country.

Conservatives had been badly shaken by the war and occupation—many had collaborated with the Vichy regime; they suffered a marked defeat in 1945, obtaining only 13 percent of the votes. Efforts were made to streamline groups which had been profoundly divided, mainly on personality lines, as they represented the "notables" in the constituencies. A first attempt was made under the name of *Parti Républicain de la Liberté,* but this soon proved a failure. A second effort led to the creation of the *Centre National des Indépendants et Paysans,* a rather loose federal body which most conservative members of Parliament did indeed join. The CNIP won almost a hundred seats at the 1951 general election, though largely as a result of the change in the electoral system, since the number of votes cast for its candidates did not increase (due to Gaullist competition). Yet Conservatives were soon to attract more supporters in Parliament, by achieving, under Antoine Pinay, the break-up of the RPF. Pinay did indeed become the symbol of French conservatism for a decade, having gained popularity almost overnight with a program of rigid financial orthodoxy and an appearance of honesty; his influence was such that de Gaulle himself felt obliged to ask him to become his first minister of finance when he returned to power in 1958. Pinay started a plan of financial solvency which was to bring the franc back into the group of strong currencies. Meanwhile, the

Conservatives had succeeded in breaking yet another extreme right-wing group, the Poujadists, whose strong words during the election campaign of 1956 were followed by much weaker deeds when they came to Parliament in the wake of the shopkeepers' and other small men's discontent. Independent Conservatives seemed therefore likely to break the Gaullist party again in the early 1960s as they had broken the RPF in the 1950s.

Indeed, Independent Conservatives, as much as the UNR, seemed to have won the election of 1958. They returned 130 to the smaller chamber of the Fifth Republic and won almost a quarter of the votes—nearly as many as the Gaullists. More conservative than the Gaullists in home affairs (and definitely favoring capitalism in the classic sense), pro-American in foreign affairs, they were markedly divided over Algeria. Being unable to adopt a clear policy on this issue—after 1958 as well as before—they were obliged to follow de Gaulle's lead. As most other parties, they accepted in fact the sinuous tactics of the president, though some became bitterly opposed to the idea of independence which began to appear inevitable from 1961. When this eventually occurred, the occasion seemed bound to reunite the independent party, as most of its members had tolerated but not liked de Gaulle. The bulk of the Conservatives indeed came to see an opportunity to ally once more, as under the Fourth Republic, with the parties of the Center, Radicals and Christian Democrats, and even with the Socialists, to oust the government and effectively return to the old system. But, in 1962, unlike 1952, they could not split the UNR; it was de Gaulle who split the Conservatives. Most of those Conservatives who had voted against the government in the censure motion which preceded the dissolution were defeated: 108 left the Assembly and 28 returned. Those who had remained loyal, primarily under Giscard d'Estaing, were recompensed, though they, too, suffered a minor setback, since 8 out of 28 were defeated at the polls. Despite occasional strains with the Gaullists, this group of Conservatives, renamed *Républicains Indépendants,* was to remain loyal throughout the following decade; they were also to be the only Conservatives to participate in policy-making.

The Independent Republicans, however, have come to be so close to the Gaullists that it is difficult to distinguish their policies from those of the UDR. On the whole, Giscard d'Estaing has been more orthodox in his financial policies than Gaullists would have preferred; he is possibly also less anti-American. But differences are fine, particularly after de Gaulle, in part because of the difficulties experienced by Giscard d'Estaing when he first launched a program of stabilization in 1963 which led to a decrease in economic growth and was one of the causes of the 1968 turmoil. Dropped from the government by de Gaulle, he remained for several years at the border between support and opposition. Yet possibly because of the gradual influence of the new institutions, Independent Republicans supported Pompidou for the presidency and their leader returned to head the French treasury, though having become less orthodox financially, and more of a nationalist in foreign policy. The Independent Republican party is therefore little more than a satellite, though it does maintain a separate organization and concludes "electoral pacts" with the UDR. A major setback for the UDR would have to occur for the Independent Republicans to become more autonomous from their major ally and for Conservatives in general to become once more a strong component of the French party system.

THE LEFT

THE COMMUNIST PARTY

France is one of the four countries of Western Europe which has a large Communist party, the others being Italy, Finland, and tiny Iceland. This situation has always puzzled observers, both French and foreign, and it is becoming daily more puzzling. Simple economic explanations are obviously not sufficient; the standard of living is as high in France as in other Western European countries, indeed higher than in some; development is as fast, and expectations should be similar. Those who in the late forties hoped that an improvement of living conditions would be accompanied by a substantial Communist decrease have been disappointed. The Communist vote was somewhat reduced, but not at the time and not for economic reasons. While countries with medium-sized Communist parties after the war (such as

Belgium or Sweden, where the electoral strength of the Communists was in the region of 10 percent) saw this support dwindle, the countries where the Communist party received between 20 and 25 percent of the votes experienced great stability on the extreme Left. In France, the only inroads in the Communist electorate were due to de Gaulle; the Constitution of 1958 was adopted by 80 percent of the voters, among whom were perhaps a fifth of the Communists. At the general election of 1958, the Communist vote slumped from 5.5 to 3.9 million, but it remained stable in 1962, the party receiving just over 4 million votes; as abstention was higher, the percentage of votes cast for the CP (Communist party) rose from 19 percent in 1958 to 22 percent in 1962 and 1967. It fell to 20 percent in 1968 and remained almost static in 1973. The Fourth Republic started with 28 percent of the votes cast for the Communists; after a quarter of a century of opposition and after considerable changes have taken place in the social and economic structure of the country, the party has lost only a quarter of its votes and there are still no signs of a further fall.

As we noted in Chapter Three, one reason for the strength of the Communist party is historical; the party benefited from the "law of leftward movement of parties." The Socialist party was somewhat discredited in the eyes of left-wingers at the end of World War I. Discontent was widespread among members of Parliament and in the rank-and-file. The break took place in 1920, at a congress at Tours, over the question of joining the Communist International. A majority of members of the Socialist party, anarchists as well as Communists, followed the minority of members of Parliament who created the "French Section of the Communist International." But the beginnings were difficult; numbers slumped by the late 1920s and results at the polls were discouraging. As we shall see in Chapter Seven, the electoral system benefited the Center parties, and electors preferred to vote Socialist or Radical on the second ballot—disregarding tactics of isolation put forward by the Communists. By 1932—a good election year for the Left—the Communists had little to be complacent about. They had ten seats in Parliament; they were in a splendid and impotent political isolation, and had found little support among the organized workers.

Recovery came from a change of tactics—and from the fact that the Socialists agreed too easily to these new tactics. From 1934 onward, the Communists began a campaign in favor of "working class unity." They disbanded their trade union, the CGTU, as we saw in Chapter Four, and advised their members to join the CGT which was under Socialist influence at the time. They brandished the "fascist menace" and succeeded in convincing Socialists and Radicals to agree to a popular front alliance for the general election of 1936. This was to be the real Communist starting point. Gaining 15 percent of the votes, over eighty members of Parliament, an almost entire hold on the Red Belt (a heavily Communist-controlled area immediately outside Paris), some successes in the countryside, as well as a foothold in the trade unions and the opportunity to hold the newly created Socialist government to ransom (by supporting it though refusing to participate in it), the Communist party suddenly became a power in the land, which it had never been before, but which it has not ceased to be up to the present day.

The *Résistance* provided a second boost to the extreme Left. Up to 1941, when the war was labeled "bourgeois" and "imperialist" by Russia, the French Communists refused to participate in the defense of the country (their members of Parliament were dismissed in 1939) and even supported the Germans in the early period. But, after the Nazi invasion of the Soviet Union, the Communist party took a leading part in the *Résistance*. It gained considerable prestige as a result (nicknaming itself the *parti des fusillés*, the Party of the Shot), successfully infiltrated the underground trade union organizations, and made inroads in parts of the countryside (particularly in those regions which the *Résistance* had freed from the Germans and had controlled long before the Liberation). De Gaulle had no alternative but to offer them posts in the government which he created in the summer of 1944 on his return to France. At that time, however, the Communists appear to have genuinely believed that they could take over power by legal means, and their secretary-general and leader, Maurice

Thorez, who became vice-president of the Council of Ministers, made unceasing efforts to boost production and reconstruction. By the end of 1945, however, troubles arose over de Gaulle's refusal to give them one of the key ministries; a year and a half later, in May 1947, they left the government, never to return. With the intensification of the cold war, they used trade union strength to harass the government (the strikes of November 1947 were among the most difficult episodes of postwar French politics). But the government won, and the Communist challenge became less and less effective, and proved increasingly unpopular among the working class. By the end of the Fourth Republic, the Communist party was a nuisance, not a menace; it could help anyone, Gaullist, Conservatives, even Poujadists, as much as Socialists, to overthrow governments, but it could do little to achieve its own aims.

By then, the French Communist party had come to be criticized for its complacency, its total lack of life, as much as for its own internal dictatorial methods. Purges had taken place from time to time; these had enabled Maurice Thorez to remain at the helm of a large machine (potential successors were successively "shown" to be wrong or traitors to the party). But vitality seemed missing. While the Italian Communist party under Togliatti's leadership gave signs of independence and vigor, the French counterpart remained Stalinist for years after the death of Stalin, felt no official worries over Hungary, urged no liberalization; it simply repeated the theory of the impoverishment of the proletariat in capitalist regimes, a classic, though by then wholly inaccurate, part of the Marxist-Leninist doctrine. This enabled the party to weather its defeat of 1958 without much trouble, but it did not make for a very rosy future. In the early 1960s, however, signs of liberalization became more numerous, though they remained limited and lukewarm and have always been followed by a return to doctrinal rigidity. Ideological troubles arose among Communist students, particularly in Paris. The strength of left-wing groups fighting against de Gaulle or against the Algerian war, the loosening of the grip of Maurice Thorez (who died in 1964) and his replacement by Waldeck-Rochet, a leader endowed with the qualities of the fox rather than those of the lion, accounted for the slow unfreezing. Above all, perhaps, the appearance of a majority government on the Right brought home more clearly than before the fact that the Communists were condemning both themselves and the whole of the Left to remaining perpetually in the wilderness if they maintained a rigid doctrinal purity. At the presidential election of 1965, the dilemma was clear, and Waldeck-Rochet gave in. Faced with having to choose between launching a Communist candidate, who would gain only Communist votes and show the isolation of the party, and supporting a Center Left candidate, the Communists finally took a momentous decision: no Communist candidate was to be run, while the party was to support actively the common candidate of the Left, Mitterand. It was the first time since 1932 that a major contest was to take place in France without a Communist in the field.

Yet later developments remained slow and hesitant. Admittedly, also for the first time in its history, in August 1968, the French CP dared to voice a criticism of the Soviet Union and (though in a somewhat lukewarm manner) attacked the occupation of Czechoslovakia, not to come back to the subject again until four years later when some disquiet was voiced at the political trials which took place in the same country as a result of the "normalization" process. This latter criticism was probably due more than in part to the need to placate the Socialist party, with which the CP had just allied with the Socialists to form not merely an electoral part, but a governmental alliance based on a "Common Program of the Left."

POPULAR SUPPORT AND STRUCTURE

Why, thus, is the French Communist party so strong electorally and what do Communist electors think they do when they vote for the party? Tradition plays a large part, of course, but one of the most potent political factors has been the fact that the Communist leadership has succeeded in draining to its advantage the anarchistic tendencies of the disgruntled working class and the antigovernment ("anti-them") attitudes of sections of the peasantry and the petty-bourgeoisie. On the one hand, manual workers have long felt that the CP was the only party which was irrevocably prepared to stand for them. Whatever the palinodes of the Soviet Union (the Soviet Union is the "land of the working class" and it has to be defended, although the same apparently does not apply to China!), the manual workers felt that only by voting Communist could they protest against the government, the employers, the bourgeois system in general. These feelings, on the other hand, are linked to the antiestablishment and egalitarian tendencies of other sections of the community. They are naturally more marked in the parts of the country which are more individualistic, less prepared to accept organizations, such as the Center and the Southeast (all along the Mediterranean coastline), than in the East and West. They do account for the paradox that the most anarchistic or individualistic of Frenchmen can conceive of the Communist vote as a natural mode of expression.

It is often said that the Communist vote is a protest vote, and that it is only that. It is clearly a protest vote, but it is an exaggeration to see in the Communist voters just Socialist electors who vote in another way. Surveys by the French Institute of Public Opinion have shown conclusively that there was a "Communist conscience," to take the expression of the author who analyzed them, Pierre Fougeyrollas. All other groups in society (including workers) believe that it is not possible to increase wages and salaries without affecting the price levels, but Communist voters do not. All other voters have supported European integration for a long time; as early as 1950, electors of all social groups (including workers) were favorable, but Communist voters were strongly opposed. Very few (5 percent) of the Communist voters felt any indignation at the Hungarian repression of 1956, while 22 percent were happy and 28 percent relieved. A majority of Communists have consistently felt that the United States was preparing an aggressive war, while the percentage of voters of other parties who condemned the United States on this score has always been minute. This is not to say that Communist voters disagree on all matters with the rest of French electors and that there is no consensus on any problem; there is consensus on a "neutral" policy, among all parties, as there was consensus against the governmental instability of the Fourth Republic and on some other, rather negative, attitudes. But the cleavages between Communist voters and the rest of the population are sharp on many important issues, and these are far from being concerned only with foreign affairs.

The existence of such a self-contained group having attitudes which conflict, in many ways, with those of the rest of the population, must be accounted for. It seems that the fact that the Communist party has been both a large and tightly knit organization for over a generation has much to do with it. The Communist party is the only French party which can be deemed to have created a "society," and a very disciplined and hierarchical one at that. Not that the membership is exceptionally large, at least by world standards (although by French standards it is considerable); there are about 300,000 to 400,000 paid-up members (or about 8 percent of the voters). But these members have been, for long periods in the case of many, tied to the party through the network of cells (of a few members, mostly on the basis of residence, despite the somewhat unsuccessful efforts of the party to create large numbers of factory cells), of section, departmental (county), and national organizations. Decisions are taken on the basis of "democratic centralism"—the classic Communist expression which is alleged to mean that proposals are discussed but that no criticism is allowed once the measure has been adopted. In fact, the system makes for little democracy and considerable centralization, since most members have no opportunity to know how decisions have been taken, reports being always fragmentary and designed to *explain* decisions taken rather than inform (a "bourgeois" notion) on debates and viewpoints. The Party Congress meets in principle every two years though not in fact (with a smaller conference called in the years in which the Congress does not meet); it is not a forum for discussion but a place where the members of the two inner bodies, the Central Committee (a body of about 100 which meets every month) and the Executive (a body of about twenty which meets every week), expound the problems, trounce deviationists, and rally support to the cause. Most important of all, as in the other CPs, is the Secretariat, headed by the secretary-general, who is the leader of the party. Never has there been any major rank-and-file revolt, nor indeed any trouble from the parliamentary party.

Nor, indeed, would a revolt be possible. This is not only

because the heads of the federations and sections, as well as of the cells, are devoted to (and controlled by) the leadership, and aim at "explaining" problems to the mass of followers. It is also because the Communist society is such that any one who leaves the party, after having spent years within the fold, finds himself an outcast, without friends and leisure activities. This, of course, is not the case for very top people who, after leaving the CP, may write about their experiences, be sought by other politicians, or indeed create another party. But the ordinary faithful are not so well placed. Indeed, in most cases, the idea of leaving does not even enter their minds, whatever disagreement they may have with the Party line. The Communist society, with its newspapers (*L'Humanité* in Paris and others in the provinces form the largest party press in France, though it has declined markedly since World War II), its young people's and women's organizations, its hold on many trade unions, its grip on a tenant association, its network of specialized periodicals for various groups (in particular farmers), its sporting and recreational activities (the *Fête de l'Humanité* is a big yearly event), can take up the life of the faithful and isolate them from the rest of the community.

Thus it can be understood why the Hungarian repression was not seen *as such* by French Communists; thus it can also be understood why supporters of smaller Communist parties, in other Western countries, have been more exposed to non-Communist ("bourgeois") views than the voters of the French or Italian CPs. Indeed, this environmental influence of the Communist party can be noted within France itself, since areas of CP strength, whether in the cities or in the countryside, are proportionately more Communist, among all social classes, than the percentage of workers would warrant on the basis of the national average. There are clusters of Communist influence: as we saw, peasants of the Center and Southeast are often Communist. However, Communist manual or white-collar workers are also clustered, for instance, in the Paris Red Belt, in some mining areas of the North, and in the Marseilles and Le Havre areas. Overall, the Communist party does not obtain much more than half its votes from manual workers (and somewhat less than half of the manual workers vote for the party); one-eighth of its voters are white-collar workers, about 6 percent peasants, and 4 percent small shopkeepers. But fluctuations can be very large. The socialization in the Communist party is a lengthy process, which, for many, starts from family and childhood. It tends to be almost indelible.

The Communist party is thus the epitome of the successful organization, particularly in relation to other French political organizations, but of an organization which had little real political effect. One cannot say with certainty how much the Communist party has helped the French working class by leading employers and governments to agree to concessions for fear of the CP's increasing its strength. But the debit side of the balance sheet is perhaps more apparent. The French Left has been torn; it has devoted much energy to discussing problems of ideology, of "line" in relation to the Communists, and consequently has been unable to work out the problems of opposition to the Right. Left-wing governments have been paralyzed, as in 1936, or even prevented from coming into being after World War II by the presence of the Communist party. The discussions with the Socialist party had led to greater formal ties between the two parties of the Left in the 1960s and 1970s. Yet the test of a genuine agreement still has to be made, as the two parties have a habit of coming closer to each other at election time, to go apart again when they become, once more, the opposition. Only if this markedly changes will the difficulties of the Left be overcome permanently.

THE SOCIALIST PARTY

The French Socialist party looks like a poorer brother of the CP. Born as a united party in 1905 and named for over half a century the "French Section of the (Second) Working-Class International" (SFIO), it originated from two socialist groups created in the 1890s, one led by Jean Jaurès, which was humanitarian and liberal, and the other by Jules Guesde, which was Marxist. Up to 1914, the party practiced noncollaboration with bourgeois governments, and it looked as if it was gradually moving toward a commanding position. After the 1914 general election the party had about 100 deputies, or one-sixth of the chamber. Jaurès, the great humanitarian leader, tried with all his strength to rally the antiwar forces, but he was assassinated just before the conflict started and French Socialists, like their German colleagues, were made to accept the *"Union Sacrée."* Even Guesde entered the cabinet.

The Communist split of 1920 had little effect on Socialist strength in the first few years; the war was more instrumental in bringing about changes in attitudes. Noncollaboration with the "bourgeois" State ceased to be the rule. Socialists did not participate in cabinets, but they supported them more often. The trade unions, led by Socialists at the time, were called more often to advise and participate in decisions; old-fashioned capitalism was being replaced by a mixed economy. Socialists became more bourgeois, noting perhaps that socialist parties abroad were coming to power or participating in governments, but seeing also that in many other countries, and in France as well, other enemies of the Republic might be more dangerous than capitalism. By the 1930s, however, the economic depression, the threat of fascism, and the change in the Communist tactics led to a return to a more purist left-wing attitude. After the 1936 general election, at which the Socialists did reasonably, though not outstandingly, well (they obtained 147 seats—or about a fourth of the total—a small increase over the 1914 result), the party appeared as the great winner, having led to victory the Popular Front coalition which included the Radicals (liberals) on their right and the Communists on their left, as well as various splinter groups around the SFIO. For the first time a Socialist, Léon Blum, was called to head the government; for a few tense spring days, the dream seemed to have become reality.

But the victory was hollow. Expectations of manual workers had been increased so markedly by the election result that sit-down strikes soon became the norm in large factories. The Communists pushed for take-overs while the liberals were already backing out. Blum, a follower of Jaurès, a *grand bourgeois* who strongly believed in both equality and liberty, made a number of important reforms (the forty-hour week, paid holidays, collective bargaining), but he did not succeed in retaining the confidence of the workers nor, of course, in acquiring that of the employers.

Financial difficulties grew and the government, in trouble with the Senate, resigned after a year in office. The Socialist party was never to have such an hour of glory, though Blum did again head two cabinets, both short, in 1938 and 1946 (the latter having been somewhat successful in stabilizing prices at a difficult juncture), and though Guy Mollet, the secretary-general of the party for two decades after World War II, was to head in 1956–57 the longest government of the Fourth Republic. Divided over Pétain in 1940, the Socialist party did take an important part in the *Résistance,* though far behind the Communists. It became central to the first coalitions of the Fourth Republic, but, having soon to fight on two fronts, and particularly against the Communist threat, it found itself obliged to acquiesce to measures and policies with which many of its voters disagreed and which even its ministers hardly condoned. Support in the country dwindled: from about 25 percent in 1945 the party fell to about 15 percent at the end of the Fourth Republic; it had 145 deputies in 1945—as in 1936— but only 100 ten years later; there were to be only 40 Socialist deputies after the 1958 general election (and 67 in 1962).

Popular Support and Structure

The Socialist party had ceased to appeal to the new and expanding sections of the community; its electorate was still mainly based on manual workers, white-collar employees, and peasants (respectively about a third, a fifth, and an eighth), but its share of the younger generations was smaller than that of any party except the Radicals (liberals), and of the residents of large towns it had the smallest share of all parties. Its membership had declined drastically from over 300,000 in the first few years after the Liberation to probably not more than 50,000 in the early 1960s. It had suffered from splits and expulsions, the major one having taken place in 1958, when, after years of opposition to the Algerian policy of the party (Guy Mollet had promised autonomy at the 1956 general election but found on becoming premier that the only line he could or dared follow was that of stepping up the military buildup against the insurgents), a section of the party, including some members of Parliament, withdrew on the occasion of de Gaulle's coming to power. The Autonomous Socialist party, later renamed United Socialist party when it joined with other small socialist splinter groups (it enlisted for a while the support of the popular liberal leader Pierre Mendès-France, who had stopped French involvement in Indochina) took only a fraction of the Socialist electorate (2 or 3 percent of the popular vote), but for a declining party the blow was serious and even for a while appeared mortal.

Yet, despite its failing, and though its leader for twenty years, Guy Mollet, has been branded as a dictator of the party, the Socialist party is perhaps the only large political group which remained consistently democratic. Members, organized in sections and in *fédérations départementales* (at the county level), are represented through an elaborate system of proportional representation at the council, which meets once a year, at the national council, which meets once an emergency arises, and even on the executive committee (*Comité directeur*), which runs the party on behalf of the congress. Debates at the congress and national committee are open and frank. Votes are taken often, indeed on all major issues, admittedly not without some manipulation by various leaders; Guy Mollet was renowned for exercising much patronage over his own *fédération,* that of the Pas-de-Calais in the North of France, and the mayor of Marseilles, Gaston Defferre, for years the *de facto* contender to the leadership and for some months a candidate for the presidency of the Republic, can be said to have run almost single-handed the *fédération* of his *département.*

THE CREATION OF A NEW "PARTI SOCIALISTE" AND THE REGENERATION OF THE PARTY

By the mid-1960s, the Socialist party began to show more resilience. Its support of the Gaullist government had ended in 1959 when a stabilization program of a conservative character was launched. The party seemed to use this opportunity to build itself into the mainstay of the opposition; for the first time in decades, and thanks to the electoral system, it had more deputies than the Communists (forty-five against ten in 1958, sixty-five against forty-one in 1962). It could thus be the main opposition group in the chamber. At the 1962 general election, Guy Mollet developed a subtle policy of arrangements with the Communists whereby in most constituencies, but not in all, the weaker of the two parties would withdraw for the stronger at the second ballot; meanwhile, he concluded a full-fledged agreement with the Center parties, which was buttressed by a promise of governmental accord if they were to win the election (an alternative which no one took very seriously, however).

From the mid-1960s, more serious efforts were also made to broaden the base of the party and to change its image. Hopes were entertained, in the first instance, around the creation of a "federal" organization which was to be substantially larger than the Communist party. The Radicals (liberals) and the Christian Democrats, as well as representatives of some of the political clubs were to belong to the new grouping, sometimes viewed as a potentially large "umbrella" for the Left. The small United Socialist party, worried at not being at the center of a Communist-Socialist arrangement, and the Christian Democrats, unsure of their conservative voters, opposed the proposal, while the old anti-Catholic reflex grew in the Socialist party itself. A smaller and looser grouping, the *Fédération de la Gauche Démocrate et Socialiste,* comprising Socialists, Radicals, and some tiny organizations, was for a while to be a more modest, but influential, alternative. Its presidential candidate in 1965, François Mitterrand, polled 45 percent of the vote at the second ballot; it returned 121 members of Parliament at the 1967 general election. But it did not survive the crushing electoral defeat of 1968.

Mitterrand was to prove stubborn in his aim to unite and indeed lead the Left, however. Helped by the disarray caused by a further defeat at the polls in 1969 in the presidential election which followed de Gaulle's resignation, Mitterrand campaigned for the reconstruction of the Socialist party—now known simply as *Parti Socialiste*—and even succeeded in replacing the aging Guy Mollet as the leader of the party (though the best known leader of the Left, he had not previously been a member of the Socialist party). He entered a series of negotiations with the Communist party designed to expand the collaboration between the two organizations. The "Common Program of the Left" of 1972 was markedly socialist (and listed several nationalizations);

it was nonetheless much more moderate than the Communists would have wanted. The leadership of Mitterrand on the Left as a whole is thus exercised more forcefully than that of any Socialist politician since World War II, and it has led to more concessions from the Communist party than at any time since its creation. It even succeeded in increasing Socialist votes in the country, for the first time in twenty-five years, at the 1973 general election.

Yet the full unity of the Left remains a distant goal; and its governmental success is even more distant. Much weaker in votes than the Gaullist block, the Left is divided into a variety of small sects, alongside Communists, Socialists, and members of the United Socialist party. The Communist party is anxious to stop the development of groups on its own left, and has been therefore ready to attack the "agitation" of the *gauchistes* in order to appear "respectable." Its leaders also worry that the *gauchistes,* who have sharply criticized the authoritarian tendencies of the CP, might undermine the hierarchy of the Party. But these differences contribute to the division of the Left, while for the majority of Frenchmen, the Communist party remains unprepared to play the parliamentary game. Mitterrand's efforts have unquestionably brought France nearer to an alternative program of government, as the 1973 general election showed. But the CP will have to transform markedly its character—or to be reduced in strength electorally to the advantage of the Socialist party—for the odds to be more balanced between Right and Left.

THE CENTER

THE RADICAL PARTY

Probably the most French of all the French parties is not a party at all. For many, and not only abroad, the resilience of the Radical party is a baffling phenomenon. Together with a number of small groups at the Center-Left of the political spectrum, the *Parti Républicain Radical et Radical-Socialiste* managed to dominate the governments of the second half of the Third Republic and was almost as successful during the Fourth. Bitterly riven by the vote of 1940 which gave full powers to Pétain, and seemingly doomed to the wilderness, the party recovered and produced from its thinned ranks scores of premiers and prominent ministers.

Far to the left in the early days of the Third Republic, the Radical party's real period of glory was just before World War I, when, after having been organized as a united party in 1901, it was prominent in its fight against clericalism and achieved the separation of Church and State in 1905. From then on radicalism was on the decline; the religious question was the main issue which still united—at least in words—all Radicals, but the sources of division began to increase as problems connected with capitalism and the development of the welfare state created cleavages between the *"grands bourgeois du radicalisme"* and some of its more obscure petty-bourgeois elements. Its greatest figure of the interwar period, Édouard Herriot, epitomized almost all the characteristics of the Radicals. Brilliant, somewhat literary in his instincts and interests, prone to considerable oratory, Herriot was probably more the victim of the system which he adored than he himself realized. In a situation of stable and disciplined parties, Herriot might have conducted foreign policy, and even financial policy, on the basis of sound principles. But he used his principles mainly in his speeches; his presence in the government was associated with troubles and with problems which he could not solve. He gave the world and France the image of an impotent government, an impotent chamber, and an impotent system.

It seemed for a while that the Radicals would never recover from the events of World War II. They left 130 members in 1940; they returned 28 in 1945. They were then the smallest of all parties, even smaller than a new party which had been created as a result of the *Résistance,* the *Union Démocratique et Socialiste de la Résistance* (UDSR), which elected 29 members. This party, allied in the first instance to the Socialists, with whom they shared the desire to rejuvenate French social structures without being as tainted with anticlericalism as the Socialists or Radicals, came to be nearer to the Radicals in the course of the debates on the Constitution of 1946. The Radicals succeeded in realizing their first great *coup* of the postwar period by concluding negotiations with the UDSR and building a federal organization, the *Rassem-*

blement des Gauches Républicaines, thus losing some of the opprobrium resulting from their war record. They managed to return, jointly with the new group, 70 deputies at the election of November 1946. The road to recovery was open. With ministerial coalitions becoming shakier as a result of the Communists' being pushed into opposition, the Radicals came back to power, and in 1948, France had once more a Radical prime minister in the person of Dr. Henri Queuille, who ran the country for over a year and achieved stabilization, both political and financial. For many, the return of the Radicals symbolized the return to normalcy and showed that the *Résistance* had been only a brief interlude.

Despite the influx of new blood coming from the UDSR (of which Mitterrand was a member at the time), "normalcy" was not to last long. The Radical party was becoming increasingly older, its electorate being mainly drawn from small towns or as a clientele of a few well-known politicians. Yet, for a short period, it seemed that even that image would be modified. One of its leading members, Pierre Mendès-France, who left de Gaulle's government in 1945 because he advocated a policy of austerity, and who had been mainly prominent for his criticisms of French policy in Vietnam, became popular overnight, not only in the Assembly where he seemed the only one who was prepared to take the responsibility for a peaceful settlement, but in the country where he practiced a style of politics which the French had not been accustomed to seeing in their premiers. His "fireside chats," direct and devoid of rhetoric, were immensely successful, and he promised a regeneration of politics, not only in foreign affairs, but in internal matters as well. In order to accomplish this, he began considering the possibility of streamlining the Radical party, and when he came to be defeated in Parliament, partly thanks to the passionate speech of another Radical, he tried to do what no Radical had ever done before; he wanted to create a rank-and-file membership which would pay dues, go to meetings, and discuss politics in broad national terms. He also wanted to make the parliamentary party obey the orders of the national organization. For some months, he seemed on the verge of winning, and of achieving the impossible. He was helped by the general election of 1956, called by yet another Radical, Edgar

Faure (since turned Gaullist), who had succeeded Pierre Mendès-France as premier and had also been defeated in Parliament at the end of 1955, thanks to the votes of many Radical members! At the polls there was a considerable upswing of the Radicals; in such unlikely places as Paris and other large towns, the young, the white-collar workers and skilled engineers, even the women started to vote radical. The popularity of Mendès-France had led to an unprecedented success of the party, which gained over a million votes above its previous level. But the old radical spirit prevailed in the end; Mendès-France failed to streamline the party, which first split, then expelled him (on the occasion of his joining with anti-Gaullist forces in 1958), and eventually came back to its ways. By the beginning of the Fifth Republic, the Radical party had returned to being the Radical party of the past, but with one difference. The presence of de Gaulle at the helm made it impossible for the party to think, at least for a period, in terms of parliamentary manipulation.

Thus, of necessity, the Radical party became part of the opposition. It turned toward an alliance with the Socialists and entered the Federation of the Left (mainly for electoral reasons). But the defeats of 1967 and 1968 and the old Radical individualism led to the party becoming once more independent, but now pulled more than ever between Right and Left and in no position to manipulate political forces. In desperation, the party elected to its leadership a successful journalist, Jean-Jacques Servan-Schreiber, who was once a follower of Mendès-France, and seemingly popular in the country by the youthful image he projected. But the old divisions soon came to the surface, almost in the same way as, nearly twenty years earlier, they had come to emerge in the Mendès-France period. Servan-Schreiber wanted to reorganize the party, give it a clear "reformist" image, and make members of Parliament subservient to the organization, whereupon members of Parliament resigned from the party and allied to the Socialists, for straight electoral reasons. Torn between Center and Left, torn between individualism and the need for organization, the Radical party seemed to have outlived its usefulness and only to represent a vestige of the past.

THE CENTER-RIGHT: PROGRÈS ET DÉMOCRATIE MODERNE

Servan-Schreiber's efforts to reorganize the Radical party are paralleled by similar attempts by other Center groups to find a way of avoiding the apparent trend toward "bipolarization" in French politics. Indeed, Conservatives and Christian Democrats have perhaps suffered more than Radicals from the new alignments. As we saw earlier, the Independent Conservatives who refused to ally with Gaullism in 1962 suffered a major setback. Meanwhile, the Christian Democrats, who had entered into a coalition with Conservatives and Radicals, suffered an equally disastrous defeat. De Gaulle had had his revenge of a party which had been prominent in stemming the tide of Gaullism in the 1940s and 1950s. By 1967, the Christian Democrats returned fifteen deputies only, and the party—known as the *Mouvement Républicain Populaire* (MRP)—officially ceased to exist.

Thus ended the short history of the French Christian party. France had indeed been the last Roman Catholic country of continental Europe to have a Christian-based party; if it had not been for the war, the defeat, and Vichy, the MRP probably would never have existed. Traditions of anticlericalism are stronger in France than in other Catholic countries; Catholicism is also laxer, and only limited sections, either geographically circumscribed (Alsace-Lorraine and parts of Brittany) or defined in narrow social terms (Christian Social progressives among workers and farmers), have had a long-standing tradition of Christian democracy. It is indeed symbolic that the French Christian Democrats should have avoided the word "Christian" in the title, though the MRP never concealed its Christian philosophy.

Starting from obscure origins in the early part of the century, moving slowly in the interwar period, and mainly in its regional outposts, the MRP emerged suddenly, at the 1945 general election, with almost 5 million votes, a quarter of the electorate, and 150 deputies; it had swept all over France, replacing the Independent Conservatives where they used to be strong, but allegedly supporting a program of social reform which Conservatives never advocated. The success was brief. The MRP found itself almost immediately faced with the contradiction of remaining in power against de Gaulle, in 1946, after having presented itself as a "faithful" Gaullist party, of opposing Socialists and Communists on the first draft of the constitution while remaining in the government with them, and, more dangerously for its future at the polls, of agreeing to progressive social policies while relying mainly on a conservative electorate. Divisions started inside; some members of Parliament left to join the Conservatives, others became Gaullists. The Assembly of 1946, where the MRP had 169 deputies, was to be the last where the party was to have a commanding position. Reduced to 96 seats in 1951 (and only remaining that large thanks to the electoral system), the party declined further at each successive election.

In many ways, the MRP was an unlucky party. It supported liberal institutions against the unrealistic and possibly dangerous first draft of the Constitution of 1946 which was rejected by the voters, and by its stand in the Assembly, it did, perhaps, save the Republic. It defended the Fourth Republic in its difficult early period when it was subjected to the combined violence, not only oral in the chamber, but physical in the streets, of the Communists and the Gaullists; it did much to reintegrate the Church in the nation, educating the hierarchy, the mass of the Catholics, and especially the young to thinking in liberal and even somewhat progressive terms; it was the first to preach European unity (and the name of Robert Schuman will probably be for a long time a symbol of European integration). It was one of the main proponents of the idea of modernization in the economic and social fields. Yet it gained little credit in the minds of Frenchmen and has been constantly assailed by politicians of all sides. In the nation as a whole, it has been associated with the stigma of the Fourth Republic; the last prime minister of the regime, Pierre Pflimlin, was a member of the MRP. In Parliament, it came to be attacked by the Socialists because of the latter's long-standing anticlerical animosities as well as because of the fear that it might not want to be sufficiently progressive in social terms; it came to be attacked by the Radicals and the Conservatives because it was felt to be too progressive; Gaullists competed for its electors, and the quarrel over subsidies for Church schools was at least in part revived in order to embarrass the MRP. Accident prone, the MRP thus found itself in the unenviable position of appearing more responsible than most other parties for the fall of the two popular prime ministers of the Fourth Republic, Antoine Pinay, whom it felt to be too conservative, and Pierre Mendès-France, whom it felt to be not European enough.

Since 1958, the MRP has continued to have the same unhappy destiny. It first supported de Gaulle firmly (though the new president did not rate its support very high), but it became more and more estranged from the new regime. Gaullists and Christian Democrats competed for the same electors; the social policies of the Fifth Republic appeared too conservative for the progressive wing of the MRP; the foreign policy was too nationalistic. Opposed to the "confederal" twist given by de Gaulle's government to the new Europe, Christian Democrat ministers resigned in 1962, the MRP joined the opposition, somewhat half-heartedly, but the electoral decline was not stemmed. Yet MRP militants refused to join the Federation of the Left, and though they drew some comfort from the fact that their presidential candidate, Jean Lecanuet, obtained 13 percent of the votes in 1965, this was a far cry from the 25 percent of the late 1940s.

Indeed, Lecanuet's relative success had been due to the creation of a new political grouping, the *Centre Démocrate*, on which high hopes were placed for the 1967 general election. The result was so discouraging that the MRP itself was dissolved and Christian Democrats and some Conservatives came to ally in a new party, *Progrès et Démocratie Moderne* (PDM), under the leadership of a new man, Jacques Duhamel. Though the electoral appeal was limited, the new party benefited from the fact that when de Gaulle resigned, the temporary president, Alain Poher, was constitutionally to be the president of the Senate up until the election. He was an ex-MRP who belonged to the PDM. During his short period in office, Poher tried to project an image of greater liberalism while campaigning as the candidate of the Center. Though he benefited from the division of the Left, he was decisively defeated by Pompidou at the second ballot and the Center came once more to be torn between the lure of office (many joined the government in 1969, including Duhamel himself) and the desire to be a reformist alternative.

The future of the Center seems unpromising. Though Servan-Schreiber tried to organize the Radical party, most of the Radical members of Parliament deserted him; though some members of the PDM remained outside the Gaullist orbit, many of its leaders are attracted to office. At the local level, members of Center parties have often done well in medium-sized cities; among the electorate, a fraction—perhaps 15 percent—refuse to be associated with either Right or Left. But this is not a base on which to start credibly to replace the government, nor is there much prospect for attracting able politicians for more than a short period. The new French party system seems to leave little place for men in the Center, except as useful interest groups able to suggest ideas and act as a brake on the major parties.

The French party system changed markedly in less than two decades. The underlying social change accounts in large part for the simpler, more "national," more disciplined party system. But de Gaulle's new institutions helped to speed up the pace. Thus de Gaulle, and later Pompidou, formed a majority party prepared to follow their lead, while traditional French individualism seemed to vanish almost overnight from the parliamentary scene. Yet, as long as Communists and Socialists do not unite or otherwise coalesce to form a strong party of the Left, the chances of a return to a complex, Center-dominated form of parliamentary game are not wholly remote. The 1973 general election led only to a reduction in the Gaullist appeal; but, as long as the Left is not a truly credible alternative, the disintegration of the UDR remains a possibility. Much depends on the general support for the institutions. If these are allowed to alter slowly while being accepted by the people and politicians, the pressure on the Left to unite will increase, Gaullists will constitute a "real" French conservative party, and the Center will be permanently reduced to being a small "junior partner" in any government. Thus we need to turn to institutions, and in particular to the presidency, to see how they can provide a framework for the stable development of French party politics.

PART THREE

THE GOVERNMENTAL AND LEGISLATIVE PROCESSES

6

The Executive

The Constitution of 1958 was introduced primarily in order to strengthen the executive. From 1870 to 1958, French governments had been weak and unstable, except during a period of about a decade at the turn of the century when the campaign against the Catholic Church gave cohesion to the majority and some real strength to the leader of the government. De Gaulle was convinced that chronic instability was one of the major causes of the decline of France; he felt that only by a change in the institutions could the man at the top be able to take a long-term view of the interests of the country, and thus based his cure on constitutional remedies. But the medicine was somewhat unorthodox. De Gaulle did not adhere to any of the constitutional models devised in the eighteenth and nineteenth centuries and broadly adopted in the major democracies. He wanted to ensure governmental stability and executive authority; he was not anxious—to say the least—to give representatives of the people effective means of supervising this executive, nor did he wish to devise an equilibrium between executive and legislature. Thus he neither proposed a revamped cabinet system nor a presidential system; he plumped for a hybrid system which gives marked preponderance to the executive. Yet, as the cabinet system and the presidential system are the only two forms of constitutional arrangements (together with a streamlined party system) which proved effective elsewhere in sustaining liberal democracy, the new French institutions were attacked from the start as both authoritarian and impractical. Few expected that they would last beyond de Gaulle; indeed, though they were kept alive under

Georges Pompidou (thanks in large part to an obedient Assembly inherited from de Gaulle, at least up to 1973), the long-term future of the constitution still remains in question.

The new organization divides executive authority between two sharply distinct segments. On the one hand, the president has the somewhat lofty and almost undefinable task of looking after the long-term interests of the nation; on the other, the government, headed by the prime minister, is in daily charge of the affairs of the country, both for detailed questions and for general matters. This raises two main difficulties. First, there is a large "gray area" of divided responsibility, particularly because the constitution does not define precisely the respective "sectors" of president and prime minister; one can thus foresee possible clashes between the two men. And lest it be assumed that this could be avoided through the power of the president to appoint the prime minister, a second set of problems arises from the fact that the prime minister has to have the confidence of the legislature. Only if the president has the greater authority of the two will conflicts be resolved in the president's favor. Election by universal suffrage goes some way toward providing the president with this authority, but as presidential elections do not coincide with those of Parliament, strains on the institutions seem unavoidable.

THE PRESIDENCY OF THE REPUBLIC

The legal powers of the president of the Republic are relatively limited. According to the letter of the constitution, the president is not much more than a head of state, at least in normal times. In the summer of 1958, when the constitution was drafted, de Gaulle had to agree to compromises with Fourth Republic politicians anxious to retain most of the parliamentary arrangements which had prevailed in the past. "Presidentialism" seemed to many to be dangerous. As de Gaulle apparently cared more for some of the "exalted" aspects in political life, he seemed to become concerned almost exclusively with powers for the president under emergencies. He wanted to avoid the repetition of the 1940 situation when the last president of the Third Republic could not intervene when the government was conceding defeat. Whether de Gaulle wanted the presidency to be run on American lines was never clarified; he settled for a president who was to be concerned with the "long-term interests" of the country rather than with "daily politics."

Thus the president of the Republic, elected for seven years, as under the previous republics, has only a limited set of powers in normal times. The bulk of these existed in the Third and Fourth Republics, and, at best, the Constitution of the Fifth Republic simply marked a return to the situation of the Third Republic on a number of points where the Constitution of 1946 had trimmed the powers of the president to the benefit of the prime minister. There is nothing unusual, by French republican standards, in the following eight powers being granted to the president: (1) appointment of the prime minister and of the ministers on the proposal of the prime minister (but not the power to dismiss the premier); (2) promulgation of laws voted by Parliament (the president may ask Parliament to reconsider a law within two weeks of its having been voted, but he has no power of veto); (3) signature of decrees, including those appointing some higher civil servants and officers of the armed forces (but the decrees must be approved by the Council of Ministers); (4) chairmanship of the Council of Ministers; (5) chairmanship of the high councils of the armed forces; (6) right to send messages to the National Assembly; (7) ratification of treaties, which are negotiated in his name; (8) power of pardon.

All these powers existed in the Third Republic, a regime which was not conspicuous for the authority of its presidents; practically all of them existed in the Fourth. The president of the Fourth Republic had lost the power of formal appointment of the prime minister, but he had the power to designate the candidate who was to be formally appointed by the National Assembly; the substance and practice were not modified. He had lost the power to sign decrees (which had been given to the prime minister in order to increase his status, not so much vis-à-vis the president as vis-à-vis the rest of the government). Moreover, in all three republics, presidential decisions have had to be countersigned by the prime minister and, where appropriate, by some of the ministers. The technique of the countersignature is basic to the operation of the parliamentary system. The "seal of authority" of the State is given to a decision in the form of the presidential signature, but the only persons who are deemed to be responsible are the members of the government and not the Head of State. No particular significance must therefore be attributed to the fact that the president of the Fifth Republic signs decrees or ratifies treaties; this is deemed simply to mean—in the tradition of French constitutional practice—that the president gives State authority to measures decided by others who have countersigned them.

The New Powers of the President
since 1958: Dissolution

There are four powers which are new to the Fifth Republic and which are the prerogative of the president alone. However, by their very nature, and by the restrictions to which they are subjected, they are powers which can be exercised only at rare intervals or in emergencies. In these cases, the president does not require the countersignature of the prime minister; they are truly and substantively presidential acts. First, the president can dissolve the National Assembly. In most parliamentary systems, and in particular in Britain, the right of dissolution is entirely open to the executive, and thus deadlocks in the governmental machinery can be solved by an appeal to the people. This was not the case in France, and it had indeed always been argued (wrongly, as the analysis of political parties has shown) that one of the main problems of the French Republic was the fact that the executive could dissolve the Assembly only in special circumstances or with certain guarantees. In the Third Republic, the right of dissolution could be exercised, but only after approval of the Senate. The prerogative was used only once, in 1877, in order to maintain a conservative government in power, and the result was the return of a progressive majority, the eventual resignation of the president of the Republic, and a customary *modus vivendi* whereby the right of dissolution was no longer used. In the Fourth Republic, the right of dissolution was, rather as it is in the Federal Republic of Germany, limited by rigorous conditions and linked to two cabinet crises occurring under certain conditions within eighteen months of each other. It was used once, in 1955, but had little effect on the nature of the political game. Since 1958, the constitution has allowed the president to dissolve, not more than once a year, after having consulted the prime minister and the presidents of the two chambers of Parliament. Thus the president can, if he so wishes, try to solve a deadlock between cabinet and Parliament by asking the people to adjudicate, but he cannot repeat the process within a year nor can he use the procedure in order to force a government on a reluctant Parliament. Unless he wishes to resort to a *coup d'état*, the president must accept the verdict of the people or resign. When, in 1962, de Gaulle dissolved the first Parliament of the Fifth Republic (after four of the five years of the Assembly had elapsed), he acted in a perfectly constitutional manner. The government had been defeated by a vote of censure (over the procedure adopted by the government to change the method of election of the president of the Republic, a procedure which was clearly not constitutional, as we shall see), and the president decided not to accept the resignation of the government, but to dissolve the Assembly instead. The people vindicated de Gaulle's decision to dissolve by increasing the Gaullist representation in the house. Similarly, the people vindicated de Gaulle's decision to dissolve in 1968, since the Gaullist majority was markedly increased over that obtained in 1967.

REFERENDA

The second and third new powers give two opposite opportunities to the president in relation to the submission of bills to the people. On the one hand, the president may decide that a constitutional amendment proposed by the government to Parliament need not be approved by referendum after it has been adopted by Parliament (which is the normal procedure). In this event, the proposal is sent to a joint meeting of the two chambers instead of going through the two chambers separately. This provision is designed to accelerate the procedure in cases of technical amendments; it has been used in 1960, in order to loosen the links between France and her African ex-colonies and to allow them to become independent states; the procedure was used again in 1963 to change the timing of the sessions of Parliament.

On the other hand, the president is entitled, on the basis of Article 11 of the constitution, to refer certain government bills to the electorate: bills dealing with the organization of public authorities; carrying approval of a community agreement; or proposing to authorize the ratification of a treaty which, without being contrary to the constitution, would affect the functioning of institutions. This article has led to the clearest cases of unconstitutional action on the part of de Gaulle, both in spirit and in letter. Controversies arose at three levels. First, the article states that the president "may, on the proposal of the Government during parliamentary sessions or on the joint proposal of the two assemblies" use the referendum procedure. In all the cases in which the article has been used—over Algeria in 1961 and 1962, over the method of election of the president in 1962, on regionalism in 1969—the initiative came clearly from de Gaulle himself, not from the government. Similarly, the initiative came from Georges Pompidou in 1972 when the procedure was used to approve British membership in the Common Market. The *form* of a proposal by the government was rejected, but no one doubted who the real originator was. A power which was meant to be one of "arbitration" (to take a favorite Gaullist expression) had been transformed into one of positive action.

Second, the article certainly intended, though it did not expressly state, that the bill be discussed and adopted first by Parliament. Never had there been before, in French practice, any suggestion that a bill might be adopted *either* by Parliament *or* by the people; clearly, the latter procedure has the effect of leaving no opportunity for amendment of the governmental proposal at any stage of the public discussion. Yet, in all cases, the bill was submitted to a referendum and was not discussed by Parliament.

Third, and this time without any shadow of doubt, a bill presented in this way to the people cannot be a constitutional amendment. Though Article 11 says that "the president of the Republic may . . . submit to a referendum any bill dealing with the organization of governmental authorities," this is unquestionably to the exclusion of the constitution itself, since Article 89 provides for a special procedure which includes a referendum, except in the case mentioned above. Yet de Gaulle used Article 11 to introduce the proposal that the president be elected by universal suffrage, which entailed a modification of Article 6 of the constitution. This proposal, which led to the referendum of October 1962 and created considerable stir (including, as we saw, the fall of the government and the dissolution of the National Assembly), was possibly the one case of unconstitutional action by the president which can in no way be exonerated. The Council of State, asked about the procedure, declared that the use of Article 11 was improper; the Constitutional Council, in one of the several cases in which it appeared to be "subservient" to the executive, declared itself incompetent. The people did approve of the change, however, and the discussion about the unconstitutional character of the action has thus become somewhat academic.

EMERGENCY POWERS
The fourth new power of the president is the one which created most controversy at the time of the drafting of the constitution (unlike Article 11 which passed almost unnoticed). Article 16 allows the president to assume full powers in certain emergencies:

> When the institutions of the Republic, the independence of the nation, the integrity of its territory, or the fulfillment of its international commitments are threatened in a grave and immediate manner, and when the regular functioning of the constitutional governmental authorities is interrupted, the President of the Republic shall take the measures commanded by the circumstances, after official consultation with the Premier, the Presidents of the Assemblies and the Constitutional Council.
>
> He shall inform the nation of these measures in a message.
>
> These measures must be prompted by the desire to ensure to the constitutional governmental authorities, in the shortest possible time, the means of fulfilling their assigned functions. The Constitutional Council shall be consulted with regard to such measures.
>
> Parliament shall meet by right.
>
> The National Assembly may not be dissolved during the exercise of emergency powers [by the president].

Article 16 was hailed by de Gaulle's supporters as the means by which constitutional catastrophes such as that of 1940 could be avoided; opponents saw in it the means by which a legal dictatorship could be established. In fact, neither seems to be the case. The article bears the stamp of de Gaulle's initiative, but it is handicapped in two ways: first, the guarantee given to Parliament is somewhat ludicrous if one really thinks of emergencies of the kind mentioned in the first part of the article; second, powers of this type are no substitute for authority as the fact that the president is mandated to act in this way ("The President shall take the measures . . .") does not give him the effective power to command the armed forces, the civil service, or any other body. Indeed, one wonders whether de Gaulle did not in fact come to have second thoughts about the article, after he had the experience of its use in 1961, following the *putsch* of four generals in Algiers. Article 16 was set in motion; a number of measures were passed (including one setting up a court of justice). Very quickly, however, various problems arose. Was Parliament entitled to discuss the measures, and only the measures? Or could it discuss anything *but* the measures? If so, what is the value in having it meet? What is the responsibility of the government in connection with these measures (which are presidential)? When Article 16 ceases to be invoked, do the measures taken lapse *ipso facto?* Must one distinguish between temporary and permanent ones (e.g., the creation of a court)? The operation of the article proved so cumbersome that it was a great relief for the government (more than for Parliament!) when at the end of the summer of 1961, Article 16 ceased to be operative. The ones who seemed to have benefited most from the emergency were the farmers, whose lobby was able to make itself more felt, thanks to the chamber being in permanent session.

THE ROLE OF THE POPULAR ELECTION IN ENHANCING THE AUTHORITY OF THE PRESIDENT

Such are the powers of the president. The new ones clearly point to the main preoccupation which de Gaulle had in overseeing some of the provisions, namely that the president should have authority to act in grave situations. This is probably why, after having accepted in the first instance, as a matter of compromise, that the president of the Republic be elected by a limited electoral college, de Gaulle insisted on seeing through the amendment of 1962 aiming at the election of the president by universal suffrage (with a two-ballot or "run-off" system, the second ballot taking place two weeks after the first between the top two candidates). Opposition to a popular election of the president (the president was elected by the members of the two houses of Parliament in the Third and Fourth Republics) was largely due to the fear of "Bonapartism." As we noted, the only popularly elected president, Louis-Napoleon, turned himself into an emperor after a *coup d'état* in 1851. In 1958, the political leaders insisted that the president should not be elected by the whole people. A compromise was found, which led to the creation of an electoral college of about 80,000 delegates, mainly representatives of local authorities, but this had the effect of overrepresenting the rural areas. De Gaulle was elected under this arrangement in December 1958 (he obtained 80 percent of the votes). But the system was unsatisfactory; the size and composition of the electoral college were difficult to justify, and, more important, de Gaulle probably feared that after his disappearance Parliament might want to return to the old system which, in his view, did not give enough authority to the president and led to the election of parliamentary manipulators rather than "guides," "stewards," or even "arbiters." He cunningly thought that if popular election was established, it would probably be more difficult for Parliament to come back on the reform, particularly if it had proved successful. It was indeed successful; not only did the people approve of the reform (though unconstitutionally presented) by a majority of over three to two (61.7 percent voted "yes"), but the first election of the president, in December 1965, led to a very active campaign. De Gaulle's reelection was somewhat difficult (he received only 44 percent of the votes cast at the first ballot and 55 percent at the second), but this difficulty indicated the popularity of the contest.

Thus, when de Gaulle resigned in 1969 on having lost the referendum on regionalism, no one questioned the election of the president by universal suffrage. The parties presented candidates, Georges Pompidou being the first to be chosen. The disunity of the Left led to the candidate of the Center, Alain Poher, being second to Pompidou at the first ballot and thus the only competitor to Pompidou at the second. On a much lower poll (abstention jumped from 22 to 31 percent, mainly from Communists), Pompidou obtained 57 percent of the votes at the second ballot. The regime had succeeded in providing a transition and the procedure had been shown to be working without any danger of "Bonapartism." The presidency did acquire as a result an authority which it did not have in the past.

THE GOVERNMENT

While the role of the president is to ensure a guardianship of the nation, the role of the government is to govern. Article 20 of the constitution states:

> The Government shall determine and direct the policy of the nation. It shall have at its disposal the administration and the armed forces.

And Article 21 continues:

> The Premier shall direct the operation of the Government. He shall be responsible for national defense. He shall ensure the execution of the laws. . . .

It is difficult to be less ambiguous. Though the president of the Republic, according to customs dating back to the Third Republic, chairs the Council of Ministers, it is the government as a whole, and in particular its leader, the prime minister, who is responsible for the policy of the nation.

THE PRIME MINISTER AND THE COLLECTIVE CHARACTER OF THE GOVERNMENT

As in many other countries, the position of the prime minister grew gradually in the course of the last hundred years. The Constitution of 1875 did not formally recognize the premier, but in practice all governments had a head who was known then (rather illogically since the president of the Republic chaired the meetings of ministers) as the "President of the Council of Ministers." However, because French governments tended to be uneasy coalitions of prima donnas and representatives of weak parties, the premier was more often a compromiser and a manipulator than a leader. The Constitution of 1946 sought to increase the authority of the "President of the Council" by an increase of powers (hence the trimming of some of those of the president of the Republic) and by the introduction of provisions designed to give the premier more influence over the government. The premier alone was to be designated by the chamber, and he was to appoint freely the rest of the cabinet. But these measures were of no avail, as the traditions of compromise and weak coalitions remained the rule. There was little difference between a premier of the 1930s and a premier of the 1950s.

The Constitution of 1958 did keep, nonetheless, some of the provisions of the Constitution of 1946 which aimed at buttressing the power of the premier (now named prime minister for the first time). Hence, the statements of Article 21 (leadership of the government, responsibility for national defense, exercise of the *pouvoir règlementaire*—i.e., the power to implement the laws—authority to make appointments to the posts which the president of the Republic is not specifically designated to appoint). Moreover, throughout the constitution (and we have noted some examples already) the premier is called for advice: this happens in cases of dissolution, in cases of use of emergency powers (Article 16), and for constitutional amendments. The constitution stresses the leadership role of the premier as much as is compatible with the position of the president of the Republic (which the constitution wishes to establish firmly) and with the collective character of the government (which was maintained from the previous two regimes).

As in most parliamentary democracies (though not in all, Germany being an example of the opposite practice), the French government was and remains legally a collective organ. This means that decisions of the French government are deemed to be decisions of all its members. Collective decision-making is shown by the fact that the important measures of the government are taken in the Council of Ministers (we noted earlier, for instance, that decrees are signed by the president of the Republic after they have been approved by the Council of Ministers). While the premier can and does give advice to the president on some matters, it is the government which is empowered to "determine and direct the policy of the nation." Collective decision-making is also associated with collective responsibility; this operates through the mechanisms of the vote of censure, which entails, if adopted, the resignation of all the ministers. As in other parliamentary democracies, the conflict between the prime minister's leadership and collective decision-making is a difficult one to solve. Clearly, there has been less collective decision-making since 1958 than before, but this is much more due to de Gaulle's (and Pompidou's) intervention than to the strong leadership of the prime minister, as we shall see in the next section.

Moreover, constitutional provisions and formal arrangements have not modified very markedly the internal structure of the French government in the Fifth Republic. Names of ministries change from time to time, but the only major reconstruction concerned the armed services (the three separate service departments have been abolished), and it followed an evolution which began in the Fourth Republic. Typically, a government would have about twenty ministers (slightly fewer than in the last years of the Fourth Republic); it would also include a number of secretaries of state, with a somewhat lower status. The first government of the Pompidou era, that of Chaban-Delmas, had more secretaries of state, but the second, that of Messmer, returned to the more normal practice of the de Gaulle period.

Behind generally similar formal arrangements, however, some important differences affect the decision-making processes and the whole nature of the cabinet. At least three of these need to be mentioned. First, ministerial instability has sharply decreased. From 1958 to 1973, France had only five prime ministers: Debré, Pompidou, and Couve de Murville under de Gaulle; Chaban-Delmas and Messmer under Pompidou. Only two premiers of the Fourth Republic lasted for over a year and no prime minister since 1875 lasted continuously in office as long as Pompidou. But stability is not in danger of becoming immobility, as was shown by the changes from Debré to Pompidou and from Pompidou to

Couve de Murville under de Gaulle, and the change from Chaban-Delmas to Messmer under Pompidou. Ministers, moreover, move fairly frequently. Before 1958, prime ministers changed more often than ministers, as if the chairmanship of the cabinet rotated while the membership remained fairly stable. The rate of change of ministers has not diminished. While Couve de Murville remained in charge of foreign affairs for almost ten years, other departments had a fairly rapid turnover: four different persons held the post of minister of finance between 1958 and 1966.

Second, attempts were made in the first phase of the regime, though with rather mixed results, to effect a "depoliticization" of the government. De Gaulle was very anxious to bring about a change, partly on the grounds that the government should in some sense be (like himself!) above the daily turmoil of political life; the government should run the State, and de Gaulle seemed to conceive of politics as an activity which somehow can be divorced from State policy-making, a view which probably stems from the part played by the civil service in the running of modern France. The Fifth Republic has thus been characterized by various attempts at introducing into the government more administrative practices and more administrators. On coming back to power in May 1958, and before the new constitution was drafted, de Gaulle appointed to his cabinet members of the civil, foreign, and colonial services, a practice which had been abandoned, except in time of war, for over half a century. The minister of foreign affairs, Couve de Murville, was from the career foreign service. Pompidou himself was a teacher and a banker and had never participated in politics before 1962 except as a personal adviser to de Gaulle in the early postwar period. Overall, in the early 1960s, cabinets were composed from a quarter to a third of ministers coming from the administrative corps. Yet this tendency has been checked, because, as we saw in Chapter Three, these administrators slowly became politicians, and joined a new political class of UDR politicians which emerged in the 1960s. The fears commonly expressed that France would be run by men aloof from politics proved unreal and are no longer expressed.

Third, and in order to give the executive more independence,

Article 23 of the constitution, introduced at de Gaulle's specific request, forbids ministers to remain in Parliament once they are appointed to the government. This provision does exist in some other parliamentary democracies (Holland, Norway), but it does contravene the general idea that the executive stems from the majority of the Assembly and aims at leading it. De Gaulle wanted precisely to detach ministers from the legislature; ministerial crises did occur in the past to help the personal careers of some ambitious men. Though they can come and speak (but not vote) in Parliament, ministers no longer belong to the legislature and thus can be expected to take a loftier view of daily politics; they are nearer to the president and thus more likely to follow his leadership. Yet the procedure did have some clumsy consequences (such as the appointment of a substitute for each member of Parliament in order to avoid a cascade of by-elections at each ministerial reshuffle) and any variations which occurred in the attitudes of ministers is probably due more to the streamlined party system which made coalitions and deals in Parliament unnecessary in the Fifth Republic.

PRESIDENT, PRIME MINISTER, AND GOVERNMENT IN THE FIFTH REPUBLIC

Institutional changes are therefore insufficient to account for the transformations of the structure of the French executive. The constitution calls for collective government, yet effective arrangements are more hierarchical. The president is not constitutionally entitled to determine policies, except in emergencies, yet, from the very start, de Gaulle did intervene, and Pompidou followed the lead. Fluctuations in decision-making patterns and cabinet arrangements point to the temporary nature of the executive structure.

THE EXTENT OF PRESIDENTIAL INTERVENTION
As the years passed, more, rather than less uncertainty tended to prevail over the role of the president in policy-making. In the early period, de Gaulle's involvement was seemingly due to the

special problem of the Algerian war and was held to be confined to some special "sectors." The notion of "sectors" was indeed suggested by the then president of the National Assembly, later to become Pompidou's first prime minister, Jacques Chaban-Delmas. On one hand, in a presidential sector, composed essentially of foreign affairs, defense, Algeria and overseas France, and some key institutional problems, the president would initiate policy and the government merely implement it. The second sector was to comprise all other matters, and in particular economic and social matters; in this the government, led by the prime minister, was the initiator.

This conception of "sectors" was never officially recognized by de Gaulle as marking the limit of his area of intervention; yet it went beyond the letter and spirit of the constitution. All assumed that de Gaulle would be the initiator of Algerian policy; few seemed to raise objections to the president's involvement in foreign policy. Yet, after a few years, the distinction became blurred and de Gaulle seemed to intervene in many important aspects of internal affairs, possibly because, indirectly, some problems touched on foreign policy or because, also indirectly, they may have an impact on the stability of the political system. But the links could be tenuous, as when the president pressed for a solution of the bitter coal strike of the winter of 1963 or ensured that steps were taken to help the build-up of a French computer industry. The involvement seemed general, as the president himself said in 1964: "Clearly, it is the president alone who holds and delegates the authority of the State. But the very nature, the extent, the duration of his task imply that he be not absorbed without remission or limit by political, parliamentary, economic, and administrative contingencies." The idea of a separation between fields seemed replaced by a more hierarchical distinction, leaving the prime minister to deal with these contingencies which are "his lot, as complex and meritorious as it is essential."

It seems therefore that the president—de Gaulle and later Pompidou—has come to view his role as one of steering on many important matters which affect the well-being of the nation, either directly or by implication. Hence the many instances of direct action of the president in financial matters: it was de Gaulle who, in 1968, decided not to devalue the franc; it was Pompidou who, less than a year later, reversed the decision. Many aspects of regional or cultural policy, and of economic development and social security reform, can clearly be ascribed to the president's steering.

Yet it would be wrong to conclude automatically that members of the government are in a truly hierarchical position in relation to the president. The system is only half-presidential in that, on many issues as well, the president remains an arbiter, rather than an actor. On various important economic and social problems, under de Gaulle and under Pompidou, prime ministers and ministers have initiated policies with the president of the Republic being seemingly neutral. Price stabilization in 1963, educational reform in 1968, social policies in the late 1960s and early 1970s, are clear instances of governmental policies which cannot easily be ascribed to the president himself. De Gaulle and Pompidou appeared to remain spectators, arbitration being more designed to give the Head of State an element of distance from the executive. Policies are suggested by ministers and adopted by the government, while the president, rather as an umpire, draws the conclusions once results can be seen. He may part with a minister; he may part with a prime minister if the key coordinator of the executive has seemingly failed to lead the government or has been exhausted by the task: thus Pompidou was dismissed by de Gaulle in 1968; thus Chaban-Delmas was dismissed by Pompidou in 1972.

THE INSTRUMENTS OF INTERVENTION

Intervention on such a scale implies the development of a network of committees and advisers which can be counted on to inform the president, first, to counteract, if necessary, measures which are opposed to the somewhat ill-defined line taken by the Head of State. This became imperative from the early years of the Fifth Republic as the official networks were based on the prime minister and on the government. In the Fourth Republic, as indeed in the Third, meetings of ministers regularly took place without the president (they were known as *conseils de cabinet*); these prepared the meetings of the Councils of Ministers, chaired by the president, and obviously came to take a major part in decision-making. De Gaulle quickly put an end to such cabinet meetings, insisting that ministers met only in his presence. Indeed, he went further, and councils of ministers came to be occasions of "presidential guidance." Though proposals were and still are often presented by ministers at full cabinet meetings, ministers have also been *told* of decisions by the president; in one extreme case, a speech made by de Gaulle provoked resignations (these however were from members of the Christian Democrat party and the event occurred before the hold of the Gaullist party had been fully established).

Going further in this direction, de Gaulle seemed even for a while to be about to dismantle the Council of Ministers and to create in its place a number of committees chaired by the president. In 1960, not only defense matters, but Algerian and foreign policy questions came to be decided in these smaller bodies where the relevant ministers, and also civil servants, appeared to be a task force for presidential action. Perhaps emergency conditions created the need for these "hierarchical" arrangements, which were gradually disbanded in the 1960s—except for defense matters, where the constitution gives official recognition to the president's committee. Ministerial committees have tended to return to the more normal pattern, where, under a minister or the prime minister, a particular problem is being examined on the full cabinet's behalf.

But the president did maintain throughout the Fifth Republic a large specialized staff which kept him informed of developments, enabled him to intervene at an official level when the matter was of no great concern, and gave factual evidence to back future interventions at ministerial level. The numerous *chargés de mission* and *conseillers techniques* constitute a parallel organization to that of the prime minister, with which they are frequently in conflict. They do not have power; they cannot decide, they can simply suggest that the president's views may well be different from those which are proposed. They cover most important fields of government action; and the size of the staff in a particular field indicates the interest which the president is currently taking for a given problem.

PRESIDENTIAL LEADERSHIP, DUAL LEADERSHIP,
COLLECTIVE LEADERSHIP?

The structure of the new French executive thus has evolved in a complex and somewhat tortuous fashion since 1958. No one truly forecast at the origin what the relationship between president, prime minister, and government would become, largely because, as we said in the opening paragraphs of this chapter, views which were put forward were based on one of two models—the parliamentary model, where the Head of State typically does not become involved at all, and the presidential model, where the Head of State directs the policy of the nation. There seemed to be no middle way (at least no democratic middle way) between, broadly speaking, the role of the British queen and that of the U.S. president. It was conceded that the president might have a special function in emergencies; this was what the constitution stated and, in the late 1950s, the Algerian problem seemed to present a clear-cut example of an emergency.

As de Gaulle increased his involvement in foreign affairs and internal matters, it seemed that the parliamentary model would have quickly to give way to a presidential model. Yet over a decade has passed, and the "hybrid" system has remained a feature of the Fifth Republic. It is clear that the authority of the president is superior to that of the prime minister and of the government, but it is nonetheless also clear that the government exists and that the prime minister plays an important part in decision-making. The arrangements seemed to have become stabilized around a model of a dual executive, where the president is ready to allow important—though ill-defined—segments of the governmental activity directed, and not merely implemented, outside his direct involvement.

Yet, though this system remained stable through two presidents and five prime ministers, the prospects for the arrangements appear markedly uncertain. In the first place, systems of dual leadership are rare and unstable. They have been the common way in which monarchies gave way to popularly based government, as in Britain at the end of the eighteenth and the beginning of the nineteenth centuries. Though the evolution has at times been slow, the transitional character of this system is its very essence. In the contemporary world, the only other form of dual leadership which appears to recur with regularity is that of the Party general secretary and of the president of the Council of Ministers in Communist states; but this is often held by observers to be temporary, and it has indeed often led to serious power struggles and to the dismissal of the weaker leader.

The French system of dual leadership has indeed helped the nation to go through a transitional period, where presidential leadership was rejected by many because of the historical dangers of Bonapartism while the absence of strong parties made prime ministerial leadership an impossibility. Under de Gaulle and Pompidou, the loyalty of prime ministers has been remarkable; they have accepted the authority of the president, to whom they have tacitly acceded the right to decide, not only major matters of policy, but even their political fate as when de Gaulle dismissed Debré or when Pompidou dismissed Chaban-Delmas. The duration of the presidential mandate—seven years—has been instrumental in giving the Head of State more aloofness, while compelling him to look beyond the current prime minister and the current Parliament.

Yet this dual system presupposes that, *indefinitely*, president and Parliament will be of the same party, even though the election of the president does not coincide with that of Parliament. Of course, a variety of short-term solutions can be found if the president and Parliament happen to be, occasionally, of a different party. The president could dissolve the chamber and hope that a new majority will emerge from the polls. The president could resign and the country could elect a new president of a different party. But such partial solutions can constitute only temporary expedients; if the alternation of majorities were to be a regular feature of future French politics, the system of dual leadership would have to disappear.

Hypotheses about the future of the presidency and the whole executive may prove unrealistic, as many of the forecasts made in the early period of the Fifth Republic were contradicted. Georges Pompidou did act more as a "Gaullist" president than had been expected; his use of the referendum—however ill-fated—and his dismissal of Chaban-Delmas in 1972 showed that Gaullist habits had become more embedded in the Fifth Republic than had seemed possible under the personal rule of his predecessor. The UDR showed loyalty, and the French people at least did not question the actions of the president. But the smaller majorities of the mid-1970s appear to limit the scope of the president's action, while the shadow of de Gaulle on the French executive gradually diminishes as the founder of the Fifth Republic retreats in history. Though the "Gaullist" phase of the executive has endured surprisingly well the early succession problems, France still seems to be lacking the permanent and effective institutions which she has been seeking since the days of 1789 when the *ancien régime* was overthrown.

7

The Legislature

The stepchild of the Fifth Republic is the legislature. In the past, French political life swirled around the lobbies and paneled chamber of the Palais Bourbon, seat of the National Assembly. Not only was the greatest share of political business of the Third and Fourth Republics conducted in the lower house of Parliament (called the Chamber of Deputies during the Third Republic, but renamed the National Assembly in 1946), but on more than one occasion political battles were fought in the streets surrounding the Palais, as Frenchmen sought by direct action either to influence the legislature or to destroy it. The Chamber came to symbolize the Republic and all its works; it finally became the focus of all criticisms aimed at the shortcomings of French politics. Careers were often fashioned on the basis of learning and perfecting the intricacies of political behavior as traditionally practiced in the Assembly; those who did not learn to practice these techniques well were often frustrated at having to remain on the sidelines, with little more to do than to play Cassandra or attack the "system." Sometimes, however, the Chamber experienced dramatic moments in the competition between great orators, immersed in critical issues and exercising almost total freedom of debate.

Perhaps because it was the arena where the "Rights of Man" were first enunciated and defended, the Assembly became in time the repository of republican legitimacy—in theory the cockpit where the representatives of the people jousted for public recognition of their views. In the nineteenth century, the highest duty of the members was to preserve the rights and liberties of

their constituents against the encroachments of potentially tyran-
nical State officers. Inevitably, however, confusion over rights and
privileges developed; members became more and more parochial
and tended to regard their function as the defense of advantages
which had accrued to their district by circumstance, natural good
fortune, or government action. From protectors of civil liberties,
the members of the National Assembly, the deputies, were slowly
transformed into the champions of vested and often purely local
interests, a development which is not uncommon in many
legislatures, particularly in the United States Congress, whose
mores resemble in many ways those of the French Parliament
before 1958. The relationship between the legislators and the
premier and his ministers, however, remained essentially the
same. The ministers were constantly called on by indignant
legislators to justify or explain actions of the government or its
servants which threatened the individual dignity or the economic
privileges of the Frenchman.

In these circumstances, the mark of a promising premier was
his ability to deflect or postpone the demands which poured in on
the government for the extension of special privileges, or to blunt
the biting criticism of legislators who regarded the government as
the plunderer of local treasure, if not the epitome of reactionary
obscurantism. At the same time, the premier who wished to
survive was constantly forced to nurse along the coalition that
constituted his majority, pleading with his own ministers (or their
friends) not to lead the attack against him, while compromising
the integrity of his legislative program in order to maintain the
cohesion of his cabinet. To compound his difficulties, the premier
had to submit the various plans of his legislative program to the
committees of the house, often hostile, whose chairmen were
usually more anxious to further their own careers (perhaps by
replacing the relevant minister) with brilliant critiques of the
legislation under discussion than to contribute to the forward
progress of public business. Here, too, parallels can be drawn with
the committees of the United States Congress, though the French
Parliament never resorted to the kind of public grilling through
hearings which have characterized its American counterpart.
Perhaps most important, though—and this time in contrast with

the United States, where the administration remains in office, whatever happens, for four years—the chamber could, virtually without notice and always without fear of reprisal, since the right of dissolution had been customarily abolished after 1877, yank the rug from under any government. Deputies would either defeat legislation on which the premier counted, or, by using the procedure of interpellation, discuss any problem which was deemed to be important, but one which could sometimes be trivial or parochial and thus force the resignation of the premier and his ministers.

In all this there was a supporting philosophy to which the parliamentarians of the Third and Fourth Republics clung doggedly. Since the Revolution the enemies of republicanism were believed to be lodged in havens where they could exercise influence disproportionate to their numbers. These havens included the Church, the bureaucracy, and the armed forces. A kind of rampant anarchism (*"le citoyen contre les pouvoirs"*—"the citizen against the powers"—all the powers, whatever they were, to take the expression of the philosopher and essayist of the Third Republic, Alain) prevailed among the French people in general and among their elected representatives in particular. This harassment of the government operations could be justified as a republican virtue. There were also some more personal reasons for the antiministerial attitudes of many deputies: the faster the pace of government change, of the rise and fall of cabinets, the greater the opportunities for numerous deputies to win the coveted title of minister, and if the actual chance was not greater, at least the expectations were great; periods of cabinet crisis were intense, as deputies expected to be called, were disappointed if they were not, and felt even more bitter if some of their enemies were. The main skill needed to win office was to build a reputation for compromise with no trace of arrogance. One had to have the grace to desist. Thus cardinal sins against the Assembly were committed by those who tried to appeal to a higher court (in this case the people) against the Assembly. Because Pierre Mendès-France talked to the people in 1954 in a language which was convincing, deputies felt that he was not playing the game; because Edgar Faure used a miscalculation of some of the deputies which gave him the opportunity to dissolve the Assembly at the end of 1955, he was never forgiven by the old guard of the Fourth Republic.

Yet the "system," despite its faults, had given France a long period of liberal government. Only defeat led to its downfall in 1940 and only major colonial problems led to its downfall in 1958. It had been helped also by the administration which the kings and Napoleon had given France and which the Republic modified, wisely enough, only slowly and piecemeal. Transfer of legislative responsibility to the executive also took the form of decree laws enabling the government to act on behalf of Parliament. Criticized and even attacked as unconstitutional under the Third Republic, indeed made unconstitutional under the Fourth, decree laws renamed outline laws in the 1950s helped the government to bypass the legislature and helped the legislature to find a comfortable way out of its own political deadlocks. To that extent, the regime showed resilience and a sense of adaptation. It did not, however, go further; though numerous schemes were proposed to increase the stability of the government (through automatic dissolution of Parliament at each government crisis, for instance), none was ever adopted. The personal stakes were too high; the life of a parliamentarian was too often punctuated by the ritual of the governmental crisis; reform could not come from inside. Only because the framers of the Constitution of the Fifth Republic operated outside the atmosphere of Parliament could some drastic measures be taken to curtail parliamentary privileges. But only because de Gaulle was there were the rights curtailed in fact as well.

GENERAL PRINCIPLES OF ORGANIZATION OF PARLIAMENT IN THE FIFTH REPUBLIC

In order to bring about a change in the behavior of parliamentarians, the framers of the Constitution of 1958 decided to introduce a number of technical devices generally designed to enhance the position of the government and to give the chambers the possibility of controlling, but not of blocking, executive action.

These devices can be analyzed under five headings. First, there are general provisions aimed at reducing the harassments and at diminishing the opportunities for conflict in the general organization of Parliament. Second, the scope of legislation is reduced and that of the governmental prerogative correspondingly increased. Third, opportunities for "guerrilla" and "open warfare" during the debates over legislation are reduced by the introduction of a number of restrictions. Fourth, the operation of censure motions is severely restricted and the classic procedure of the interpellation abolished. Fifth, an overall control of parliamentary activity is provided by the possible intervention of the Constitutional Council. To these five types of devices, one should add the extended power of dissolution given to the president of the Republic, since, provided it remains effective as it clearly was in 1962 and 1968, the members of the National Assembly are likely to feel less disposed to show vindictiveness against the government if they know that they might rock their own boat by trying to sink the executive ship.

THE ELECTORAL SYSTEM

Parliament is composed of two chambers, the National Assembly and the Senate, the upper house having regained the title, but not all the powers, which it had under the Third Republic, while the lower house kept the name which the Constitution of 1946 had given it. The National Assembly is elected for five years (if it is not dissolved before) by direct universal suffrage; the electoral system is known as the *scrutin d'arrondissement à deux tours,* that is, a two-ballot (or run-off) system within single-member constituencies (taking place on two successive Sundays). This type of electoral system was used during most of the Third Republic, but it had been replaced in 1945 by proportional representation which was kept during the whole of the Fourth Republic, though with considerable modifications in the direction of the majority system. Proportional representation was advocated by the Left (and to some extent the right-wing and Christian parties) as the two-ballot system traditionally favored Center parties. At the first ballot, only candidates receiving 50 percent or more of the votes cast in the constituency are elected. In a country which has had numerous parties and splinter groups, the number of candidates elected at the first ballot has been small: at the general election of 1936, the last before World War II, only 185 out of 618 deputies were elected at the first ballot; at the general election of 1958, the first of the Fifth Republic, only 39 out of 465 deputies for metropolitan France were elected at the first ballot. With the streamlining of parties, however, this number has increased (to 96 in 1962 and 166 in 1968). Between the first and the second ballot (at which the candidate who gets most votes is elected irrespective of his percentage, but at which only candidates who obtained more than 10 percent of the votes at the first ballot may stand), deals take place and candidates withdraw voluntarily, sometimes without further ado, sometimes in favor of other candidates better placed in the race.

In the past, this kind of arrangement had benefited Center parties, as these could receive votes from the Right in left-wing areas, and from the Left in right-wing areas. This is why Center parties favored it in 1958 and de Gaulle agreed to reintroduce this system as a form of compromise. Moreover, the Fourth Republic had tampered so much with proportional representation that a widespread feeling of unjust manipulation of the electoral system had prevailed. The two-ballot arrangement may not be as mathematically fair as proportional representation, but it is simpler, and it brings the members of Parliament nearer to their constituents. In practice, the two-ballot system did not have in the Fifth Republic the results which had been expected. Far from favoring the rather inchoate Center groups of the traditional type, it benefited the Gaullists; the Left being disunited in 1958, it was crushed. Since 1962, the Left has recovered, but the exaggeration effect of the majority system (which is well-documented for Britain and other countries) has played a large part in helping the UDR. With about half the votes, the Gaullists and their allies had nearly 66 percent of the seats in 1968, while the Left obtained only 20 percent of the seats for one-third of the votes.

The Senate, sometimes nicknamed the "Grand Council of the French Communes," is elected for a much longer period (nine years, as in the Third Republic), with one third of its members retiring every three years. The electoral college, composed of representatives of local authorities, is complex in detail; it does not include all the municipal councillors of all the local authorities (of which there are nearly 38,000—some of them being very small, as we shall see in Chapter Eleven). Overall, the college is biased in favor of the small villages, as even the tiniest local authority has one delegate, with the resulting effect that the third of the population which lives in places under 1,500 inhabitants has slightly over half the delegates. Senators are themselves elected on the basis of the *département* (county) and the number of senators per *département* varies according to the population. There are also two ballots, with the delegates coming to cast their vote at the county town and the two ballots taking place in succession on the same Sunday. Rural overrepresentation led to an entirely different complexion of the Senate from the National Assembly. The big winners in the Senate are the Center-Right parties, mostly Conservatives or Radicals, while the Gaullist party, which swept the towns and big cities, did not succeed in having more than a small minority of senators at each successive election to the Senate since 1958. Hence a considerable tension between the two chambers and between the government and the Senate; hence the fact that the Senate did not see its status increased in practice as a result of the new regime, in contrast with what had been expected. Indeed, de Gaulle tried by referendum to curtail the power and to change the composition of the upper house in 1969 at the same time as he was proposing a regional reform. One of the reasons for this failure was the apparent support of many (on the Right and Center) for the Senate.

THE LIFE OF THE NATIONAL ASSEMBLY
The change in the electoral system of the National Assembly in 1958 was designed to decrease the size of the opposition in Parliament, since it was hoped that the center, rather than the extremes, would benefit from the new arrangements. But several other devices written into the constitution tend to create a better climate and to give the government more breathing space (the

electoral law is not part of the constitution, which simply states that the deputies "shall be elected by direct suffrage" and that "the Senate shall be elected by indirect suffrage"—Article 24).

First, both houses of Parliament sit only about six months in the year, in the autumn and the spring, unless the government decides to call for a special session or unless Article 16 is invoked. Article 29 also says that "Parliament shall be convened in extraordinary session at the request . . . of the majority of the members comprising the National Assembly . . ." but de Gaulle interpreted this restrictively when the question arose for the first time in 1960, as if the article had stated that only when a majority of the members requested such an extraordinary session *might* Parliament be recalled. He also argued that it was up to him to grant the request and refused to do so in the circumstance (on the grounds that Article 30 says that extraordinary sessions, unlike ordinary sessions, are opened and closed by a decree of the president of the Republic).

Second, the president of the National Assembly is elected for the duration of the legislature, instead of once a year, as was the case before 1958; this had led to tensions and conflicts before the Assembly had started its business, thus creating climates of ill feeling. The president of the Senate, however, is elected after each partial reelection of the Senate, every three years. The president of each house is assisted by what is known as a *bureau,* which is composed of several vice-presidents and secretaries drawn from the various parties with some regard to their strength in the house; they continue to be elected every year, but, as there is quasi-proportional representation, troubles are less common and arrangements usually take place beforehand.

The president of the Assembly (for ten years Jacques Chaban-Delmas, before he became prime minister) and the president of the Senate (at first Gaston Monnerville, a radical member strongly opposed to de Gaulle, and later Alain Poher, the unsuccessful presidential candidate of 1969) are among the top politicians and they are consulted by the president, according to the constitution, in various circumstances (such as dissolution or the use of Article 16). They conceive of their role more as speakers of the United States House of Representatives than as speakers of the British House of Commons; though of necessity impartial in the actual conduct of debate, they do attempt to influence the conduct of business by informally talking to members. Before 1958, these offices were stepping stones to the presidency of the Republic, where indeed the same qualities of informal advice and backstairs influence were necessary; hence the fact that contests sometimes tended to take place when the time came to appoint the president of one or the other house.

Finally, a third arrangement—which brings us nearer to the actual process of lawmaking—also tends to increase the role of the government in the organization of Parliament. It stems from the fact that the Constitution of 1958 decreased the powers of the *Conférence des Présidents*, a body which plays a similar part to that of the Rules Committee of the House of Representatives (and indeed resembled it in its behavior before 1958). It includes the chairmen of the committees and of the parliamentary "groups" (the parties in the chamber). It is chaired and called to meeting every week by the president of the house and its function is to decide the business for the coming sittings. Before 1958, the government had obtained the right to send a delegate to the *Conférence,* and this delegate could state which bills or problems the government wished to see debated, and in what order, but he had no vote; the decisions taken by the *Conférence* were often at considerable variance from the wishes of the government. The tactics consisted in trying to avoid debate on the matters which the government wanted to put forward but deputies disliked and thus create embarrassment through inaction. Since 1958, these tactics are no longer possible, through the combined operation of the apparently innocuous Article 43 of the constitution, which states that "Government and Private Members' bills shall, at the request of the Government or of the Assembly concerned, be sent for study to committees especially designated for this purpose" and of the more sinister looking Article 48, which states that "the discussion of the bills filed or agreed to by the Government shall have priority on the agenda of the Assemblies in the order set by the Government." Thus the government can disregard whatever feelings there may be against bringing the bill forward in the *Conférence des Présidents* and make sure that this bill is sent first to a committee and then extracted from the committee and presented to the floor of the house.

SCOPE OF LEGISLATION

THE TRADITIONAL SUPREMACY OF THE LAW

Traditionally, as is logical in a country which adopts a parliamentary system, the French Parliament could legislate on any matter. The constitution merely regulated the principles of organization of the public powers; there was no Supreme Court to rule laws unconstitutional or to prevent Parliament from interfering in certain fields. The Constitutional Council established in 1958 now has some powers (which we shall examine later in this chapter), but these are based to a large extent on an entirely new conception of the law which has been introduced by the new constitution. In the past laws (*lois*) were defined merely as texts adopted by Parliament, by contrast with decrees (being texts adopted by the whole government) and *arrêtés* (being texts adopted by a minister or a local authority). These documents derived their legal power from each other; the government could not make decrees, and ministers and local authorities could not make *arrêtés* unless a law (and if necessary a decree as well) had given the authority the legal power to do so, in most cases specifically (for instance, by stating that "the Minister of ——— shall adopt by *arrêté* the rules implementing the present Article") but sometimes generally (it had always been recognized that the government had general powers to issue decrees to implement legislation, this being known as the *pouvoir règlementaire*). This hierarchy meant that, in practice, decrees and *arrêtés* tended to deal with less important matters than laws. But, formally at least, the distinction among the three types of documents simply came from the type of public body which was empowered to issue the text.

This situation was felt to be doubly disadvantageous. On the one hand, it meant that Parliament was always free to invade, if it so desired, the field which had been previously dealt with by *arrêté* or decree. Nothing prevented Parliament from legislating on trivial matters, and such instances did occur if there was some powerful electoral reason which compelled the deputies to do so, but once some matter had been regulated by a law, it was difficult to go back, as only a law can amend another law. Thus parliamentary interference increased indefinitely, time could be wasted on small matters, and occasions for action by private lobbies were multiplied. On the other hand, this expansion of legislative action had in fact the effect of diminishing the real role of Parliament in important matters, as if Parliament had been weaving around itself a spider's web which could no longer be cut to size but had to be destroyed; it became common for governments to ask for a wide delegation of the power to modify laws by decree (hence the expressions of decree laws or outline laws). In a country where the authority of the government is sufficient to prevent the chamber from overstepping its rights, as in Britain, the legislative supremacy of Parliament has fewer disadvantages; in a country such as France, where the executive was traditionally weak, many felt, understandably enough, that a restriction of the scope of legislation could have beneficial effects.

LIMITATIONS OF THE POWER OF PARLIAMENT IN THE LEGISLATIVE FIELD

Hence the complex Article 34 of the Constitution of 1958 which purports to prevent undue parliamentary interference by defining the scope of legislation in detail. A detailed definition is indeed necessary if the limitation is to be effective, but the problems which are raised by this limitation are difficult to solve and the interpretation of the clause has proved tricky on various points. After having stated that "all laws shall be passed by Parliament" (which also means that laws are passed by Parliament only), the article proceeds to elaborate what laws are by stating that "laws determine the rules" (*règles*) relating to a number of listed matters: civil rights; the fundamental guarantees of public liberties; the obligations of the citizens for purposes of national defense; nationality; personal status; property in marriage; inheritance; the definition of crimes and penalties attached to them; criminal procedure; the organization of the judiciary; taxation; the electoral system; the fundamental guarantees of civil servants and of members of the armed forces; the creation of categories of public corporations; the nationalization of private property. The article then adds that "laws shall determine the fundamental principles" relating to certain other matters: the organization of national defense and of local government; education; social security; the law of property and commercial law; labor and trade union laws. Finally, the article states that its provisions "may be elaborated and completed by an organic law."

The list is fair; it includes all the important matters which one would expect a parliament to be concerned with. But three difficulties have to be faced. First, what is meant by "rules" (*règles*) in the first part of the article is not entirely clear; the word *règle* has no precise meaning in French law. Second, and a potentially more worrisome source of trouble, there is no way of being sure of what a "principle" is, and yet the article argues that only the "principles" of education law, for instance, have to be defined by law. Conflicts have arisen, as was to be expected. The arbiter, on this point, is the Constitutional Council, but the matter has clear political undertones: if Parliament were to delve into the details of legislation, the government would have to conduct a difficult series of battles in the Constitutional Council which would undermine its authority, perhaps as much as previous battles aimed at preventing Parliament from legislating on trivia. Third, the last provision, which mentions the possibility of "elaboration and completion" by an organic law, can also be quite ominous for the government.

The drafters of the constitution tried to buttress the system by introducing yet another distinction, this time not between laws and other types of texts, but among the laws themselves. Before 1958, there were only two types of laws: "ordinary" laws and the constitution. The latter had a higher status than ordinary laws, though, there being no Supreme Court, the practical effect was small; the main one was that the procedure of constitutional amendment was longer and more difficult. In order to strengthen the government in relation to Parliament, in order also to bring some realism to the question of delegation of legislative power to the government, the Constitution of 1958 introduced two new types of documents, named "organic laws" and "ordinances."

Organic laws (of which we mentioned one example in relation to Article 34) are laws which are passed by Parliament with a somewhat more stringent procedure than that of the ordinary law: a delay of fifteen days must elapse between the moment it is submitted and the moment it is passed by the chamber to which it was first presented; opposition by the Senate entails another vote by an absolute majority of the members of the National Assembly (except if the organic law concerns the Senate, in which case both houses must pass identical texts); finally, and most importantly, organic laws must be deemed constitutional by the Constitutional Council before they can be promulgated. Thus it is hoped, for instance on Article 34 (as well as on matters concerning the organization of Parliament and various other constitutional bodies which are regulated by organic laws), that the Constitutional Council will prevent Parliament from overstepping its powers. On the other hand, if Parliament wants to delegate its legislative powers (or if the government asks for and obtains powers of delegation from Parliament), any amendment of legislation made by the government in this way takes the form, not of a decree law as before 1940, but of an ordinance, which has to be ratified by Parliament at the end of the delegation period. Thus governments cannot go too far and be granted too many powers by a Parliament overburdened or frightened by a sudden crisis, as was often the case in the 1930s, and the government hopes to have the Constitutional Council on its side in cases of parliamentary encroachments.

The machinery is therefore complex; it needed to be if it was to meet the problems at all satisfactorily. On balance, it has worked reasonably smoothly, contrary to expectations, largely of course because the government could control its majority. Other aspects of the regulation of the powers of the Assembly, to which we now come, have led to greater difficulties.

THE LEGISLATIVE STRUGGLE

In a parliamentary system, the two main activities of a parliament consist in voting laws and in controlling the government. But the two are intertwined, as previous analyses have already shown.

Before 1958, it was indeed through the development of the legislative struggle that the patience, wits, and skills of ministers were being tested, since, in the last resort, a government needs laws to implement its program and needs in particular one law, the financial law, merely to survive. Thus, though we shall see that the question of the control of the executive leads to certain specific problems and certain particular arrangements, it was naturally on the legislative process that the drafters of the Constitution of 1958 concentrated a large part of their "engineering" talent. In order to understand the purpose of the reforms, the best way is to follow the sequence of legislation, note the traps which deputies used to set for the government, and see how the Constitution of 1958 intervenes on the side of the executive.

A bill debated in the French Parliament goes through the following sequence—not very different from that which bills go through in the United States Congress. After having been laid on the table of either chamber, by a member of that chamber or by the government (with the exception of finance bills which must be presented first to the National Assembly), the bill is sent to a committee which then reports to the house (each bill has a *rapporteur* from the committee which reports on the bill as amended). The house discusses the bill first in general, then article by article (and if necessary paragraph by paragraph), and votes on each article. There is then a final vote on the bill as amended. At this point it goes to the other house, which follows the same procedure. If both houses agree on the same text, the bill is sent to the president for promulgation (we saw that he could ask for a second deliberation and has fifteen days to do so, but has no veto power; requests for second deliberations are very rare, and are normally aimed at correcting technical errors which had been overlooked). If the houses disagree, the bill goes again to each house; if there is still disagreement, a joint committee comprising an equal number of members of each house is set up, with a view to coming up with a common text. Only if the government intervenes, as we shall see, is there a possibility of preventing deadlock if the two chambers still disagree (in the Fourth Republic, the National Assembly could always override the opposition of the upper chamber).

PARLIAMENTARY COMMITTEES

We have already noted that the Constitution of 1958 eliminated two sources of potential antigovernment action, one at the very first stage, when the bill is sent to a committee, and the other at the report stage, when the bill is due to be debated in the chamber. But there were many other possible sources of friction. As can be expected, committees constituted very powerful hurdles. Organized, as in the United States but not in Britain, on the basis of specialist subjects (finance, foreign affairs, interior, etc.), the twenty or so committees of the pre-1958 parliaments had great opportunities to make trouble for the government. They comprised the members of the parliamentary groups (elected on the basis of proportional representation) who were most interested in the problems concerned, or had electoral reasons from their constituency's point of view to appear interested. Their chairmen, elected every year together with vice-chairmen (the seniority system never took roots in France, though some chairmen did remain for long periods), were naturally men of influence within their sphere of competence. They were natural leaders of any opposition in this field; they were the real "shadow ministers," and indeed behaved like shadow ministers, often hoping to acquire the minister's job at the next governmental crisis (and thus unlikely to be keen on preventing the occurrence of such crises). They were recognized as shadow ministers by all, both by the government who always took care to listen to what they said and by the chamber which always gave committee chairmen the right to speak in reply to ministerial points.

Committees made life difficult for the government because they were built as if oppositions were to be maximized, but they also made life difficult because the procedure of the chambers gave the committee full responsibility in relation to bills. When a bill, whether coming from the government or from a private member, went to a committee, it became in effect the committee's bill. The committee could so alter its substance that it could emerge unrecognizable. But, whether this happened or not, the committee's bill, not the original document, was reported to the house, and any return to the original text technically had to take the form of amendments to the committee's bill. This procedure, which might be acceptable in relation to private members' bills, many of which were drafted very quickly and without much technical help, was disastrous for the government. The government constantly had to make sure that the economy of the bill was not upset by a whole series of changes which had taken place in committee and which might have to be opposed, one by one. The outcome was always uncertain particularly if, as a result of a protracted discussion, the debate on the floor went far into the night.

The Constitution of 1958 sought to reduce drastically the power of committees from one of complete control of the legislative process to one of advice given to the house on the line to take on the bill in general and on the various clauses. Hence two sets of provisions, one of which was perhaps too clever to be really successful. On the one hand and at first sight rather cunningly, Article 43 limits to six the number of permanent committees in each house. It was perhaps hoped that, like the British House of Commons committees, they might not be specialized; it was certainly hoped that they would become so large that they would include more than merely experts aiming at fighting private battles with ministers (they are from sixty to 120 strong). But, despite various rulings from the Constitutional Council, the government could not avoid the setting up of informal subcommittees, which tend to correspond to some extent to the old committees and are better able to discuss legislation in detail; the effect of Article 43 seems therefore to be small. On the other hand, and more successfully, committees are no longer empowered to substitute their bills for those of the government, as Article 42 states that the discussion on the floor has to take place on the government's text; changes approved by the committee are submitted to the house, but as amendments.

THE WEAPONS IN THE HANDS OF THE GOVERNMENT

During the discussion on the floor of the house, harassment of governmental legislation often took place in many other ways. A very common one, which consisted of withholding amendments until the bill came to the floor (so as either to embarrass the government and its supporters at the last moment, or lead to delay by forcing a reference back to the committee) is now forbidden. Only amendments which have been discussed in committee need to be discussed on the floor, unless the government is prepared to see them discussed. But the most drastic arrangement, which was attacked from the start for being potentially dangerous and which provoked anger from time to time as it was being used, is the procedure of closure. Article 44 allows the government to request each chamber to vote by a single vote on the text under discussion (this has been known as *vote bloqué*). As the article stands, it is clearly vulnerable to abuse; there is no restriction on the moment at which the government can use the procedure, or indeed any safeguards at all. It is difficult to see, however, what safeguards could be written into the constitution which would not at the same time so limit the operation of the article as to make it of little use. Safeguards have to come from the chamber itself, which should not tolerate abusive requests for closure and is in a position to rebel (by rejecting the bill) if the government insists on very quickly bringing the debate to a close. Though the procedure has been used fairly frequently when the government's majority was relatively small (and over 100 times in the first ten years of the Fifth Republic), it has not given rise to real abuse; the government does accept amendments and does incorporate them in bills for which it eventually asks for a single final vote. If one takes into account the obvious excesses of the previous system, the changes in the legislative procedure were probably necessary (the British government does, after all, use the guillotine) if the new system of government were to function effectively.

The constitution gives the government two other sets of powers relating to the legislative procedure. Finance bills have to be treated differently from other laws, since they have to be passed by a given time. Before 1958, French parliaments were notorious for their delaying action in respect to the budget; indeed, the budget was customarily one of the hurdles which few governments passed safely, and this in turn increased delays, as a new government had to be formed and rethink the budget before the finance bill could be approved. In order to redress this situation, the Constitution of 1958 limits to seventy the number of days during which Parliament can discuss and decide on the budget; if it has not settled matters by the end of the period, the government becomes entitled to promulgate the finance bill by ordinance. In fact, this stringent weapon has not had to be used, and budgetary procedure has taken a much more normal turn than before the Fifth Republic; debate over specific items is often long and sometimes tough, but budgets are now voted on time and the techniques of either holding the clock at midnight on December 31 (the end of the financial year in France) or of voting "provisional twelfths" (the granting of money for a month while the debate went on) have wholly disappeared.

Finally, the government, and the government alone, can end a deadlock between the two houses by asking for yet another reading by each house of the text adopted by the National Assembly. If there is still disagreement between the two houses, the National Assembly is called to vote again, and this decision is final. Thus the Senate is not in a position to do what it was criticized for having done before 1940, namely to block governmental legislation, particularly of a progressive kind. But the government can benefit from the Senate's legislative veto if it finds it convenient; only if both houses agree is the government forced to accept legislation of which it does not approve.

The legislative struggle thus goes on with wholly different weapons in the hands of the protagonists. The government is not permanently on the defensive. Many have said that the 1958 Constitution went too far in tilting the balance in favor of the government. This is, in the light of past experience, very arguable. The executive had to be strengthened; but as all means of procedure were used with great skill, very strong procedural checks had to be built to prevent the game from following its "normal" rules. In reality, the danger does not perhaps so much arise from the fear that the measures might be too strong, as that they might be ineffective, if the authority of the government were once more to decrease. The political "engineering" of the Constitution of 1958 is a brave effort. It has clearly been very useful, even though harsh criticisms have been made about the "voting machine" character of Parliament. But its permanent success does depend on the strength of the parties of the executive, as "procedural engineering" cannot be expected to do more than reduce the opportunities of challenge; it cannot avoid challenge altogether.

THE VOTE OF CENSURE

Only in a relatively recent period has the question of the vote of censure, in France and in other parliamentary systems, appeared to constitute a major problem. Traditionally, as can be seen by the British practice, parliaments were entitled to censure governments at will; this was assumed to be a fundamental right of parliament, though censure might immediately be followed by dissolution. But, in France and in some other countries, ministerial instability led to a questioning of this "inalienable" right. If the parliamentary system were to die because governments fell too often, it appeared reasonable to limit the right of censure so as to preserve the parliamentary system as well.

There are serious difficulties, however, if one is to limit the right of assembly to censure of the government. The first concerns legislation. If the government cannot be censured easily, but if the Assembly can easily reject bills proposed by the government, and in particular reject or delay financial bills, the Assembly might well obtain, indirectly, what it would have wanted to obtain directly through a vote of censure, namely the fall of the government: the cabinet may simply resign. Thus, if governmental stability is to be achieved, procedures have to be devised which limit not only the conditions under which the motion of censure can be operative, but also the conditions under which legislation can be rejected without a vote of censure. Only if both problems are solved will governments be given the means to achieve their policies and thus not be tempted to resign frequently of their own free will.

Procedures limiting the right of the Assembly to censure the government must therefore also cover legislation. This had not been the case in the 1946 Constitution; only the censure motion was regulated. Thus governments continued to fall between 1946 and 1958 because the Assembly did not pass the bills which these governments wanted, though they did not technically lose the "confidence" of the Assembly. Various schemes were therefore proposed, usually linking the fall of cabinets to an automatic subsequent dissolution. But the Assembly was too strong before 1958 and no reform succeeded.

The framers of the Constitution of 1958 did introduce a reform, but it is drastic and somewhat clumsy. First, Article 49 of the constitution states that motions of censure have to be proposed by at least one tenth of the deputies; forty-eight hours must elapse before the vote can take place, presumably in the hope that some might rally to the government on second thoughts. And if the censure motion is defeated, those who proposed it cannot propose another during the same parliamentary session (of which there are two each year). Second, as in 1946, abstainers are counted on the government's side; an absolute majority of the members of the Assembly is needed to defeat the government. But—and this is the clumsy aspect, as it would indeed be strange if a government were maintained in office with more deputies against it than for it (though not an absolute majority against it), the constitution stipulates that only those voting for the censure motion (i.e. against the government) will record their votes. Supporters of the government simply do not vote at all. Third, if the government wants to see a bill through, but encounters difficulties, it can "pledge its responsibility on the vote of (the) text." In this case, the text becomes law without a vote, unless a motion of censure is tabled; if the censure is not adopted (and the procedure is the one which has just been described), the government is safe and the bill is adopted.

Perhaps such drastic arrangements were needed for the system to be foolproof. Thus the government has the upper hand. No "interpellation" can be tabled, as in the past; governments cannot be suddenly overthrown. Deputies have only two means to curb the executive. They have the question, which was introduced by the Constitution of 1958 allegedly on the British model; however, instead of being short exchanges between a deputy and a minister, in France these questions have tended to be small debates without a vote, taking place on one day every week. The other curb is the motion of censure. The government may also initiate debates on its program or on a "declaration of general policy"; if it so wishes, it can stake its responsibility and set the procedure of censure in motion. But these are the Assembly's only means of supervision and control of the government; the rest of its activities are legislative and budgetary. Clearly, the constitution went too far; the excesses of the Third and Fourth Republics may have led to the introduction of a stringent procedure, which also had to be clumsy and even bizarre. But the weapon is too heavy; it is difficult to use because, somehow, it seems unfair. Under the Gaullist phase of the system, the technique has been used in a number of cases; in September 1962, as we noted in Chapter Six, a censure motion was even passed. But the procedure is so harsh that it reduced sharply the number of policy debates, and this prevented the Assembly from airing major questions, except occasionally. Thus the main criticism against the new system is not so much in the field of legislation; laws are discussed, and opportunities for amendment are probably not very different in the French Parliament than in other Western European parliaments. But the censure motion is such a straitjacket that broad foreign, defense, or economic policy matters are rarely debated. Previous assemblies were so prone to overthrowing governments through interpellations instead of just airing questions that restrictions had to be imposed; but the medicine has been strong. Over time, when old habits are forgotten, greater opportunities for debate will have to be introduced.

The real solution might indeed be different. The Fifth Republic showed that even a strong government, backed by a strong president, could only exceptionally use Article 49. Pre-1958 governments fell largely because the assemblies laid traps for the executive; but they also fell because the executive was overanxious to see all its bills pass through Parliament. This does happen in Britain, but even the British government, though relying on a tight party discipline, does have occasional problems with its legislation; a century ago, this insistence on legislation was not the practice of parliamentary systems, any more than it is the practice in presidential systems such as the United States, where the veto power and various means of pressure do not give the president more than a limited say in the bills which pass through

Congress. If French governments were more prepared to let Parliament exercise some legislative initiative, governments might not need so often to use their authority; by not dissipating their power over too many matters, governments might be more effective in really crucial cases.

THE CONSTITUTIONAL COUNCIL AND EXECUTIVE-LEGISLATIVE RELATIONS

We already mentioned some aspects of the role of the Constitutional Council, which has played a large part in the transformation of executive-legislative relations. One of its powers—not the most important—related to referendums and national elections, both presidential and parliamentary, which it must officially declare and settle in cases of disputes. There have indeed been disputes after each election, particularly in very close contests (before 1958, disputes were settled by each house), and the council seems to have been somewhat overprone to quash elections and impose by-elections, while showing perhaps some slight prejudice against opposition parties. Its second set of powers relates to the standing orders of both houses which, though not organic laws, have to be submitted to the council before coming into force. This provision led almost immediately to a sharp conflict between Parliament and council, as various clauses had been reintroduced in the standing orders along lines of pre-1958 arrangements, which the council rightly felt contrary to the new constitution and quickly proceeded to quash; one of the arrangements quashed allowed for a vote following debates on questions and thus would have indirectly brought back, though in a limited way, the practice of interpellation. This was wiped away, not surprisingly, by the Constitutional Council. Third, the council periodically intervenes to interpret and implement Article 34 on the scope of legislation. Though its decisions usually favored the government, the council also on occasion sided with the legislature, particularly in the latter part of the Gaullist period, as if either the council felt that the political situation might be about to change or if the moral pressures had tended to diminish.

France thus experiences a new form of parliamentarianism, labeled "true parliamentarianism" by its supporters and condemned as the end of Parliament by its opponents. Clearly, the legislature has lost many of its old rights. The game of politics is no longer practiced according to the rules which prevailed for three quarters of a century and had therefore become the norm for both members who reveled in the system and those outsiders who criticized democratic government on the grounds that it was synonymous with irresponsible parliamentary behavior. Many of the attacks against the new arrangements are, perhaps not surprisingly, based on an old system which seems to have acquired virtues since its disappearance. In fact, the French National Assembly is not particularly sheepish, and the moderation of its attacks against the government does not come only—indeed, far from it—from constitutional changes.

Whether one considers the first legislature (1958–1962) or the second (1962–1967), one finds numerous instances of restiveness, rebellion, and executive retreat; the third (1967–1968) was very short, and the fourth (1968–1973) had a very large Gaullist majority. The government often gave in. It gave in on the details of many budgets; it gave in on substantial sections of many bills, as on the turnover tax reform where opposition came from all quarters, for purely electoral considerations, and resembled closely pre-1958 practice. When the government did not give in, as on an amnesty law after the Algerian war, it had to use all resources of procedure and apply the "whip" strongly to its supporters; yet over thirty Gaullist deputies and nearly forty other followers of the government did not vote for the bill in the final vote. Admittedly, as has often been noted, the government gives in mostly on less important questions. Admittedly also, debates on defense or foreign affairs have been infrequent and occurred almost exclusively in the context of censure motions; they scarcely affected the course of policy. But foreign affairs is typically not a field where parliaments are strong: neither the U.S. Congress nor the British House of Commons can be said to have achieved much either in the whole of this area. Since 1958, the pendulum has swung too far against the Assembly—though not quite as far as critics and parliamentarians are usually ready to claim.

What is indeed needed is a recognition by all that the legislature has the right to discuss, to supervise, to suggest, while the government has the right to lead and to be subjected to fears of early dismissal. This can only happen if attitudes of deputies are transformed. Thus the new party system is at least as critical as constitutional rules. The loyalty and discipline of UDR deputies and the overall trend towards a more "national" form of party politics have helped to induce deputies to exercise their functions in a new perspective. Time has been important; members have begun to learn about the new system, about the limitations to their power as well as about their possible role. Members have learned about their constituency functions, about their possible scope as middlemen (perhaps too much, indeed, in view of some scandals); they have learned about their scope for action in various campaigns for the extension of individual rights. The French National Assembly has changed since 1958. Unlike members of the old Parliament, Fifth Republic deputies have been drawn from business, medicine, the civil service, less from legal professions and teaching; this has been a net gain, as Parliament has become more representative of the real interests of the nation, though workers, and especially manual workers are grossly underrepresented: the dozen or so manual workers are almost exclusively in the Communist party. With a smaller majority than in the 1968–1973 Parliament, with members more accustomed to parliamentary work, the French Parliament may engage more actively in its function of scrutiny and information, both at the level of general policy and at the level of more detailed constituency matters in which it can play an important part (and already does to a large extent). If this does happen, the Gaullist strait jacket will have proved profitable in helping Parliament out of the irresponsible, at times even childish, forms of behavior in which it was engaged and in moving toward a more mature recognition of the role of a legislature in a complex society.

THE ADMINISTRATIVE MACHINERY OF THE STATE

PART FOUR

THE
ADMINISTRATIVE
MACHINERY
OF THE STATE

8

The Bureaucracy

The counterpart to the weakness of the French executive was traditionally the strength of the bureaucracy. Indeed, as we noted in the previous chapter, the civil service was so strong that this seemed to justify the vigilance of parliamentarians, though this vigilance usually turned to irresponsibility. Not surprisingly, many felt that the advent of the Fifth Republic would lead to the complete dominance by the technocracy. Shielded from the people's representatives by the popularity of the president, indeed pushed to give the country the internal economic strength and technical excellence which was needed to achieve externally the aims of French "greatness," members of the French bureaucracy were naturally seen as the main beneficiaries of the new arrangements. They would, at least, be able to do as they pleased, unencumbered by various forms of control; the "enlightened despotism," which had characterized the French administrative system for several centuries but had suffered some setbacks in the second quarter of the twentieth century, would be given a new lease on life.

These fears (or hopes) did not materialize in the long run. As we saw, the most obvious sign of influence of the civil service, the entry of some of their members in the government, soon turned into a mere manifestation of the arrival of a new type of politician, by a different route from before, into the new Gaullist party. Despite its weaknesses, French local government did not give way to the centralizing tendencies of the bureaucracy; quite the contrary, demands were gradually made for various forms of decentralization and for regionalism. Not many have succeeded, as we shall see in Chapter Ten, but the era of administrative ascendancy is clearly of the past. Particularly since 1968, though already to some extent before, civil servants have begun to worry about their own power vis-à-vis groups and the population at large. It would be highly exaggerated to speak of a crisis in French administration, but it would be wrong not to pay some attention to the elements of disquiet, rethinking, and questioning which have become noticeable in many quarters of the civil service, and in particular in the younger age groups. Some and possibly many civil servants are unsure of their position in a democratic state, especially if greater emphasis is to be given to participation. Administrators are no longer so sure they should run the State *for* the citizens and impose decisions for the public good.

Yet these attitudes emerge in a context which is—and has been for centuries—that of a modernizing State. The French administrator may be cross-pressured in the present day, but he is cross-pressured because the support for the idea of "social engineering" is strong in the framework of French bureaucracy; it stems directly from a long-standing tradition. Born from the *dirigisme* of the kings and later of Napoleon, French social engineering was given its intellectual stamp of acceptability by various writers, philosophers, or sociologists. The aims and the role of civil servants, specifically of higher civil servants, have to be related to the influence of men such as Saint-Simon and Auguste Comte, who were, in particular the former, the promoters of social engineering in the early years of the nineteenth century. Society has to be molded; it is, in the true sense, a machine, which can be perfected by appropriate means. Progress is equally important, and equally feasible, in social and technical fields; indeed, the two are linked, not merely because the conditions of social progress lie in technical development, but because methods of technical achievements should be imitated in the social fields. In this the *École Polytechnique* is a key element, and, characteristically, Saint-Simon and Comte were associated with teaching at that school. And while "*saint-simonisme*" faded out as a doctrine, its influence on attitudes was profound, indeed determining, during most of the nineteenth century (Napoleon III was a *saint-simonien*), particularly in those periods when economic development took place at a rapid rate. Clearly the planners of the second half of the twentieth century were not *saint-simoniens* in the strict sense; but they were affected—infected, so to speak—by similar ideas. Their goals, their mode of operation, their arrogance also, were in large part inherited from the same tradition.

This tradition has a variety of consequences on the role of the bureaucracy in the nation, which we shall examine throughout this chapter. The most important is the centralization of the French State, which includes as its corollary the spreading of the services of the State over the whole nation. But another, perhaps not sufficiently stressed, is the greater concern for economic than for social well-being, as the happiness of men is viewed as clearly dependent on the better organization of society for the *production* of goods and services; the approach is expansionist. Ideas might change as the potential dangers of economic growth for the health of citizens and the protection of the environment become more widespread, but the process will be slow. If, then, the expansion of goods and services leads to the happiness of men, the problem is to find, not just how many of the goods need to be produced to create happiness, but the distribution which will maximize the happiness of all; this is viewed as a technical point which needs to be solved by those who know about techniques of social organization. Liberals assume that citizens will make demands; technocrats of the French tradition try to find out what demands might be, should be, or could be. Thus, while a liberal democratic approach leads naturally to rather more emphasis on social problems, since demands are likely to be for a change in the social arrangements, the French technocratic line will come to social questions as problems of distribution, stemming from the expansion of the production of goods and services and raising technical questions, rather than compassion or the recognition that the people at large have a right to make their views felt and see them, at least in part, implemented. Such a philosophy clashes unquestionably with the participationist view which has come to be voiced more strongly both in and outside the bureaucracy. Thus some civil servants at least may be somewhat cross-pressured in the present context.

Yet the philosophy of social engineering prevails. Economic development still plays a greater part than does social welfare. The plan only became recently concerned with both economic and social development. Moreover, in the plan for instance, social rearrangements are tackled on lines of prediction and subsequent action which contrast markedly with the neutrality and passivity of the liberal democratic State. Though in particular in the 1970s, the weight of groups and the impact of the ideology of participation limit the extent to which classic forms of social engineering can be applied in practice, the philosophy is deep-rooted enough to emerge at crucial points in the French bureaucracy. It has been so powerful for so long—and had so much influence both at home and abroad—that it is unlikely to be undermined easily in the coming decades.

THE CIVIL SERVICE

On the surface, the French civil service may seem almost identical to its counterparts in other countries. It includes hundreds of thousands of jobs in a whole variety of fields, most of which are routine and lowly. There are typists, secretaries, technicians of all kinds. Yet even these low-grade employees of the State, by being *fonctionnaires* (from the expression *Fonction Publique* which applies to the civil service), have privileges and generally possess a status which differs more markedly from the status of private employees than it does for their counterparts in Anglo-Saxon countries (if not Germany or Italy). Some of the differences have decreased because private employees gained similar advantages; pension rights and annual holidays are no longer a privilege of civil servants. But some have remained untouched, as the security of tenure which is very much higher than almost in any other form of employment and gives to civil servants (at least once they are *titularisés*, that is, have passed their probation period) an almost full assurance to remain for life in the employment of the State. Conversely, civil servants used to be forbidden to strike and even to join unions; this has mostly disappeared and civil service strikes are quite frequent, though these are mainly token one-day strikes, except among industrial civil servants, and in particular postmen, where they last at times much longer. But the procedure by which one becomes a civil servant is longer and more complex than in other walks of life. Typically, competitive examinations have to be passed to ensure equality for all, and candidates are many; typically, too, requirements for entry are more stringent than in other walks of life, either because the service always believed in diplomas or because, through the examinations, the level of entry naturally increased.

Because of these status advantages and the benefits which they gave, the civil service quickly became a pole of attraction. This was possible only because the service was very large with respect to the whole population from very early on. It had 200,000 members in 1871, about four times the size of the British civil service at the time; it was over a million in 1950, while the British civil service did not reach 700,000 at the same period, though the French population was smaller. Size differences were due in part to the fact that French teachers are civil servants, while English teachers are not; but part of the difference was also due to other branches of the local government service being much less well staffed in France than in other European countries. This is not merely a legal distinction, it means also more centralization. It means a comparatively greater attractiveness of the civil service because of better career prospects than in the smaller local government service. It means that the French civil service is present everywhere in the country. Opportunities offered by civil service careers are therefore better known to all. The service is more likely to cream off a large part of the talent (which it might eventually send to Paris, and thus the difference contributes to the importance of the metropolis).

The Grands Corps

Yet these characteristics would not have given the French civil service a sense of mission had not its structure been shaped vertically for centuries, and more systematically by Napoleon, by a number of "*corps*," each in charge of a particular segment of the service. Indeed, until 1945, there scarcely was *a* French civil service. Admittedly, all the *fonctionnaires* had some common rights, given by special laws (as on pensions), but there was neither a general "code" of the civil service (this was passed in 1946 under the title of *Statut de la Fonction Publique*), nor was there a general set of arrangements, for instance for the grading of civil servants; these were appointed by the various ministries to fill certain jobs, and they were, for the more technical or specialized jobs (not necessarily senior, but at least skilled), recruited on the basis of *corps*. These *corps* constituted the basic cells of the service and were supposed to have a spirit of their own (*esprit de corps*) which would mark them differently from other branches and divisions and would give each of them a desire to excel. Napoleon saw the point clearly, and it was he who was to make sure that these *corps* could have privileges and a tradition. As these divisions were prejudicial to the unity of the service and fostered inequality, postwar reforms tried to abolish the *corps* and replace them by general grades. But the "spirit" dies hard, and, perhaps more importantly, the 1945 reforms of the civil service did not abolish the most prestigious of the *corps*, the *grands corps*, which in the economic field (Inspectorate of Finance), the administrative judiciary (Council of State), the home and local government sector (Prefectoral Corps), various technical branches (Corps of Mines, Corps of Roads and Bridges), have been for generations the pole of attraction of aspiring civil servants. With their prestige and power, they managed to survive. The reforms tried to link them to the rest of the service, but this was to no avail. Up to the present day, the French civil service continues to be run, in most of the ministries, by members of these *grands corps*. Though each of them has barely a few hundred members, they run the civil service and give it its tone.

The Grandes Écoles

The domination of the *grands corps* occurs through the peculiar training given in a few elite schools. In order to recruit the best possible candidates, the civil service sets up difficult examinations. But, in order to achieve a standard of technical excellence (as we noted earlier, some of these *corps* are technical or need a training in law), it became natural to train the new recruits in special schools of the *corps* itself. These schools used to take also some outsiders to the *corps*, but the main purpose has always been to provide the special training of the elite, which was from the start an elite of intellect and education, not a social elite.

There are many "*grandes écoles*" of this type, some of them old (School of Mines, for instance), some of them recent (School of Taxes). Two are particularly important because of their general impact on the civil service. One is the *École Polytechnique*, created in 1795, originally to provide officers for the artillery and engineering branches of the army; it gives the nation its best technical administrators. The other is the *National School of Administration* (ENA) created in 1945 as part of the effort to unify the civil service and prepare candidates for higher management jobs in all government departments (including the foreign service). Moreover, a school of similar status, the *École Normale Supérieure*, trains the most brilliant of the future secondary school and university teachers. Competition for entry is fierce. The School of Administration is a postgraduate school, which provides students with one year of training in the field ("stage") usually in the provinces, a year of study in the school itself, and a further stage usually in a large firm, before the new administrator is posted where he has chosen to go (in fact, only top candidates can choose, as the others are left with the remaining places). The final examination, which leads to the posting, decides in particular whether students are to become members of a *grand corps*; typically, the first twenty can do so, while the rest become *administrateurs civils* and will not normally reach the very top posts of the civil service. A sign of the current malaise has been the refusal, in 1972, by some of the best students to enter the *grands corps*; the generation of 1968 chose to become *administrateurs civils*, on the grounds that the career of a civil servant should not be decided by the rank obtained at twenty-five in a series of examinations.

THE ROLE OF THE GRANDS CORPS IN THE NATION
Except for the diplomatic corps, which is left somewhat separate and whose members typically remain in the foreign service (the

service still has some of the aristocratic flavor which it had in the past), members of the *grands corps* do not stay in the original service for more than a few years. The *grands corps* have acquired such prestige that those who belong to them are transferred to head divisions all over the service. Thus, after a period in their original organization, members of the *grands corps* are "detached" (the official expression) to be posted over a wide range of public bodies (including nationalized corporations). Inspectors of finance do not merely serve in the Inspectorate; they are in charge of practically the whole of the Treasury, of many sections of the Planning Commissariat, and of numerous other divisions and branches in which financial or economic expertise is required. The situation is broadly similar on the technical side; graduates of the *École Polytechnique* who have achieved particular excellence enter one of the two technical *grands corps*, the Corps of Mines and the Corps of Roads and Bridges, and are later detached to run, not merely mining or roads and bridges divisions of the ministries, but other government departments and various nationalized industries. In the Planning Commissariat, "miners" (as they are called) and inspectors of finance collaborate to form the core of the top decision-makers.

Technical excellence and skill can thus be achieved; this is at some cost, however. Not only is the selection based on examination and competition to an excessive degree, but it tends also to create too permanent and too rigid a distinction between the potentially very high fliers and the bulk of the members of the higher civil service. This is not because the service has undemocratic attitudes; as the administrative and particularly diplomatic sides of the bureaucracy had a bourgeois and even somewhat aristocratic tone before the war, the School of Administration was created precisely to broaden the basis of recruitment and it achieved this aim to a substantial extent. Besides, the *École Polytechnique* and the *École Normale Supérieure* have for the most part drawn young men from the lower middle class. Moreover, the setting up of "second" or limited competition examinations enabled other civil servants to move to higher ranks. But the emphasis on examinations rather than experience as a basis for selection tends to lead, if pushed to extremes as is sometimes the case, to a wastage of early efforts and to disillusionment with the job obtained. It also creates an undue sense of security; of course, the civil service, in France as elsewhere, institutionalizes security, but if one gives a near certainty to reach the very top to those who are successful in examinations at twenty-five, many civil servants will become "mandarins," a widespread accusation made against the civil service before the war. The fact that private enterprise does attract many civil servants who have gone through the *grandes écoles* is thus of great value, since it provides many of the fliers with an added incentive and many of the disappointed ones with the chance of a new career.

The move from the civil service to various sectors of private enterprise (or to nationalized industries) is common, fashionable, indeed almost expected. Its name, *pantouflage*—putting on one's slippers—has even become part of the politico-administrative vocabulary. It exists because of the reputation of the service and of the reputation of the training schools (which normally insist on successful candidates either staying a few years in the service or paying a fairly large sum). As a result, the private sector finds itself in the intellectual dependence of the civil service (rather than the other way around, as in the United States). It also clears the way for younger men in the various *corps* and accounts for the fact that in France, unlike Britain, men at the top of the service are usually in their forties. And it provides for many personal links between business, the nationalized industries, and the bureaucracy. Thus, before the war, employers' organizations were in part unnecessary; even in the more complex world of the 1970s, the personal links, forged during years at the training schools, play a considerable part, as links between those who went to the same "public school" in Britain and, though less so, at Ivy League colleges in the U.S. More profoundly, leading businessmen who were previously civil servants will understand more easily (though they may well criticize) the constraints on the public sector. Before the war, the weight of the civil service was perhaps too heavy in the Malthusian climate of the great depression; with the rejuvenation following the Liberation, dangers of stultification of the private sector have disappeared. Thus the civil service is at the center of things; it can lead the economy directly and indirectly.

It can endow its members, as a result, with a sense of the importance of their role, which increases in turn even more the feeling of mission which has characterized the French civil service, even though it might also spread throughout the service—and perhaps at the lower echelons more than at the top—an exaggerated sense of power and the will to play with it.

THE STRUCTURE OF THE CENTRAL GOVERNMENT

A detailed examination of the organization of ministerial departments and of their outposts in the provinces would go much beyond the scope of this book. Moreover, as might be expected, French ministries tend to follow the same hierarchical rules as bureaucratic organizations everywhere, with some variations over time and from department to department. But a number of broad characteristics of the structure of the central government administration go deeper and combine to create a spirit which is peculiar to the French bureaucracy.

THE RELATIVE AUTONOMY OF THE VARIOUS SERVICES

First, the structure of the ministries tends to reflect markedly the old existence of the *corps*; each department should probably be viewed more as a "federation" than as a single hierarchy. Ministries were often created after the *corps*: the Corps of Roads and Bridges, for instance, existed almost a century before the Ministry of Industry was created. The setting up of a new ministry has often consisted in placing a number of *corps* under one political head (the minister). As branches and divisions expand, reorganizations take place, but each of the subsections remains somewhat autonomous; there is usually no merging of personnel nor of traditions. Consequently, there is very rarely one civil service head of a ministry. While British departments all have a permanent secretary, French departments are composed of a number of *Directions Générales* (five or six), plus some autonomous *Directions* and branches (*bureaux*). Above these units, all equal in status, there is no civil servant, only the political minister.

The relative independence of these *Directions Générales* was so great before the war that attempts were made in 1945 to break up the compartments and to unify the service. The School of Administration was created to train a uniform class of civil administrators who were to be posted in any ministry. But these have remained subordinated to members of the *grands corps*, as we have seen. The overall aim was therefore only partially achieved, though there is less autonomy of the *Directions Générales* than in the past and more exchange of personnel. In a small number of ministries, a post of *secretary general* in charge of the whole department was even created. But, except in the Ministry of Foreign Affairs, where it has long existed, the experiment was not successful and did not spread.

THE ROLE OF THE "EXTERNAL SERVICES"

Second, the "missionary" and centralizing role of the central government imposes a large deployment of the French bureaucracy in the provinces. This did indeed contribute markedly to increasing the attractiveness of the civil service to large numbers of Frenchmen aspiring to move up the social ladder. In the original Napoleonic model, the distinction between central and local government did not even fully exist; all public institutions were viewed as part of the State (and still are technically in law). As the demand for democratically elected councils grew throughout the nineteenth century, and as liberal governments came to power after 1870, local authorities became increasingly distinct from the central government. But this was never followed by a clear-cut division of fields between central and local authorities. Nor did this lead to the gradual reduction of the outposts of the central government in the provinces; quite the contrary, these expanded as the central government wished to supervise local authorities or induce them to run services in an efficient and dynamic fashion.

Thus French ministries have typically a relatively small core in Paris and large tentacles in the provinces, known as "external services." Until recently, these were organized by each corps in the way thought most appropriate: some services were subdivided into a small number of large regions; others adopted the *département* as their basic unit; yet others used smaller districts. These differences resulted in a serious lack of coordination, an ironical situation since Napoleon had implanted in each *département* a prefect, who, rather like a colonial governor, was to be the *general* representative of the government and whose mission was to coordinate the policy of the external services under the guidance of the minister of the interior (the Prefectoral Corps is a *grand corps*, as we saw). In fact, though prefects continued to have authority and prestige throughout all the successive regimes, and though they were always recognized as agents of the government as a whole, their effective powers of coordination decreased gradually, particularly in the technical fields. They came to be bypassed by many officials of the external services who discussed projects with and received orders directly from their own ministry in Paris. Indeed, in many services, the organization of the external services was such that the *département* was not even the main unit.

Problems of coordination between the external services have become one of the main concerns of the central government. The development of new services, and of planning in particular, have created serious and further difficulties. Though a number of steps have been taken, the question remains open. First, efforts were made in the 1950s to reestablish the preeminence of prefects; officials of the external services have been instructed to communicate with Paris through the prefect. This unrealistic order was in fact bypassed as it is quite natural for members of technical services to refer to the members of that service in Paris. However, as part of the problem stemmed from the smallness of the *département* (of which there are ninety-five in France), the central government tried to solve the difficulty by embarking on a process of "regionalization" of its services—to be distinguished from the demand for self-governing regional units to which we shall refer in Chapter Ten. The idea was to create a basic geographical unit larger than the *département* into which all the services of the State would be divided (though some would be further divided at a lower level). Slowly, the principle prevailed, and there are now twenty-one standard regions for all administrative purposes. Coordination at regional level is ensured by a "super-prefect," known as *Préfet de Région* by whom conflicts are solved and through whom demands made to Paris take place. The prefects of the *départements* remain and they are in charge of coordination at a lower level. Thus external services have indeed been modified and, as a result of better transportation, some services at the lowest levels have even been abolished. But the increase in the demand for participation has made the whole question more sensitive than in the past. As we shall see in Chapter Ten, the problem of the role of prefects and of the nature of the regions is in the balance.

THE INFLUENCE OF TECHNICIANS

Thirdly, also directly in line with the missionary role of the administration, the status of technicians has always been high in the decision-making process of French administration. British and other Anglo-Saxon central governments emphasize the distinction between technical experts and managers, management being indeed conceived as a special, technical skill. In the French administrative tradition, on the contrary, services are self-contained units run by technicians. Thus an engineer of roads and bridges will become the head of an external service in the provinces (already an administrative job) before being put in charge of a *Direction* in Paris. Managerial skills are learned on the job; it is assumed that anyone can become a manager with the consequence that, while France has prestigious technical schools, it has a very poor record in the management training field. Admittedly, students learn some elements of law at a *grande école* and, though more recently, some economics and sociology as well, but these are side aspects of their training program.

The fact that technicians are in charge (in sharp contrast with the practice of the British central government, for instance) has had important consequences for the spirit of French administration; the expression "technocracy" can therefore probably be used with some justification. Unlike managers, technicians are relatively insensitive to costs and quite insensitive to public opinion; they believe in their service, which they view as of utmost importance and in need of expansion, almost by definition. It has sometimes been said that French railways have achieved technical efficiency because they are considered as toys by the *polytechniciens* who run them! Even if the remark is exaggerated, this approach applies at least in part to most technical services. Hence, in contrast with the British civil service, which is conscious of what public opinion will tolerate, the French civil service has always been enthusiastic about such projects as the *Concorde* jet carrier, the airbus, or the Channel Tunnel. Administration is viewed as the creation of things, not the management of men; civil servants are anxious to put their stamp on the physical landscape of the country rather than to reconcile differences between segments of the community.

THE PROBLEM OF CIVIL SERVICE CONTROL

Fourthly, however, the dynamic character of the French bureaucracy, which technicians and others display, leads precisely to a reduced role for the elected government; it also leads to clashes among the various services, each of which makes demands which go far beyond what the nation can afford. Thus the double problems of supervision of the bureaucracy and of coordination among agencies remain permanent difficulties which can only be solved by a strong executive. Not surprisingly, suspicion between politicians and civil servants grew: hence the need for vigilance often expressed by members of the legislature; hence the creation of a variety of controls enabling ministers, first to be better informed of the activities of civil servants, and second to be in a position to follow up the implementation of government policy.

Control thus plays a crucial—and often very frustrating—part in French administration. It takes many forms, some of which are internal to the civil service structure itself and date back in part to Napoleon. In each corps, an inspectorate supervises the service, both in Paris and in the provinces. But these inspectorates are often weak, in part because the inspectors-general are older men who stayed in the service while most of their colleagues in the same age group found in private business a more active life and a better remuneration; their status is therefore relatively low. Their main effective role has indeed become, not one of inspection in the strict sense but one of inquiry; they are often charged by those who run the service to examine long-term problems and thus act in a way similar to a royal commission in Britain or a presidential commission in the U.S. A second type of control is by the administrative courts, headed by the Council of State, which we shall examine in some detail in the next chapter; these courts started as internal organs of supervision on the model of inspectorates and, indeed, like inspectors, they still conduct inquiries and have advisory functions (on bills and decrees, the Council of State advises the government about legality, opportunity, and effectiveness). But they are now real courts and are at some distance from the administrators.

Internal controls seemed insufficient to liberal governments issued from Parliament and suspicious of administrators. Hence the development, around each minister, of a ministerial *cabinet*, which is both his personal staff and his eyes and ears in the department. Members of the *cabinet* (to be sharply distinguished from the "cabinet" or government) are appointed by the minister; they help him to keep in touch with constituents and with Parliament; they help to prepare plans for legislative and other reforms and to see that, once adopted, they are implemented. Perhaps above all, at least traditionally, they inform the minister about the activities of administrators and see that these are not at variance from the minister's ideas. They are thus a protection against civil servants anxious to have their way as well as a brain trust making suggestions to a harassed minister.

In the postwar period, and especially since 1958, *cabinets* have changed, as a result of the changed relationship between bureaucracy and government. Originally chosen by the minister among his "loyal" friends, they have come to include also technicians, drawn from no other source than the civil service itself, as the minister is increasingly in need of technical advice. A minister of transport will thus staff his *cabinet* with an engineer of roads and bridges, an inspector of finance (to examine costs), a member of the Council of State (to help draft legal documents), etc. Of course, these men, usually young, are loyal to the minister, and are likely to follow him if he goes to another post; their career depends in part on the help which they give. But they are civil servants, and part of their loyalty is to the civil service and especially to the *corps* to which they belong. As other civil servants, they are anxious to foster development rather than control other civil servants on behalf of constituents or politicians. *Cabinets* thus provide only a limited check on bureaucratic impulses.

The structure of the civil service and the attitudes of civil servants combine to foster tendencies toward development of enlightened despotism rather than toward the democratic implementation of ministerial decisions. The tendency is too deep-rooted for a change to come about in a short period—and a change might mean, of course, less dynamism. While French political structures are prone to periodic and even dramatic upheavals, French administrative structures have shown, on the contrary, considerable resilience.

THE SCOPE OF THE PUBLIC SECTOR: THE PLAN AND PUBLIC ENTERPRISE

Naturally enough, the dynamic orientation toward development which characterizes the French bureaucracy led to a considerable expansion of the public sector. This was also due to the comparative weakness of business which has always seemed to need to be pushed, and helped by government funds and which was traditionally protected by fairly high tariffs (though these have fallen as a result of the Common Market, French business is still given a variety of advantages). Hence the marked development of the activities of the central government; hence, perhaps even more characteristically, the development of a large, complex, and almost indescribable network of public corporations, legally autonomous from the State itself, and often linked to private enterprise in the form of "mixed" companies (*sociétés d'économie mixte*). This, together with the large-scale nationalizations which took place in 1945–1946, explains the relative ease with which the idea of an economic "plan" was adopted and its provisions implemented in the postwar period.

The Plan
The remarkable development of the French economy in the last twenty-five years owes so much—and owed so much in the early

period—to the activities of the *Commissariat général au Plan* that it is difficult to appreciate that this operation started only as a small brain trust of key experts, with only some telephones, little effective power at their disposal, but much enthusiasm, who worked under the leadership of Jean Monnet, a strong-willed ex-civil servant and ex-businessman, who was to be crucial to the psychological success of the idea and who was later, much in the same vein, to foster European unity. From the start, the plan was to be flexible; it was to be run by a team, not by a hierarchical and bureaucratic organization. Its strength was to come from the intellectual authority of the men, who were to attract to their views businessmen and workers, farmers and industrialists, private and public enterprise. At the beginning, of course, the *Commissariat* could count on the prevailing socialistic mood of the country and of its leaders; but this was not to be for long. The first move was in the area of basic investment and therefore on nationalized corporations, whose cooperation was easier to obtain. But the planners were never given powers to order (hence the expression "indicative planning"); only the treasury could direct investment. Gradually the *Commissariat*'s strongest weapon came from its ability to forecast; by providing employers with trends in the various branches of industry, it gave them, free, a basis on which they could decide the direction of future growth. And, as employers did follow forecasts, the plan became, in many ways, a self-fulfilling prophecy; this, in turn, increased the authority of the planners.

Between the First Plan of the forties and the Sixth Plan of the early seventies, however, major changes did take place. First, naturally, the objectives became different. The First Plan had been concerned with the reconstruction and development of basic industries. Those which followed were concerned with the whole of the economy; the end of the Second Plan (1957) coincided with the end of the period of rapid inflation which France had known after the war, and thus the emphasis of the Third Plan was on greater stability. Indeed, the government seemed so concerned with monetary rectitude in the early 1960s that the whole planning machinery seemed for a while in jeopardy. However, after 1962, from the Fourth Plan onward, new objectives began to emerge; the drafters of the scheme emphasized regional development and expansion of the social (and not simply economic) amenities offered to Frenchmen. From that time dates the concern with decentralization and the effort to rejuvenate provincial and local government life.

Second, the preparation of the plan became more complex. The First and Second Plans were drawn by officials and with little discussion, even in Parliament. Gradually, during the Second Plan and more so during the Third and Fourth, the idea of involving large segments of the community came to be regarded as normal. The Planning Commissariat divided the preparation of the specialized targets and programs among numerous committees, at first because the planners could not do the work alone; twenty-seven commissions were thus created for the Fourth Plan, which included representatives of industry, commerce, and the social services. Thus employers, leaders of nationalized industries, and trade unionists have come to be associated with the preparation, though the latter have always complained of underrepresentation and of the advisory character of the committees. Yet, increasingly, plans have given rise to debate, not so much in Parliament, as in the Economic Council, in the regional economic committees (which were created in 1964, as we shall see in Chapter Ten), and among the public at large. The targets of the Fifth and Sixth Plans were heavily criticized for being too restrictive in terms of growth and for not being concerned enough with social investment—though social investment became, in the 1960s, one of the main targets of the plan.

The plan was attacked at the beginning by employers who feared that it might straitjacket private business; it has been criticized by many on the Left for being merely indicative. In fact, French plans have been a rather interesting blend of an empirical approach to social and economic change and of social engineering in the stronger sense. It is a modern experiment in that it uses the latest mathematical techniques in order to understand and forecast trends; but it is also empirical and Fabian in that, unlike Soviet planning, it is flexible and realistically adapted to a complex economy. Whether the planners aim at socialism is debatable; this suggestion would certainly be rejected by many planners, by the trade unionists, and by the employers. Yet, whether socialist or not, the French plans helped to make French society more public-minded. By switching their objectives gradually from basic economic growth to social development, the planners slowly made the French bureaucracy more conscious of the importance of social issues. It has thus helped to modify the conditions of the economic, social, and political confrontations, indeed not only in France, but, through its influence, in many foreign countries as well.

PUBLIC ENTERPRISE

In the middle of a climate of guidance by planners and of modernization of the economy, French public enterprise scarcely suffered from the attacks against the public sector which took place in many Western countries, and in Britain in particular. From a base which included, already before the war, the post office, the railways, some shipping lines, and miscellaneous undertakings, such as potash mines in Alsace, electricity production in the Rhône valley, and luxury china at Sèvres, the public sector expanded in 1945–1946 to include the whole infrastructure of the economy. The coal mines, major banks, insurance companies, gas, electricity, much of aircraft manufacturing, were nationalized out of principle. Renault, the largest car manufacturer, was nationalized as a penalty, as the owner had collaborated with Germany during the war. Much of air transport and more of the shipping lines came under direct control of the government. As private radio stations were no longer allowed after the war, the State acquired a *de facto* monopoly of radio and television within France; as radio stations at the periphery of the country were operated on a private basis, the French State acquired majority capital in a number of them; the major French news agency, the *Agence France-Presse*, replaced the private prewar *Agence Havas*. As the demand for oil was increasing and France had very little within its territory, the State created companies, typically as a major shareholder, which engaged in research, production, and distribution of oil and natural gas on a worldwide basis. There are few important sectors of the French economy in which the State does not have a share, not merely because it helps with funds, but as an active entrepreneur.

This was possible because the French bureaucracy developed, after World War I, a panoply of juridical forms of participation. Originally, of course, the State acted directly, in its capacity as a central government; this was the formula adopted for the post office when the kings made a State monopoly. But a second technique was quickly found, that of the *établissement public* in which the funds are public and control is tight, but where a board takes decisions and contracts with third parties on behalf of the agency; this is the formula adopted in local government as well. But the method was not flexible enough. The civil service thus came to create, almost on the private model, companies and corporations which had the same structure, the same rights, and the same obligations as private firms. In the case of the large undertakings nationalized after the war, special legislative arrangements gave the corporations a somewhat different organization; boards have to include representatives of the State, the users, and the employees, for instance. But, for many other State companies, there is simply no difference with a private business. This made it possible for State corporations to combine with the private sector, for instance to create subsidiaries. The almost infinite variety of forms adopted by the public sector and the immense network of bodies whose ramifications extend well beyond what the ordinary Frenchman knows to be public firms naturally led to a blurring of the difference between private and public sector; this helped the collaboration which, as we saw, has been characteristic of French economic life from its early period.

The French bureaucracy is strong; for a variety of reasons, it has earned this strength and deserved the influence which it acquired. Yet the dynamism and missionary zeal of planners and others have to be considered alongside some of the internal problems of the bureaucracy. As we said early in this chapter, there is, in some quarters, a malaise. As we also noted, French administrative structures are often bureaucratic; the "team spirit" of the planners is a more exceptional phenomenon than the over-legalistic refusal of the unconcerned employee. One of the paradoxes lies indeed in these two sides of the bureaucracy which are complementary: As the State needs a large apparatus and means to enforce its rules, a bureaucratic line is often needed, even by those State organizations which wish to develop and promote change. Indeed, even if the French bureaucracy is at times heavy, not all bureaucracies have the same missionary zeal, nor do their civil servants all have the competence and talent which marked, from its origins, the French senior administrators. It may have been a pity that France did not develop earlier and more widely a sense of private enterprise—any more than it developed group structures and cooperative action. This is changing, and the case for a "missionary" administration may therefore diminish. Meanwhile, and surely for many years, the French bureaucracy will continue to be one of the main instruments of progress in society.

9

The Judiciary

The character of a political system is markedly affected by the nature of its judiciary. This is well known for the United States, where the Supreme Court has played a major part in upholding civil rights, in adjudicating on the relative role of the states and the federal government, and in placing clear limits on the role of Congress by enforcing its power of judicial review. This is also well known for Britian, where, in a different manner, and without encroaching on the power of Parliament, the courts have traditionally upheld the liberty of the subject. In France, too, but again in a different manner, the judicial system has helped to give a particular shape to the political system. In many ways, the judiciary has been much weaker, and also more timid, vis-à-vis the executive than in Anglo-Saxon countries because the Revolution and the various subsequent changes in regimes led to periodic variations in the political climate in which the judiciary operated, and indeed at times to purges of the personnel. This scarcely contributed to the status of the profession and implied a considerable influence of the government and legislature, despite the principle, repeated by constitutions, that the judiciary is independent and considered as a power alongside the other powers of the State. Specifically, France never granted to judges the power of judicial review. Acts of Parliament are sovereign and cannot be challenged in a court of law; even regulations of the executive cannot be challenged in the ordinary machinery of the judiciary. In this, of course, France does not differ from a large number of liberal democracies, and from Britain in particular, but the power of judicial review might have given French judges some of the means of acquiring the higher status which they have clearly lacked.

The Growth and Importance of Administrative Justice

Yet this is a one-sided picture, in part because it would be wrong to conclude that the French judiciary is markedly dependent on the executive; it may not be assertive enough, but it is not normally subservient. But the picture is also one-sided because the French judiciary as a whole is at the same time remarkable in at least one of its facets, which relates closely to the developments described in the previous chapter; over the last two hundred years, France has created, through a slow process of adjustment, a system of administrative control through the judiciary which has been widely imitated for its novelty and its boldness. Thus, whereas the protection of the citizen in general (for instance in criminal matters) could be better organized, the protection of the citizen against the bureaucracy has been imaginatively ensured.

This development took place by accident—it was not intended by the revolutionary leaders nor by Napoleon. Indeed, it came about paradoxically; as the last years of the *ancien régime* had been marked by a long series of battles between the government and the judiciary, the revolutionary leaders wanted to ensure that the newly created courts would not harass the executive (and the legislature). It was therefore stated that the courts would no longer be empowered to make general statements—amounting to general rules—as this was encroaching on the powers of the legislature, or to interfere with the activities of administrative bodies, as this was encroaching on the field of the executive. The bureaucracy was therefore placed above the law, so to speak; it could no longer be sued for the damage which might have been caused. Such a drastic rule clearly needed some limitations in practice; it was indeed assumed that citizens would ask administrative bodies themselves to make good any damages they might have suffered. This was officialized by Napoleon in 1800, when he created a number of bodies which were to have both an advisory function and one of scrutiny of requests made by citizens against the administration. One of these bodies, the *Conseil d'État,* was to sit next to the government; the others were to sit near the prefect in each *département*. Though these were not to take the final decisions, and though the grievances of citizens were to be presented as mere requests which the government, acting on advice, might or might not grant, the effective control of the bureaucracy was born. At the same time, Napoleon had created a distinction which was to remain the basic division of the French judiciary: on the one hand the "ordinary" courts deal with conflicts between private citizens (including, of course, private firms) and with criminal matters; on the other, administrative courts deal with the conflicts between citizens and administrative bodies. We shall see that in practice the distinction is now much more fluid and is indeed quite complex. But the division of the French judicial system into two separate hierarchies is crucial and has had many consequences—not the least being that, in reality, the best defender of the rights of the citizen has tended to be the administrative, not the ordinary court.

ORDINARY COURTS

Differences between the two networks of courts do not merely extend to the structure of the two parallel hierarchies. They run much deeper and affect even the nature of the legal system and relate in particular to the role of case-law. Largely because the Revolution was adamant to abolish the chaotic situation of the *ancien régime* in which the law was unclear, varied from one part of the country to the other, and depended in large part on what seemed to be the idiosyncrasies of judges interpreting custom, it was stated that courts in the future would judge cases on the basis of codes. These were drafted mainly under Napoleon, the Civil Code of 1804 being the first and perhaps the most prestigious of these codes. As codes were promulgated, it became possible to prevent judges from deciding on problems by way of precedent; they were to refer to the code which would give the solution. In point of fact, however, as the law is never without obscurity, it was necessary to create a court which would deal with matters of interpretation of the existing law; thus precedent was to play some part. But codes do remain the basis of decisions of the ordinary courts, and the bulk of the training of judges—in the ordinary branch—is based as a result on a knowledge of the law and of the various codes in which much of it is written.

THE JUDGES

Since the Revolution, too, and in order to avoid the excesses of the previous system in which judges were wholly independent and literally owned their position, justice was organized as a public service and staffed with officials who would not be given such privileges as to make them believe that they were above the State. Reforms of the nineteenth century did give the judiciary gradually more security of tenure than ordinary civil servants, but they are civil servants; thus promotion was classically a means by which pressure was—and still can be to some extent—exercised on them. There are clearly defined ranks and schedules of promotions, as for other civil servants. Training now takes place in a *Centre National d'Études Judiciaires,* a specialized school open to law graduates successful in a competitive examination and modeled on the School of Administration. Thus the judiciary is in every sense a career service where one starts at the bottom and moves up gradually.

One peculiarity of the French system is the inclusion of the prosecuting and investigating magistrates among the judiciary. At the end of their period of training, candidates can choose whether to become judges in the normal sense or whether to become part of what is known as the *magistrature debout* (standing judges, because prosecutors stand to accuse). The original idea was to give some semblance of independence to the prosecution and to the investigation while ensuring that the government could remain largely in control. While in Britain the investigation is largely conducted by the police under the supervision of the court, Napoleon saw to it that the overall supervision of the investigatory phase remained outside the jurisdiction of the court proper. Hence the creation of a special category of judges, known as the *juges d'instruction,* who are in charge of deciding, on the basis of police evidence, whether a case has been made and committal to trial is to be allowed. These judges have long been at the center of controversies; though technically independent from the police, they are career civil servants whose reputation tends naturally to be based on good relations with the police and are therefore reluctant (despite various attempts at making them independent) to take a strict and close look at police operations. Moreover, they decide on arrest and bail and, up to the 1960s, bail was infrequently allowed by law and even more rarely conceded by the *juge d'instruction*. Appeal from the latter's decision does exist, but only recently has the appeal body, the *chambre des mises en accusation* (a separate section of the court of appeal composed of ordinary judges), had any real power to control and reverse the decisions of the *juge d'instruction*.

THE NETWORK OF COURTS

While the judicial profession is thus a career, the courts are organized hierarchically. A major reform took place in 1958 which reduced drastically the number of courts, both civil and criminal, but the principle of the hierarchy was not touched. Since the reform, the 3,000 or so justices of the peace were abolished; they used to operate in every large village (*canton*) and dispense a fairly rapid justice for smaller matters while playing a large part in solving conflicts at the village level. But the gradual urbanization of the country made most of these courts superfluous, while cases remained unjudged in the larger cities. Thus the reform decided that the lowest court would be the *tribunal d'instance* of which there are about 450 for the whole of France, averaging about 4 per *département,* but distributed in relation to population. These courts deal mainly with the smaller cases which justices of the peace used to deal with in the past.

For most important cases, plaintiffs go to the *tribunal de grande instance,* of which there are 172—less than 2 on the average per *département.* This court has appeal functions, especially from the judgments of some of the specialized courts, which have tended to multiply and which, though often criticized by experts, are usually simpler, less expensive, and more appropriate in technical cases. The most important are the *tribunaux de commerce,* which deal with commercial disputes, and the *conseils de prud'hommes,* which deal with disputes between employers and employees over the implementation of labor contracts. While the judges on these specialized courts are elected by and from among businessmen and workers, the *tribunaux d'instance* and *tribunaux de grande instance* are entirely staffed by members of the career judiciary. *Tribunaux d'instance* have one judge, who in addition to his more formal powers also acts much as a justice of the peace did in the past, settling domestic and other minor disputes by conciliation. The *tribunaux de grande instance* have three or more judges, and neither court has a jury. The specialized courts are the only civil courts in which lay members are called to decide on cases.

Criminal law is dispensed in one of three sets of courts, depending on the gravity of the offense. Police courts function in almost all localities of any importance (in fact in the same way as the *tribunaux d'instance*). More serious offenses are brought before the *tribunaux correctionnels* where judges (the same as those of the *tribunaux de grande instance*) decide on cases without juries. Finally, the most serious crimes are tried at the periodic sittings of the *cours d'assises* (one per *département*) which consists of three judges and nine jurors. Eight votes of the twelve are required for the conviction, and French judges normally bring their influence to bear on the jurors. Indeed, the French judge is not assumed to take a back seat in criminal trials; he actively participates in the questioning of defendants and witnesses (this is known as "inquisitorial" justice, while the Anglo-Saxon system, where the judge remains passive, is known as "accusatorial").

Appeal on matter of fact is generally allowed in civil cases (unless the matter is trivial), but not in criminal cases; appeal on interpretation of the law is always allowed. Appeals of both types normally go to a court of appeal, of which there are twenty-five throughout France, unless, as mentioned earlier, the *tribunal de grande instance* is statutorily competent, or unless, on the contrary, the law decides that appeal on a point of law will go directly to the highest court in the hierarchy, the court of *cassation,* which sits in Paris. This court is empowered to decide only on points of law; it can only confirm or "quash and send" for a retrial to another court of the same category, but not the same one as the court which decided on the case (the formal expression is *"casse et renvoie,"* hence the name of the court). If the court which tries the case again does not follow the lead of the court of *cassation* on the point of law at stake, the plaintiff can go to the court again. While a case which comes to the court for the first time goes only to one chamber (seven judges at least), a case which comes for the second time goes to a bench composed of judges from all the sections (*toutes chambres réunies*); if the court of *cassation* once more states that the point of law was incorrectly interpreted by the lower court and thus quashes and sends for yet another retrial, the lower court to which it sends the case for this second retrial has to follow the line of the court of *cassation*. Thus unity of interpretation of French law is maintained and the view of the court of *cassation* can prevail, though only after due attention is paid to the viewpoint of the lower courts.

THE LEGAL PROCESS

Alongside the judiciary, the other legal professions have been strictly regulated by law, though they are of course not part of the civil service. A major reform has at long last taken place in 1971 which had the effect of abolishing the cumbersome distinction between two categories of counselors, the *avocats* and the *avoués*. Up until then, plaintiffs had to be represented by an *avoué*, in charge of the written part of the procedure, and normally needed to be represented as well by an *avocat*, who was in charge of the oral part and pleaded in court (though technically plaintiffs could defend themselves). This distinction had the effect of increasing markedly the cost of justice (though technically free, the costs of representation are large, as in other countries) and of slowing up the process. But vested interests were considerable, particularly as the *avoués* bought and sold their practice and the State had therefore to compensate them. The members of the legal professions (including the *notaires*, broadly equivalent to English solicitors, who are in charge of preparing papers and dealing with wills, marriage settlements, etc.) are supervised by the courts whose responsibility it is to bar them from the profession and to approve of their general codes of conduct.

THE HIGH COUNCIL OF THE JUDICIARY

Since 1946, the whole judicial structure has been supervised by a constitutional body, the High Council of the Judiciary, but the powers of this council were substantially altered by the Constitution of 1958 and its independence from the government reduced. Formerly staffed mainly with members elected by the National Assembly and the members of the judiciary, it is now composed of the president of the Republic (chairman), the minister of justice, two appointees of the president, six members chosen by the president drawn by the court of *cassation,* and one, also chosen by the president, from a list of three proposed by the Council of State. Lower courts have no representatives and the president has considerable scope for intervention. The powers of the council were reduced at the same time, mainly in order to increase the Ministry of Justice's scope for action, particularly on promotion questions. Since 1958, the high council no longer prepares the annual promotion lists; the work is now done by a special committee composed of the prosecutor general of the court of *cassation,* six representatives of that court, and six officials of the Ministry of Justice (the high council merely gives an advisory opinion). The high council did retain, however, the disciplinary powers which it acquired in 1946, and in this respect at least, the independence of the judiciary is better ensured than before the war.

ADMINISTRATIVE COURTS

Administrative courts, as we saw, emerged only gradually from the status of advisory bodies to the government which was theirs under Napoleon. These advisory bodies had two functions. First, they were to help the government in Paris, the prefects in the *départements,* to draft regulations (decrees and *arrêtés*); in some cases the law even compelled the relevant executive authority to submit the text for advice, and in a small minority of cases, formal approval of the text had to be forthcoming. Second, Napoleonic councils were to advise the government and prefects on complaints coming from citizens about administrative actions. While the first advisory function remains almost unchanged (and it does occupy a substantial proportion of the personnel of the councils), the advice about administrative actions transformed its character; during the nineteenth century, the government came, as a matter of course, to agree with and automatically implement the suggestions made by the councils. The "advice" had become, by a process of evolution through custom, a real decision. In 1872, the situation was formalized by a law which stated that the council would have the status of courts and be competent to decide on complaints involving the administration.

THE CONSEIL D'ÉTAT

The administrative courts are thus true courts, organized hierarchically, some of which deal with general administrative matters, while others are concerned only with particular problems (special bodies tackle disputes over national assistance, for instance). The general administrative courts are by far the most important. At a lower level, the ninety-odd *Conseils de Préfecture* of Napoleon were reduced to twenty-three in 1926 and were renamed *tribunaux administratifs* in 1953, while their powers were increased to speed up cases. At the upper level, sitting as an appeal court in many cases but directly competent for the more important problems, is the famous *Conseil d'État,* about which much has been written and which has become the model administrative court in large parts of the world. Composed of over 150 members, almost entirely recruited through the School of Administration (as we saw, those who belong to it form one of the prestigious *grands corps*), the Council of State is divided into several sections, the main distinction being between four advisory (so-called "administrative") sections and a judicial section (*section du contentieux*). This section is in turn divided into a number of chambers in which normally five *conseillers* decide on cases on the report of more junior members (*maîtres des requêtes* and even sometimes *auditeurs*), but very important cases can be decided by as many as ten or fifteen *conseillers.*

THE PECULIAR POSITION OF ADMINISTRATIVE COURTS

The structure and procedure, even the judicial approach, are different from the ordinary courts, and this division between what almost amounts to two systems of law is one of the most peculiar facets of the French judiciary. In the first place, the status of the members of these courts is that of ordinary civil servants; unlike members of ordinary courts, they do not have even the special guarantees of tenure which have been introduced to give judges greater independence. Moreover, the separation between the "advisory" and the "judicial" functions is, even now, not complete, and the link is deliberate. Members of the *Conseil d'État* may move, for instance, from one section to another; they may also be detached for a period, as we noted earlier, to take a post in what is officially known as the "active" administration (i.e., the administration which takes decisions); when detached in this way, members obviously do not participate in the judicial (or indeed advisory) activities of the council. But they are likely to come back after their period of detachment is over and will sit again among their colleagues to decide on cases. These arrangements may seem paradoxical, or to have the effect of ensuring the full dependence of the judges. They are of course due to the historical origins of administrative courts, which emerged slowly—in a British fashion!—from that of advisory councils. Yet they turned in practice to give these courts not less, but more independence and more flexibility vis-à-vis administrative bodies. They acquired their influence by stages; but this influence became so large that the government has not dared to touch them. Indeed, their members have had more prestige, and even more real security of tenure than ordinary judges. Moreover, their influence increased because, being composed of administrators knowing the real problems of administrative bodies, these courts took their decisions on the basis of a realistic appraisal of the situation. In the early period, this meant probably a greater preparedness to allow the civil service some leeway. Gradually, however, this meant a much better, much less formal, approach to the examination of the bases of administrative decisions. Thus the administration is not more likely to win against the citizen. The converse is often true; civil servants are less likely to be able to cover their decisions with mystery and to deceive members of the court with a high-minded presentation of difficulties which could easily have been overcome.

THE ROLE OF PRECEDENTS

Naturally, as a result, administrative courts also have a different procedure from that of ordinary courts. The Council of State has always felt free to invoke precedents and to use general principles as grounds for its judgments. In many respects, administrative courts tend to decide cases on the basis of equity (in the literal sense of the word), of what seems honest and reasonable, rather than on the basis of the letter of the law which, particularly in the past, tended to define governmental powers loosely for emergencies. Moreover, plaintiffs find in the administrative courts, and particularly in the Council of State, some of the characteristics of the Scandinavian institution of the ombudsman; the *maître des requêtes* who is given the task of preparing and reporting on a case will do all the work himself, dig through the administration's files and find what happened, on behalf of the plaintiff who, in some cases, has nothing more to do than file his complaint and pay a very small fee. Administrative courts were created to advise (and presumably help) the government against undue complaints; they have turned out to be the citizens' best (though at times somewhat protracted) friend.

Finally and most importantly, administrative courts are competent to decide on the validity of executive decisions. The Council of State, in particular, can be asked to state whether governmental decrees are legal and should stand or illegal and be quashed. While full constitutional control is still not established, almost all the documents issued by executive authorities can be challenged in an administrative court. The procedure, known as the *recours pour excès de pouvoir,* is limited only by two general conditions. First, the plaintiff must show that he is in some way affected, at least potentially, by the regulation (and this is interpreted very liberally). Second, the case must be filed within two months of the decision, so as to limit uncertainty about the validity of documents—uncertainty which can be very worrying to others and in some cases dramatic, as can be demonstrated from United States Supreme Court decisions. The Council of State has taken very seriously this power of scrutiny and needs to convince itself, before passing judgment, not only that the text was issued by the legal authority under appropriate powers, but that the spirit of the document does not go against the real purpose of the law; the *détournement de pouvoir* (use of legal powers but in a distorted manner) is one of the grounds on which administrative courts can and often do annul decrees or *arrêtés*.

As a result of the different approach to procedure and to the law itself, administrative courts, and the Council of State in particular, have created what amounts to a really distinct judiciary. The protection of the citizen in matters of liability of the State has given rise to a whole body of case-law which is highly complex and very different from liability in private law. This in turn explains why agencies of the State may wish to have the status of private agencies, rather than administrative bodies. It became increasingly recognized, as public enterprise grew, that many commercial and industrial undertakings of the State (such as mixed economy or nationalized corporations) should be treated as private agencies, and, consequently, they have to be sued in ordinary courts. The problem of the competence between ordinary and administrative courts is thus often a difficult problem, which is solved in the last resort by a court of conflicts, composed equally of members of the court of *cassation* and of the Council of State; some difficulties of litigation are thus part of the price which has to be paid for the existence of a strong system of administrative courts.

The development of the role of the Council of State is truly remarkable, particularly in a country which took pains to limit the status of the judiciary and obliged judges to decide on cases within the rigid framework of elaborate codes of law. Administrative courts are, in many ways, the most effective counterpart to executive power and administrative centralization; this is not only because they can and do take the side of the citizen when decisions of central and local bodies are unjust or go beyond the law, but because the fear of the judgments of the *Conseil* and other administrative courts may lead central and local authorities to be more prudent. Administrative courts are thus true defenders of the rights of citizens and, though they are not mentioned in the constitution, they are as important to the real and living constitution as many of the bodies mentioned in the formal document. The appointment in 1972 of a quasi ombudsman, known as "mediator," is unlikely to change this situation markedly for many years to come.

The French judiciary is therefore a mixture of old and new, bold and timid, liberal and traditional. Its division into two branches has had a considerable impact on its character. Almost certainly, had administrative questions been dealt with by ordinary courts, the citizen would have been less well protected and the governmental machine would have remained more independent. Curiously enough for France, this development took place piecemeal in an evolutionary fashion, almost without anyone noticing what the ultimate goal of the evolution would be. The result has been remarkable, in contrast with "ordinary" justice, where progress is clearly needed to make it more liberal, more anxious to protect aggrieved citizens or accused persons, and generally to make it more prepared to assert its influence.

10

Local Government

French local government has always been one of the casualties of the centralization of the administrative system. Its organization was markedly affected by Napoleon, who, rejecting the early decentralizing schemes of the Revolution, adopted an authoritarian plan whereby local authorities were not only supervised, but indeed almost entirely run, by agents of the central government. A slow process of liberalization took place in the nineteenth century, in the 1830s and the 1880s in particular, but reforms were never radical enough to break decisively with the origins. The maintenance of a large amount of central government control was due in part to political reasons; even liberals always felt that full devolution of power to local authorities was dangerous, since much of the opposition to the government was an opposition to the regime as well. Royalists before World War I, Communists since the mid-1930s should not be given, or so it was felt, too strong a base from which to attack the institutions of the State. But part of the centralizing spirit is also due to the engrained feeling that services should be as uniform as possible, and that, if local authorities were left to their own devices, they would often let services fall to unacceptable standards. Indeed, the very system which had been created tended—and still tends—to justify national government intervention. As local authorities typically do not have the means and size to enable them to run services efficiently, it became logical to conclude that the skills of the central government should come to the rescue. Local government is thus caught in a vicious circle; only a major transformation, politically difficult to achieve, could bring about the amount of responsibility which local authorities need if they are to be trusted with the development of services, let alone show the dynamism which the central administration has shown in the last decades.

Some change has taken place, however, though perhaps in attitudes more than in the structures. Often sleepy in the interwar period, and too anxious to rely on central government help, local authorities have been caught since the 1950s by the idea of development, and they have experienced as a result the effect of their financial limitations. They have asked for more government help to run their affairs. They have begun to realize that the size of the authority was the key to change and that parochial patriotism could lead only to stagnation. They are undergoing the problems of "take-off." The reforms which have been underway since the 1960s are thus only the beginning of a long process of overhauling. Even the prospects of major structural change are no longer so remote. Regionalism, in particular, though still very limited in scope, has a potential for future major developments.

THE STRUCTURE OF LOCAL GOVERNMENT

In the Napoleonic model, as we noted in Chapter Eight, all public authorities belonged to one unit, the State, and the distinction between external services of government departments and local authorities was minute. There were four territorial divisions below the central government, adopted partly for reasons of convenience and partly because of the specifically local aspirations of the population. The effect of the evolution of the nineteenth century was to increase the importance of those two territorial divisions which were smallest and largest, and to reduce to almost nothing the role of the other two intermediate units. At the bottom, the commune, created by the Revolution, often on the basis of the old parishes, was to be the basic unit for towns and villages alike; it was the first type of local authority to acquire real autonomy, though the government retained a substantial amount of control. Above the commune, the canton and the *arrondissement* were slowly to lose any powers which they might have had and are now merely electoral districts within the highest unit, the *département*. This was created artificially by the Revolution to break the old

French provinces (such as Brittany, Provence, etc.) into new counties which would not have the old forms of particularism and thus would not endanger the unity of the nation. New names were provided for the *départements,* drawn from mountains or rivers (Loire, Jura, etc.) to deemphasize provincial ties.

TOO MANY DEPARTMENTS AND COMMUNES

The *département* did acquire a life of its own; many aspects of the life of Frenchmen are centered around activities taking place at the capital city of the *département,* the *chef-lieu.* The size of the unit was indeed appropriate to the communication conditions of the nineteenth century. Thus the ninety original *départements* remained almost unchanged for a century and a half in a country which was still largely agricultural. But the situation has altered markedly since the 1950s: depopulation of the countryside led to a marked decrease in the population of the more mountainous *départements* of the Center, the Alps, and the Pyrenees. Conversely, some of the industrial locals, in particular in the area around Paris, became "under-administered" and unmanageable. Meanwhile, new patterns of communication and new social problems made many *chef-lieus* seem like large villages rather than urban centers. Thus the question of a major overhaul arose to an increasing extent, and ideas of regionalization developed. But boundary changes took place only in the Paris area where, for the first time since the Revolution, new *départements* were created bringing to ninety-five the numbers of these units in the 1970s.

While the size of the *département* raises a problem, the small size of the commune is an acute handicap. There are 38,000 communes, with an average population of 1,300. Indeed, if one excludes the large towns and cities, such as Paris, Marseilles, or Lyons, the average communal size is even much smaller: 35,000 communes have less than 2,000 inhabitants, their average population being 450. This is unquestionably much too small to enable municipal authorities to run even a minimum of services let alone promote modern developments. Yet moves toward the reduction of the number of communes have been hard to come by. For years, the problem was not even perceived by either the government or the local authorities. The vested interests of local politicians combined with old-fashioned viewpoints of communal patriotism. The central government was perhaps not anxious to create new units which would be more able to counteract its schemes and would be less in need of technical advice. Even more surprisingly, professional discussion did not seem to suggest that a profound reform was an imperative.

Slowly, the climate has begun to change. Traditionally, communes used to create joint boards to run some services, mainly utilities. In the 1960s, laws made it easier to enable small communes in the neighborhood of large towns to form joint units for various purposes. In the wake of the housing boom which followed World War II, the need for land became acute and some of the medium-sized towns had to expand outside their boundaries. In a first step, "urban districts" were created, which did not replace the various communes around the larger towns, but at least did create a council which could handle in common some of the major social problems which expansion had raised. In the late 1960s, a further move enabled—indeed to some extent forced—large towns to join with surrounding areas and form "urban communities," after a Paris district had also been set up. Yet the old communes were still not abolished; the purpose was more to force the major cities to create new groupings in order to tackle major urban problems.

The law on urban communities had been fought bitterly by the opposition in Parliament, in the name of communal liberties. Indeed, the government had forced the proposal on reluctant local authorities rather than trying to convince and accommodate. But the new arrangements had the effect of increasing the distance between local authorities and the population, since the new authorities were "two-tier," the council of the communes electing the larger council, with no popular election in the new authority. As the idea of urban communities becomes more accepted—a variety of towns, originally not included in the scheme have come voluntarily to join it—the demand for popular elections may grow, and, consequently, the idea of a merger may be more acceptable.

Meanwhile, the government decided at last to begin to tackle the problem of the small communes and asked Parliament in 1971 to pass a law specifically designed to foster amalgamation between authorities. Once more, opposition was strong. Yet the law does not directly compel local authorities to merge, but only does so indirectly if a majority of the communes concerned agree to amalgamate. Financial inducements are added to hasten the process. Though few communes have joined in the early phase, the need to amalgamate may slowly become felt, as local patriotism decreases, as communes find it difficult to hire officials to run their services, as citizens see the benefits accruing from the larger districts. The problem of communal size, which for decades prevented local government in the rural areas from being economically efficient and socially active, seems at last on the verge of partial solution.

Since reforms which took place in the 1830s and 1880s, communes have been run democratically by a municipal council elected by universal suffrage every six years on the basis of a two-ballot majority system. The municipal councillors, from nine in the very small villages to thirty-seven in the large towns, except in Paris, Marseilles, and Lyons, where there are more, elect the mayor and his assistants. In the cities, elections are on strict party lines, but there are appreciable differences between electoral behavior at the local and national levels. We saw in Chapter Five that the UDR is still not firmly implanted locally, though the Gaullists made a more determined effort at the municipal elections of 1971. In small towns and in villages, elections still return many "notables"; they are often uncontested in the smallest units.

COMMUNAL GOVERNMENT

The municipal council is relatively weak, however, by comparison with the mayor, who is more than the head of the executive branch of the commune. In the Napoleonic model, mayors were not elected, but appointed by the central government (they came to be elected by the municipal council in 1882). The mayor was therefore entrusted with most of the executive *and* legislative powers and acted in many ways also as a representative of the *central* government. This rather authoritarian system was kept almost intact when mayors came to be elected by councils;

together with his assistants (*adjoints*), the mayor is in charge of policy-making and implementation. The role of the council (which holds at least four sessions a year, some of which are very brief) is primarily to supervise the action of the mayor and to vote the budget. Local by-laws are the responsibility of the mayor. Admittedly, as the municipal council elects the mayor, it can exercise influence indirectly, but the council does not have the right to censure the mayor and to force him to resign; the system is thus not truly parliamentary. Of course, if there is conflict between mayor and council, for instance if the council refuses to vote the budget, the mayor may be led to resign. The government is then likely to dissolve the council and call for new elections. Such conflicts do occur, but they are relatively rare; the electoral system tends to strengthen the majority party, and the mayor normally enjoys the support of at least a majority. Moreover, many mayors have considerable personal following in the commune and can distribute patronage. Although some are "compromise" candidates, they are mostly, in large towns in particular, personalities of stature, at least locally, and often nationally. The position of mayor is a normal stepping-stone toward a parliamentary career. Thus one often finds a strongly entrenched mayor able to pursue for years and decades the policy which he likes more often than an unstable and uncertain leadership unable to solve conflicts in the municipal council.

PREFECT AND COUNCIL IN THE DEPARTMENT

The organization of the commune is therefore rooted in self-government, with even a touch of "bossism" in cities where municipal patronage is large and the mayor solidly entrenched. Such is not the position in the *département*. There, little transfer of power has occurred since Napoleon; a weak elected council of the *département*, known as "general council" (*conseil général*) has been somewhat democratized, but executive power remains wholly in the hands of Napoleon's creation, the prefect.

We saw in Chapter Eight that the prefect was the representative of the government in each *département* and was indeed nominally the head of the external services of all the ministries. But the prefect is also the executive agent of the *département;* he corresponds to the mayor of the commune, but he is an appointee of the central government. He is therefore necessarily an executive agent of the county with a difference: he is more like a colonial governor than like the head of a local authority. First, he is not local; he does not come from the area. Almost systematically, the central government chooses men who are "above" local personal troubles, that is to say, from outside. Second, it is central government policy to move prefects every two or three years, precisely in order that they do not become involved locally and cease as a result to be able to impose the government's will. Third, prefects are typically chosen from among subprefects, who are men posted in each *arrondissement* to supervise the activities of mayors and if necessary block or reverse their decisions within the limits of the powers which the law gives them. Indeed, prefects, too, have, among their central government functions, that of supervising the activities of mayors and municipal councils. Thus both the way in which prefects are chosen and their prior career lead them more to defend the interests of the central government than those of local authorities; they are likely to feel uninvolved in local problems except to the extent that their career may be jeopardized if they generate much local political conflict. There is, admittedly, another side to their role. They advise and help mayors, particularly of smaller communes, in dealing with the central government. Budgets of small local authorities are for instance often drafted by agents of the subprefect, as these mayors do not have the skill, or the staff, to draft the budget themselves. Thus mayors are not necessarily antagonistic to prefects and subprefects, who are at times their mentors in the technical problems which confront them. But this is "paternal" advice, not a democratic arrangement; the problem arises only because of the smallness of the average authority, and thus in no way justifies the existence of prefects in a reorganized local government system.

The maintenance of the prefects perpetuates the dependence of local authorities on the central government. It contributes also to justify the perpetuation of a tight system of control of local authorities. Above all, it prevents the *département* from becoming truly a local government unit. Faced with the prefect, the general council is usually weak and often subservient; it engages at times in purely prestige battles which have little to do with real local autonomy. The weakness of the general council stems first from the electoral system which is antiquated. Each canton elects one general councillor on a single-member, two-ballot basis, but, since cantons were created during the Revolution and have scarcely been altered, there are thus differences of from one to a hundred among the population sizes of these districts. Rural areas are grossly overrepresented, with cities obtaining only occasionally an extra general councillor. Only a major redrafting of the map of the cantons, which would radically change the composition of councils, could bring about proper representation. As existing councillors have a vested interest in perpetuating the system, they conspire with the prefects and government to maintain the power equilibrium. Thus the general council is much tamer than it might otherwise be, and, being mostly representative of rural areas, it is likely to be composed of those very men who form the "clientele" of prefects because they need their assistance to solve communal problems. The interests of large towns, on the other hand, are overlooked, and the modern problems of local government (housing, transport, education, etc.) are simply not dealt with by the general council. This in turn reinforces the need for centralization, since central government agents can legitimately suggest that they need to advise, help, and indeed initiate if the problems of society are to be solved.

The reform of the composition of general councils is a crying need which does not, however, attract the attention of observers nor even enter the programs of parties of the Left. Only after such a reform can the problem of the reorganization of power at the county level be solved adequately; meanwhile, relations between prefect and general council clearly leave the prefect with an upper hand. The council meets for two sessions a year only; it is primarily involved in voting the budget, which has of course been prepared by the prefect and his staff; rarely does the council become involved in matters of overall planning and policy-making. The law which reorganized the general council a hundred years ago (in 1871) on a somewhat more liberal basis for the time admittedly did allow for the existence of a permanent standing committee empowered to supervise the actions of the prefectorial staff. In practice, however, though members of the committee have some influence, and though the president of the general council is often a politician of some stature, the staff of the prefecture and of the central government's external services are free to initiate programs and to implement them.

The lack of a real local government at the *département* level is further evidenced by the absence of officials who can be truly said to work for the *département*. The only local government service which exists is that of the communes. In the county, agents, even if legally on the *département*'s payroll, are appointed by the prefect or his subordinates, or by the various external services of the ministries. The situation is thus exactly the reverse of the German pattern, where federal ministries have to use the services of the agents of the *Länder* to implement their rules. In France, were the general council to take a decision of which the prefect would disapprove, and were the prefect obliged to abide because, exceptionally, he would have no veto or other forms of control, the decision would still have to be implemented by central government agents. One can imagine that the reality of implementation would be at variance with the desires of the general council.

It is indeed surprising that such a local government system should have survived for so long in a nation which has been ruled for long periods by liberal governments and where the legislature has so often claimed to wish to limit the powers of the State. It is highly symptomatic that the last major reform of the general council should date back over a century. The excuse is, as we stated early in this chapter, that liberal governments have feared the consequences of decentralization; almost immediately after decentralization was introduced in 1791 war broke out and revolts flared in many parts of the country. "Republican" governments never forgot. Moreover, a succession of less liberal regimes and recently, the advent of the Fifth Republic made the possibility of reform more remote. More profoundly, and indeed surprisingly, liberals seem to share a distrust for local autonomy, which is not expected to lead to "progressive" results. This accounts for the limited moves toward regionalism: the French have been accustomed for so long to having prefects that they do not seem to be able to envisage survival without them!

THE POWERS OF LOCAL AUTHORITIES AND CENTRAL GOVERNMENT CONTROL

At first sight paradoxically but in fact quite logically, French local government is characterized by a combination of relatively large and almost ill-defined power and of very tight central government control. Historically, this combination is understandable; as we said in Chapter Eight, local authorities were originally viewed as external services of the central government; they were therefore in charge of practically all the public services in the locality. When, in 1871 for the *département*, in 1884 for the commune, more powers were given to the councils, the counterpart seemed to be a large dose of central control. Thus, according to the law, the councils and the executives of the commune and *département* are in charge of the affairs of these local authorities; they can theoretically intervene in any area of local concern—in sharp contrast with English local authorities, for instance, who have a circumscribed area of intervention. Indeed, mayors are entrusted with powers which they exercise in the name of the central government; they are responsible, for example, for the registration of births, marriages, and deaths, as well as with electoral registration. They have "police" powers, in the French sense of "policing," which means that they can impose regulations (*arrêtés*) relating to the health and welfare of residents in almost any field. Mayors and councils have also many powers in the economic sector. Municipal undertakings are fairly common and limitations come mainly from the administrative courts which quash decisions of municipal councils setting up local monopolies or even competitive municipal enterprises when they reduce the freedom of trade and industry as a result.

CENTRAL GOVERNMENT CONTROL: TUTELAGE AND
FINANCIAL DEPENDENCE
Central government control follows logically from the very existence of this wide and ill-defined array of powers; indeed,

given that the typical commune is a tiny unit, guidance and even active central government intervention appear almost natural. Thus the granting of general powers is associated with a general form of supervision known as tutelage (*tutelle*) by which practically all important decisions of mayors and municipal councils have to be confirmed by the prefect, or, in the most important cases, by the government itself. By-laws of mayors and votes of municipal councils are not in principle effective unless approved by a higher authority. Thus the real scope of the autonomy of local authorities is markedly reduced. Yet, though the system has been criticized by supporters of local government, no major overhaul has been undertaken. Admittedly, in some cases, positive approval has been replaced by tacit approval to quicken the process; some very minor decisions can now also be taken without approval. But the bulk of the actions have still to be approved, while, conversely, the prefect can substitute himself for the authority if no decision is taken on matters in which the law says that the council must act.

Traditionally, tutelage was exercised primarily in relation to by-laws (often ostensibly, and at times really, because mayors were acting *ultra vires*—or on the basis of spite—when the Council of State could have been left to judge these matters); it was also exercised commonly for the budget, which is the most important single decision of most local authorities. Some relaxation of the rules of budgetary control has taken place, as the slowness of the tutelage mechanism made many authorities grind to a standstill. Particularly in large towns, the fear that local authorities would be inept or corrupt has somewhat given way to the recognition that they have achieved adulthood and know how to run their affairs (and the possible ineptitude of others is of course the consequence of the very small size of most communes). But much control takes place while local authorities have little means of broadening the scope of their income, the introduction of value-added tax in the 1960s having further reduced their room to maneuver. Traditionally, most local taxes were on property; as these became insufficient, a local turnover tax on commercial transactions became the main source of communal revenue. But value-added tax—a national tax—replaced local turnover taxes, some of the product being redistributed to communes on a complicated basis which takes all the decisions away from local agents. As the central government tries also to provide inducements through percentage grants for some services, local autonomy is even further reduced. The reduction of the scope of tutelage has been more than compensated by decreases in financial autonomy.

POLICE AND EDUCATION

The scope of local action is also limited by the part played by the central government in a number of fields which are usually run in other countries by local authorities. Police and education are the two main examples of this centralization. During most of the Third Republic, police forces were divided into local forces under the responsibility of the mayor (with prefectorial tutelage, admittedly) and State forces effectively under the control of the prefect (*gendarmerie*). But, since 1940, the central government has progressively eroded local police forces. First in large towns, and gradually in all urban areas, the police passed under State control, in part to increase efficiency, but in part of course also to ensure the loyalty of all the police forces. Alongside the *gendarmerie,* the government created the *Compagnies Républicaines de Sécurité* (CRS) to provide a mobile paramilitary force to be used in case of disturbances, thus giving the French central authorities well-trained national units; but this contributed further to the decrease in the influence of local authorities over the whole service.

Education has always been one of the classic examples of French centralization; the tendency has been maintained through successive regimes, the Republic having inherited—and wholly accepted—from Napoleon a network of central government agencies in charge of running the public education service. Curricula are uniform and mostly conceived in the Paris ministry. It is claimed that a minister of education could tell Napoleon III what every French schoolchild was learning at a particular moment. This may no longer be true, but if differences in curricula are introduced, they are typically suggested by Paris or at least must be authorized. In parallel, teachers are appointed by uniform standards and methods—competitive examinations for the better positions, ordinary examinations for the rest—and the ministry decides on the teaching positions. A local authority can neither choose what will be taught nor who will be the teachers. Its only involvement is in school building which has become, of course, a major planning problem in expanding cities, but is of course also controlled by government agencies. Enterprising communes are engaged in further education programs or some technical teaching, but as these expand they tend to be taken over by the State machinery, often because of lack of funds of local authorities. Yet this centralization is scarcely the subject of any controversy; neither Right nor Left suggests more autonomy for local authorities or for the schools themselves; only in universities, and indeed only as a result of the "Revolution" of 1968, has a modicum of autonomy been introduced—and this remains very modest by comparison with other liberal countries.

SHARED SERVICES AND AGENCY ARRANGEMENTS

While police and education are thus extreme cases of centralization, central government intervention is great in many other services which are shared between the State and the local authorities. In social aid, for instance, which is financed from contributions of the commune, in the *département*, and in the central government, the administration is in the hands of agents posted in the *département*; central control is thus large on the implementation of policies. A similar extent of central control has been achieved as a result of the "voluntary" association between local authorities, often "induced" by the prefect, in other fields; fire services, for instance, are in effect run on behalf of local authorities by central government agents in the *département*.

More generally, officials of the external services of the central government tend to act on behalf of communes, which find it necessary to employ them as agents. Technicians of the central government often build roads and the commune only provides the funds, as most communes are too small to employ technicians on more than a part-time basis. The roads and bridges offices of the central government are large and well-equipped; they are anxious to help, either by contracting with private builders or even by building directly. A similar process leads rural engineers to be concerned with a variety of communal schemes of rural development, such as water works, drainage, or soil conservation. Given the structure of local government, the population as a whole benefits from the arrangement; services are better run and standards more uniform. But this is more "enlightened despotism" than local self-government.

The small size of communes accounts for the extensive development of these "agency" schemes. In towns, and in particular large towns, the action of local authorities is much less circumscribed, and mayors of cities do play a large part in the shaping of services and in future planning. This has indeed become increasingly the case in the 1960s; municipal councils ceased to be concerned merely with "immediate" services (lighting, street repairs, refuse disposal, sewage, etc.) and became engaged in long-term programs ranging from the provision of industrial sites to large housing projects. These projects, which are formally entrusted to separate municipal corporations alongside other public bodies, have been financed in particular through the sponsorship of a vast State credit institution, the *Caisse des Dépôts et Consignations*. These housing schemes have transformed the physical appearance of most provincial towns and of the Paris area while creating major planning problems (and an occasional scandal). Enterprising local authorities are engaged in promotion; they negotiate directly with businesses as well as with the State. They are therefore less likely to consider themselves dependent on State external services for advice and guidance as they were in the past. From their dynamism (if at times rugged and not always artistically pleasing) stems the current pressure for greater local autonomy which French local government badly needs. This pressure has provided the main driving force behind the demand for regionalism which successive governments seem increasingly unable to stop or even to contain.

TOWARD REGIONALISM?

Regionalism is perhaps the liveliest issue in French political and administrative life. There was scarcely any interest for the provinces in the 1950s; local government affairs were typically considered petty or distasteful. Yet the urge for participation which led to the "Revolution" of 1968 was in large part responsible for the resignation of de Gaulle after the ill-fated referendum of 1969. It is perhaps ironic that a president who insisted on concentrating on lofty problems of State organization and of foreign affairs should have fallen on an internal question, so new for the French nation; it indicates the extent of opinion change, and the future of the Fifth Republic may well depend on the speed and extent of change in this field.

PARIS AND THE PARIS REGION

Regionalism was first confined to the Paris area, naturally enough since, as we saw in Chapter One, Paris is the only truly large French conurbation (it has about 8 million residents, while Marseilles, Lyons, and Lille only approach 1 million). Yet until 1958 the consequences of the spread of Paris over many local authorities had gone almost unnoticed. The administrative structure was the same in the suburban area as in the rest of France whereas, in the city of Paris proper, central government control was particularly tight. Except for a very short period in 1848, Paris never had a mayor because of the fears of revolution; all the revolutions started in Paris, and indeed the troubles of 1968 were to be much more widespread in Paris than anywhere else. Thus all the regimes, from Napoleon to the Fourth Republic, maintained an authoritarian system whereby, alongside the municipal council, broadly vested with the same powers as all municipal councils, two prefects, the Prefect of Seine (the *département* including Paris) and the Prefect of Police, appointed by the government as all other prefects, were entrusted with the powers exercised by mayors in other communes.

However undemocratic, such an organization could at least deal with the administrative problems of Paris, as long as the conurbation was not very much larger than the city and the *département*. But, by the 1950s, only about a quarter of the Paris area residents lived in the city with about half in the *département* as a whole (boundaries dated from 1860). Thus transport, housing, education, planning, just could no longer be tackled by the existing structures. Transport was a particularly pressing problem since the Paris *métro* scarcely extends beyond the boundaries of the city itself. But housing, too, was uncoordinated, while education, health, and welfare services needed overall planning if the well-being of the fifth or so of the French population living in the Paris area were to be catered to.

Thus the first French regional organization was created in 1959 under the name of District of the Paris Region. This was to be headed by a government-appointed "delegate general" having considerable status but stopping short of being a regional prefect. Indeed the agency cannot be strictly labeled a local authority, as the activities of the district resemble more those of an economic or socioeconomic undertaking than those of a classic local authority. The district is in charge of forward planning (a plan of the future of Paris was published under the title of "Paris in the year 2000") and of overall coordination between regional services, such as transport, housing, industrial and commercial development. On these, the district is an executive agency working within a budget and aims mainly at fostering the development of the outer zone of the Paris conurbation.

A council for the district was created, mainly to vote the budget of the authority while advising the delegate general on broad policy issues. But as the council is not directly elected by the population and is composed of representatives of the local authorities of the area, it lacks authority to press its point of view. The government was worried that the district would be dominated by the Left because of the strength of the Communist-controlled "Red Belt"; it played also on the parochialism of many of the smaller local authorities which, often more middle class, did not wish to see their interests lost under the weight of the city of Paris (now right-wing in a majority, admittedly) and the larger left-wing communes. The council remains remote; it raises few problems for either the government or the delegate general. The tame Paris municipal council found an even tamer counterpart in the regional council.

Yet the creation of the district did not resolve even all the administrative problems of the Paris area, since at the lower level the same local authorities did remain in charge of most of the services. The government was nonetheless obviously anxious to avoid domination by the Left at the lower level as well as at the regional level; amalgamation of local authorities was politically impossible—nor was it demanded by local politicians or administrators. Thus the reform of 1964 simply led to a reshaping of *département* boundaries; six new *départements* were formed where two existed in the past, all having the same structure as other *départements* and only one of which has a Communist majority on its general council. Regionalism will still have to wait before it begins to take roots in the Paris area.

TIMID REGIONALISM AND THE GROWTH OF REGIONAL DEMANDS
Yet even this limited amount of regionalism was not implemented in the provinces before the early 1970s. As we saw in Chapter Eight, the need to find better areas for the administration of central services led to the setting-up of standard regions; for a period, the only regional development was the appointment of a regional prefect! In part to help the planners to prepare more effectively the new plan and to improve the implementation of the existing one, and in part because the idea of provincial decentralization was gaining ground, the first semirepresentative bodies of the regions were created in 1964. These *Comités de Développement Economiques Régionux* (CODER) were to be sounding boards of opinion in the region; they included therefore prominent representatives of the various economic and social interests, as well as local councillors. Their influence remained weak: they have issued reports and occasionally acted as pressure groups. The status of some of their members is high, but collectively these bodies attracted little attention—the lack of an electoral base being largely responsible for this low reputation. Yet they were the first experiment in almost two hundred years of "provincial" representation in a country where the fear of dislocation through excessive devolution to large local authorities has always been rampant.

One of the main themes of the "Revolution" of 1968 was participation. Though mainly strong in Paris, the outburst was directed against government centralization and even the cultural dominance of the capital. In the wake of the riots, de Gaulle and his government promised to meet some demands, but they presented a scheme of regionalization which was so limited in scope and displayed so markedly the traditional features of administrative control that it failed to satisfy the most moderate of the "regionalists." First, the powers of the regional authority were to be strictly circumscribed—they were listed in the law— and the taxation base was to remain narrow; regions were not to be allowed to try out social and economic experiments which would help to enliven the provinces and attract imaginative politicians. Second, the region was to be run on the pattern of the *département*, with a prefect in charge of the executive, the council being merely, like the general council, a weak appendage of the executive. Yet, third, these councils were not to be elected, but, like the council of the Paris district, composed of representatives of a large number of bodies; they could not have an internal unity as a result, and they would not threaten the power of the prefect. Clearly, they would not interest the population or the politicians. The new structure would be merely an expansion of the 1964 regional structure—regional councils being only revamped versions of the existing CODERs. If the French wanted participation and regional autonomy, the 1969 proposals were not to satisfy them.

The reform was proposed to the people; a majority rejected it, though de Gaulle had staked his future on it and did indeed resign in view of its defeat. In fact, the reform might have been approved, had not the president chosen to attach—in the same question—a reform of the Senate which antagonized many on the Center and on the Right. But the departure of de Gaulle did not give the new president and the new government an incentive to act further, and more speedily, in regional matters. While the premier, Chaban-Delmas, insisted on a "new society" and on better relations with unions and groups generally, no move was made for almost three years to give regionalism a new and more serious try. Yet increasing pressure was applied at various levels to act more positively in the regional field. Left-wing and Center groups pressed for greater action. In many parts of the country, such as Brittany, Alsace, the whole of the southern half, cultural movements for the revival of local languages, in part, but in part also against the "colonization" by Paris and against central government control, became more vocal. In the most timid fashion, the government presented, in 1972, a regional reform which seems even weaker than that of 1969; it merely gives more official status to the regional prefects and the representative councils than had been the case since 1964. In the very short term, the government's action may suffice, as the bulk of the population and of the politicians of all parties remain—for various reasons, often due to tradition—relatively unconcerned and perhaps even frightened by full-scale regionalism. The idea of French "unity" is strong, as was noticeable when J. J. Servan-Schreiber worried his fellow members of the Radical party by starting a campaign asking for no more for regional and local authorities than is customary in other liberal democracies. Yet the regional issue is slowly gaining strength. It emerges in relation to a variety of problems; it coincides with the newly felt desire for local autonomy and responsibility. The drive of the bureaucracy helped France to achieve a rate of economic growth which is among the highest in the developed world. The very success of this policy is leading to demands for local and regional action which will surely increase in coming decades.

French local government is thus at the crossroads. For generations, it was dangerous to predict that change would occur, as demands for local autonomy were minimal in every political quarter and across the breadth and width of the country. The French seemed ready to see the whole country become a dependency of the capital and be run, albeit in an enlightened and paternalistic fashion, from the capital. They appeared to want to participate in social climbing by moving to the capital only to return to the provinces to find again some of the folklore which had charmed them in their youth. This is no longer true. Paradoxically on the surface, France is both more unified and more affected by demands for regional and local autonomy. The old inferiority complex of the provincial is slowly disappearing, and because it is disappearing, men and women from the provinces are prepared to make demands which their parents did not even conceive.

Demands will probably grow, despite the resistance of the traditional structures, of the civil service, of the parties, and even of many local representatives. A process of socialization has begun, however, and not merely in government circles. For long, as we noted, the smallness of communes was not felt as a problem; changes in the early 1970s indicate that the government has realized at least the broad dimensions of the reform needed. But local authority representatives have to go through the same process and accept that many will° lose their small base of patronage and their limited political glory. A similar process of rethinking has to take place at the level of *départements* and regions, but, in this context, the government, the central administration, and local authorities have to change habits which grew during almost two centuries and which shaped the structure of rural and provincial France. Yet the change has to occur if one of the main "blockages" of society is to be overcome. As the change may be painful, and the result uncertain, most politicians still remain on the sidelines; since 1968, they have also become aware of the dangers of delay, and local and regional reforms may be implemented, though of course very late to meet the real problems of local autonomy.

PART FIVE

FRANCE
AND
THE WORLD

11

Foreign Policy

French foreign policy in the 1960s derived its force, direction, and style from Charles de Gaulle. But it was not uniquely the general's creation; it was essentially based on an analysis and interpretation of French history by the president. De Gaulle has readily admitted at times that in the twentieth century France came to the bargaining table of international politics with no material of military substance, no assets in the accepted currency of international relations, and yet maintained her position and indeed often strengthened it. This does not mean that France dealt alone in the faded glories of past greatness—a manifest impossibility in the world of international diplomacy. What it does mean is that France demonstrated through de Gaulle that diplomatic technique, firm leadership, and world influence (if not power), although overlooked in recent decades, can (if skillfully employed) be indices of international status only slightly less formidable than vast populations, great national wealth, giant industrial complexes, and large standing military establishments. What de Gaulle has done is to emphasize the best of France's assets, all of which have their roots in the past: her worldwide cultural influence; the traditional intelligence of her people; the energy of her leaders; and a crucial geographical position at the crossroads of Western Europe. From this amalgam he created the image of a vibrant, living state with a special character and force that he was busily adapting to the requirements of an otherwise bipolar world.

There is no trickery in all this because France is accepted as a power on the international stage to an extent which nations of roughly comparable size and equivalent richness in historical tradition are not. One reason for this, of course, is that de Gaulle insisted on asserting his claim for French *grandeur*. Furthermore, he has never desisted from forcing his claim on the other nations of the world which are sufficiently endowed with the natural and tangible elements of power to make their recognition of his claim decisive. While de Gaulle has not used sleight of hand in carving out a unique status for France, he has not hesitated to capitalize on the mystique of his own personage to achieve the goals he set for his country.

Yet, although de Gaulle's efforts were instrumental in giving France a leading place among nations, his failures in his later years clearly indicated the limits of the influence of a nation which can no longer pretend to be more than middle-sized. Thus the day of reckoning had to come when de Gaulle's worldwide commitments were to seem too vast for France's internal base, unless within Europe, France, or the French leaders, could play a major part and become the spokesmen of a new community. De Gaulle's successors have clearly seen the need to extricate themselves from the complex game which de Gaulle tried to play, but failed to win, in the 1960s. Hence the somewhat tortuous maneuvers of Pompidou in the early 1970s, obliged, as he was, to manage the susceptibilities of the more rigid Gaullists, while aiming at bringing France back in the wider fold of European nations.

EARLY POSTWAR FRENCH FOREIGN POLICY

The defeat of 1940 was traumatic for France, both internally and externally. Although technically counted among the Allied victors against the Third German Reich, the country was only a shell when, five years later, the battle was over. In the process of fighting the German invader and in successive years of Allied bombings, much of the nation's wealth had been destroyed. The restoration of French sovereignty, moreover, had been largely accomplished by the force of American and British arms and, indirectly, by the Russian armies, which broke Hitler's eastern front. France played only a secondary role in these events, despite

General de Gaulle's success in fielding a liberation army of surprising size, largely composed of Frenchmen from the overseas empire in Africa, the Middle East, and Indochina.

Once the fighting ceased in Europe, France saw her holdings elsewhere threatened not by the erstwhile enemy, but by her allies and by the newly born forces of native nationalism. Under British pressure, she was quickly forced to dissolve her protectorates in the Middle East and shortly thereafter began dispatching troops to Indochina to quell the incipient native revolt in Vietnam. By the late 1940s, nationalist stirrings had begun in North Africa. Within a few years, Tunisia and Morocco had won their independence and the Indochinese war was succeeded by an even more agonizing struggle in Algeria.

Meanwhile, in Europe, France was involved in a somewhat fruitless search for security against the possible revival of German militarism, to which she had fallen victim three times in less than a century. At the same time she was seeking a means of maintaining the leadership of the continent while totally ill-equipped to do so. Preoccupation with the German question made it difficult for French policy-makers to grasp immediately the essential fact that in a world where an uneasy balance of power was delicately kept between the United States and the Soviet Union, neither of these two superpowers would allow Germany to become a pawn of the other. Hence the only solution from the point of view of *Realpolitik* was to see to it that the West's particular part of Germany did not become dangerously weak relative to the other half and, more importantly, to commit positively the weight of the Bonn Republic to the power of the West. The long detour of French policy before this fact was seen complicated and delayed the effective building of a united Europe. It also caused antagonism against France throughout Europe and the Free World.

Nevertheless, considerable progress was made in the early years after the war toward bringing Europe closer together, and France instigated most of these moves. She was instrumental in initiating international discussions which led to the creation of the Council of Europe; she contributed effectively to the international planning which produced the Organization of European Economic

Cooperation (with efficiently using American aid as its main purpose); and she launched the idea of European integration—the Coal and Steel Community was to be known for a long period as the Schuman Plan, from the name of the French foreign minister of the period. However, although France moved with dispatch and provided ingenious leadership during the formative period of these organizations, the path was by no means smooth, and considerable European suspicion of French motives resulted as long as it seemed that France was using all her power to control a renascent Germany. It was only at the end of the 1940s that French policy can be said to have been wholly committed to Western defense against Russia and to a form of European integration which would include Germany on an equal basis. But the development of both these ideas was sometimes difficult, since French prejudices still remained near the surface and since colonial problems often interfered with the general aims of French foreign policy.

THE FOREIGN POLICY OF THE FOURTH REPUBLIC

FRANCE AND THE BEGINNINGS OF EUROPEAN INTEGRATION

After France came to realize that the idea of partitioning, or even controlling, Germany could not be seriously entertained in view of Anglo-American opposition, her foreign policy came to take great pride in the construction of Europe. This became a way of integrating Germany so as to make adventures of the Hitler kind wholly impossible; this was also, in the eyes of "technocrats" such as Jean Monnet, a means of forcing competition on French industry which had been hitherto depressed through Malthusianism and protectionism. But immediate and full-blown European unity was impossible on a number of grounds. First, public opinion was scarcely ready for it. It was not even ready for it in some of the devastated countries of Western Europe, such as France or Germany; opposition was likely to be even greater in countries which were still confident of their own ability to survive alone in the postwar world, such as Great Britain. Moreover, any immediate European developments on a large scale would be dangerous for the economies themselves; protectionism had to be demolished gradually if countries were to be able to benefit fully from the change. Hence the discovery of the step-by-step method of European integration, which was at the root of the proposal made by France of a first "community" which would be limited to coal and steel. It was to be a real "community," not simply an agreement or an alliance; there were to be institutions (an executive, a parliament, a court) which would have a supranational character; members of the executive, in particular, were to take decisions on the basis not of the interests of the individual countries, but of those of European coal and steel as a whole.

Even this relatively modest suggestion for European integration was more than Great Britain was prepared to accept. While the British had taken part in the discussions leading to the creation of the Council of Europe, it became clear, when the proposal for a coal and steel community was made in the spring of 1950, that Britain was both convinced that she could solve her own problems alone and unwilling to bow to decisions taken on a supranational basis by a community organization. The Europe of the Six (France, West Germany, Italy, Belgium, Holland, and Luxembourg) was born from this refusal, which was to have serious consequences, both psychological and practical, in the years to follow. European integration, as launched and propounded by the French (and in particular by the party which advocated European unity most consistently, the MRP), was to have a continental flavor—some said a Roman Catholic flavor. De Gaulle was later to use (or attempt to use) this situation to his benefit, and he was to find allies in some quarters of French politics who had become convinced that Britain would never really be prepared to participate in the building of Europe.

GERMAN REARMAMENT

By the time the treaty establishing the European Coal and Steel Community was signed in 1951, however, the question of Germany had already been revived much more dramatically through an American proposal that the old enemy of France should be rearmed and brought within NATO. Opposition flared from various quarters—indeed it became clear very quickly that the move would not be willingly accepted by France. Various efforts at procrastination were made by the French government, but they failed against American determination. Something had to be done by the French who, by the early fifties, had recognized that NATO was necessary to their own defense (except for the Communists and a small neutralist section on the Left) and who were engaged in a war in Indochina in which American support was being increasingly sought and obtained. The French government thus conceived of a plan, the European Defense Community, which used the European idea to limit the full weight of German rearmament: armies would be merged; there would be only contingents of each nationality at the lower levels; the high command would be fully integrated. If the scheme had succeeded, France would have managed, in one move, to prevent Germany from ever recovering an army capable of waging wars, to bring forward the idea of community, and to satisfy the Americans on basic defense requirements.

The plan was accepted in Washington, but the French were to be divided on EDC in a way which resembled some of the most bitter political fights of the early part of the century about the Dreyfus case or the separation between Church and State. Except for the Communists, who were predictably and thoroughly against the idea, all the parties were divided, some right down the middle. Most Christian Democrats, many Socialists, and some Radicals and Independent Conservatives supported the scheme, not because of its intrinsic virtue, but because of its contribution to European integration. De Gaulle and his supporters were strongly against the plan, mainly on nationalistic grounds, as was a large section of the army which felt that the price was too high, since it might lead to the dismemberment of the French high command. The government procrastinated for two years (between 1952 and 1954) before presenting the treaty to Parliament, while the climate of opinion in the country became more passionate and opponents gradually gained ground. In the end, it was to be Pierre Mendès-France who, after having solved the Indochinese war at Geneva, decided that the abscess had to be opened, however painful the operation might be. After a stormy debate (as a result of which the Christian Democrats were never to forgive Mendès-France for not having come down firmly in favor of the treaty), EDC was killed at the National Assembly by a coalition composed of all the Communists, about half the Socialists and the Radicals, a large minority of the right-wing Independents, and almost the totality of the Gaullists. The consequence was to be full German rearmament at the end of 1954 with, however, the guarantee given by the British that they would maintain an army on the Rhine for fifty years and that they would agree to the creation of a much less supranational Western European union. The new treaty, though less pleasant in the eyes of the integrationists, was at least acceptable to the French nationalists.

FRANCE AND THE COMMON MARKET

European integration did indeed appear at a very low ebb at the end of 1954. It seemed that it would be impossible to bring back to the fore an idea which had been so severely shaken by the crisis of EDC and which was not based on a genuine *rapprochement* between the French and the Germans. Yet the idea of step-by-step integration was revived in 1956, somewhat surprisingly, by the new French Socialist government. After a relatively easy negotiation (in view of the problems which were at stake) and largely because it was agreed from the start that the most difficult problems would have to be solved during various transitional periods lasting up to fifteen years, a treaty was signed and ratified in 1957 by the French Parliament, and the Common Market was born (another treaty, creating the European Atomic Community, was also signed and ratified). The decision was recognized as momentous at the time since it probably prevented the European idea from dying; in fact, the decision was perhaps even more momentous than was thought in 1957, for de Gaulle's policies on Europe might well have been very different and his room for maneuver greater if the last Parliament of the Fourth Republic had not landed him with a new child which Frenchmen suddenly came to love and were to continue to cherish during the whole of the subsequent period.

The legacy of the Fourth Republic was thus far from negative. The Franco-German problem had been solved, though indirectly.

Commitment to the Western alliance was perhaps less strong than in other European countries. France never practiced a militant form of "Atlanticism"; this was perhaps because there were many Communist electors; this was also because, even before de Gaulle, the French were somewhat uneasy about the Anglo-American leadership of the alliance. But there was never any question of breaking the ties which most people agreed had been essential in preserving peace in Western Europe and perhaps in making the Soviet Union realize gradually that an aggressive policy would be of no avail. But it was in the field of European integration that the French contribution had been the greatest; despite the failure of EDC, it was the Fourth Republic which had provided leadership and started a movement which no one would be able to reverse. Admittedly, the cost had been the division of Western Europe, which became clear in 1958 when the European Free Trade Association was erected as a countermove to the Common Market, but, for the French integrationists, this cost was both temporary and unavoidable; Britain would only respond if she were made to realize that the Common Market would be a success and that her economy would suffer from remaining outside. This the continental Europeans were determined to prove. By the late 1950s, they had already to a large extent made their case, as businesses everywhere were preparing for entry into the large new market. The failure of the Fourth Republic in Algeria can perhaps be said, in retrospect, to have been more than compensated for by the success of the European idea.

COLONIAL POLICY: FROM THE FRENCH UNION TO THE END OF THE FRENCH OVERSEAS COMMUNITY

"ASSIMILATION" IN THEORY AND PRACTICE

Meanwhile, the Fourth Republic died for having been overburdened by the decolonization process. Up to 1939, the large French empire had been at times shaken by local revolts, but these were always quelled. The defeat of 1940 and the growth of nationalistic ideas everywhere were soon to have an impact on the

French colonies. Admittedly, the French had always prided themselves on practicing a policy different from that of other European powers. The key word was "assimilation." The notion was that the cultural, social, and economic characteristics of the mother country would gradually be extended to overseas dependencies. Native peoples would become French and their countries would either become part of France or be closely associated with Paris; the French assumed that the natives would want to become French—indeed that nothing better could happen to them than to become Frenchmen. In fact, before World War II, only a few Africans and Indochinese had become citizens, and most of these had acquired this status by virtue of having served in the French army. In Algeria, administrators from the mother country found the durability of Moslem customs, institutions, and practices so formidable that it was necessary to make many adjustments and to maintain the principles of Koranic law. But many Africans, Indochinese, and even Arabs were virtually turned into Frenchmen through being educated, first locally in primary and secondary schools built on the French model, and later in French universities. These constituted an elite, who often went into administration (local administration run on French lines and under French aegis) or teaching (President Senghor of Senegal was for a long period a teacher in a French grammar school). The mass of the people, however, often remained completely untouched by the "Gallicization" process, even in Algeria, where colonization lasted longest and assimilation was most pronounced.

The basic fallacy of the policy was clearly the belief that the indigenous population wanted to become French. But there were also three major weaknesses in the implementation of the idea. First, in many cases, wide gaps existed between theory and practice, between the enunciation of a colonial policy in Paris and its local enforcement. The notion of equality, when it existed, tended to be theoretical and abstract; the reality of daily life was, at best, enlightened despotism, at worst (though not very commonly, except in some quarters in North Africa), unpleasant racism. Second, French colonial administrators often found it expedient to support and identify themselves with local leaders.

When, particularly since World War II, new generations, often educated in France, came to question the right of the French to rule, these traditional leaders gradually became discredited and the colonial power was associated with this discredit. Third, the assimilation policy came too late, and at too leisurely a pace, to compete with the development of nationalism; the real drive toward complete assimilation came in Algeria when the war had already shown that demands for independence could no longer be reversed.

FROM INDOCHINA TO ALGERIA

The first real war of independence began in Indochina in 1945, although Algeria and Madagascar also experienced at the time more than minor revolts. Unable to end the war in Indochina by an early settlement, the French entered into a war of attrition, which was to last eight years, had major effects on the morale of the army, contributed to poisoning the political climate in the mother country, and ended in defeat. The Constitution of the Fourth Republic, in 1946, had created a "French union," partly based on assimilation, and partly open to association; this failed to solve the most acute problems, either in Indochina or in Africa. Troubles flared up in 1953 in the two "protectorates" of Tunisia and Morocco and, from November 1954, Algeria became the scene of increasing military actions. Although Pierre Mendès-France ended the Indochinese war by a settlement which led to the partition of Vietnam and came to an agreement in Tunisia, although his successor, Edgar Faure, disentangled France from Morocco, and although to prevent troubles spreading to Black Africa the Socialist government of 1956 initiated a law designed to give autonomy to the various territories, still the Algerian problem proved intractable to all. The million or so Frenchmen who lived there were prepared at all costs to defend their superior status, even if the cost was the end of the Republic.

By May 1958 the war was clearly proving too much for the French army, despite half a million conscripts; limited efforts were periodically made toward autonomy. These moves were so limited that the Algerian rebel government was unwilling even to discuss them. Yet the French settlers (mainly farmers, shopkeepers, artisans, white-collar workers of the "poor white" variety) suspected the government's intentions. Many of their leaders were beginning to drive the army toward open rebellion. On May 13, 1958, a "committee of public safety" was installed in Algiers when it became known that Pierre Pflimlin, a mildly liberal member of the Christian Democratic party, had been appointed prime minister by the National Assembly. Within ten days, the rebellion extended to Corsica. Within three weeks, de Gaulle had been given almost full powers by the National Assembly and the Fourth Republic had come to an end.

De Gaulle tried for four years to find ways of solving the Algerian problem while stopping short of independence. The Constitution of the Fifth Republic, meanwhile, had established a "French community," designed to give more autonomy, though not full independence, to French Black Africa; but the arrangements lasted only two years and, by 1960, de Gaulle gracefully and easily granted independence to all the territories which accounted for the bulk of the French Empire (Guinea had "taken" its independence in 1958 during the referendum campaign). The 1960 independence move proved not only inevitable, but indeed advantageous to France. Strong economic and cultural ties remained. Various bilateral agreements enabled France to retain considerable influence in, and to give large sums to, her former possessions. Though the assimilation policy is wholly dead, cultural penetration is as intense as ever. The language ties with France (French is spoken more often in the United Nations since 1960 than before) help to maintain economic and technical links. Moreover, as the Fifth Republic has taken postures of independence from the blocs and of championship of the rights of the smaller nations, countries of ex-French Black Africa, suspicious of Russian and Chinese intervention as well as of American capitalism, about which they know little, prefer French influence. Thus the image of France came to be strengthened to a point which few could have forecast in the early fifties. Coups and changes of government in the African states did little to modify this special relationship.

Meanwhile, the Algerian war proved increasingly unpopular at home and the belief that it could be won gradually diminished.

Local settlers tried to stage a coup in 1960, and some army leaders openly revolted for four days in 1961. De Gaulle emerged victorious from both crises by a mixture of cunning and assertion of authority and thus slowly drew the country—and probably reconciled himself—to Algerian independence. Long negotiations took place, designed to give French settlers some advantages and, for a while at least, dual nationality, while the home country and Algeria were marred by the bombing outrages of a newly created Secret Army Organization of the French settlers; these came in open revolt when, in April 1962, Algerian independence was at last agreed to, and approved by referendum. But the army remained loyal. When the date of independence came, the large majority of settlers left Algeria in a panic, and the collapse of the Secret Army Organization was delayed only for a while by a civil war between various factions of nationalist Moslems.

As a result of the Algerian settlement of 1962, hatred of de Gaulle on the Right became widespread (there were to be several attempts on the life of the president during the period). Many felt that they had been betrayed, and betrayed by the man whom they had brought back to power. Almost certainly de Gaulle's views did change when it became clear that integration between Europeans and Moslems was an empty concept which neither side would accept. Thus the French president showed realism in his approach to the Algerian problem, as well as a combination of toughness and skill in the realization of the goal. For the majority of the French, he succeeded in doing what no other politician was in a position to do: he solved the last colonial problem facing the country, repatriated the army and most of the Europeans, avoided a fascist takeover, and established relations with the new Algerian regime which, despite ups and downs (mainly in connection with the ownership and distribution of the large oil resources), have remained closer than could have been expected after eight years of war. The Algerian war was traumatic for a generation of Frenchmen; it will always be to the credit of de Gaulle that he found a solution which healed the wounds on all sides and allowed the page to be turned over, thus making it possible to say, a decade or so later, that few remember the Algerian war and the scars it made at the time.

DE GAULLE'S FOREIGN POLICY

Meanwhile, the French president had engaged in a new foreign policy of "greatness" which could scarcely have been expected of France in the Fourth Republic. From the start, the key to this greatness had been the leadership of the new Common Market. Thus, though he did not believe in European integration, let alone federalism, he was determined to use the instrument which the treaty of Rome gave to the French government. He therefore stated plainly, on coming to power in 1958, that he would respect French foreign obligations. Indeed, he went further and sought to lower tariffs sooner than the treaty required. Having devalued the franc (and created a "new franc" worth 100 of the old ones, partly for prestige reasons, since the franc became roughly equal to the Deutschemark as a result), he decided that France was to swim, from then on, in the same waters as the other five countries. It was indeed typical of his attitude to have anticipated, rather than followed, the first Common Market move, and it can only be surmised whether France would have followed the treaty so closely had the Fourth Republic remained in being. For de Gaulle, however, this was not out of real love for the "European idea"; it was a matter of honor—and of calculation.

An "Independent" and "Global" Foreign Policy

From the start, de Gaulle was determined to increase French independence with respect to foreign policy. Since the United States was the country on which France was, perforce, most dependent, French policy would aim at disengaging itself as much as possible from the United States. At a higher level, moreover, de Gaulle was convinced that the United States (and the Anglo-Saxons in general, as he called the Anglo-American community) were being both old-fashioned and naïve in their conduct of world affairs. They were old-fashioned in their stress on an anti-Soviet line which did not correspond to the realities of the post-Stalin world: Russia (as he always called the Soviet Union) was returning to the fold of the European nations. To emphasize the divisions between the Communist and non-Communist parts of Europe was to help the perpetuation of a division which was becoming daily more artificial. Americans were being naïve in forgetting the requirements of power politics and in giving too much prominence to ideology in international relations. For de Gaulle, nations were human beings, with their wills and passions, and whatever dress each nation was currently wearing made little difference to their real behavior. Russia's and China's traditional aims would be upheld, whatever regime currently held power. Nothing would be gained in refusing to recognize a country on the grounds that one did not like a regime or in refusing to accept that large countries needed buffer states to protect their interests. In the 1962 Cuban crisis, de Gaulle was one of the first to give full and explicit support to Kennedy; equally, de Gaulle deemed American policy in Vietnam to have been unrealistic, since it had not taken into account the traditional aims and needs of China.

The twin instruments of a foreign policy, in the Gaullist interpretation, were to be a position of basic strength and a skillful system of alliances. The position of strength was to be had through the atom bomb, viewed as a credible deterrent which would force others to negotiate with the French government. De Gaulle had not started the French atomic program; he inherited it from the Fourth Republic. But de Gaulle was to go further and give great emphasis to the *force de frappe.* He chose to reconvert the whole French army and to divert as much money as possible to the construction both of weapons and of means of delivery. The Algerian war was a burden in this respect, as it forced the French president to maintain strong conventional forces which were of no relevance to the requirements of a modern system of defense, and, more importantly, to the aims of a global policy. As soon as the war was over, and despite opposition from a large section of the military, de Gaulle took steps to reduce the size of conventional forces both from a desire to redirect funds to the nuclear weapon effort and to adapt the military establishment to modern defense concepts.

The system of alliances was to be built on the foundations of European integration inherited from the Fourth Republic. Instead of a European community, in which European countries would be merged (in de Gaulle's view a wholly unrealistic, or at best a premature idea), the French president wished to develop the "Europe of the fatherlands." The aim was indeed a little too ingenious to be really successful. Briefly, it consisted in using what integration was already in existence to make sure that alliances would not be broken and to turn to France's advantage the cultural and economic potential represented by the combined strength of the European nations. On the one hand, the idea of European integration and the already existing institutions of the Coal and Steel Community, the Atomic Energy Community, and the Common Market would make the other five members of the Six wary of making moves which might lead to a break, and only France had an atomic force (indeed, Germany was prevented by the treaty of 1954 which allowed her to rearm from ever being involved in a nuclear weapons program). On the other hand, France (and de Gaulle) would be free to decide how to use the combined European strength; this could be employed to further aims specific to the French (or to de Gaulle's vision of what France needed). In order to establish French supremacy, at least in foreign policy, over the other five countries, the French government suggested that meetings of foreign ministers (or heads of governments) should take place periodically. De Gaulle hoped to play in them the part which he succeeded in playing, for a while at least, in the French overseas community. At the same time, failing agreement of all five, a special arrangement was made with one partner; Franco-German friendship was pushed to a point which it had never reached during the Fourth Republic or before. Konrad Adenauer's passionate desire for European unity, as well as the strong influence which the French president had on the old German chancellor, led to a temporary and apparent identity of views. A curious confederation seemed to be born gradually, which borrowed some of its features from the structure of holding companies; though she had only a share in the Europe of the Six, France appeared able to make the major decisions (or at least to speak in the name of the others) and the French leader, through his control of French policy, could lead European destinies.

While these arrangements were skillfully constructed, de Gaulle was gradually disentangling France from what appeared to him to be the unacceptable constraints of the North Atlantic Treaty. In a first phase, he pushed for the establishment of a three-country directorate, in which France, Britain, and the United States would take the major decisions which other countries, not possessing nuclear weapons, would have to abide by. In the name of realism, de Gaulle claimed that only those three countries could carry out the threat of the deterrent and that a larger directorate would in any case be cumbersome and unwieldy. The American government predictably refused (whether de Gaulle believed that his idea would be agreed to is difficult to know) on the grounds that the other members of the alliance were entitled to have as much of a share as was permitted by the necessities of modern warfare. This was dismissed by de Gaulle as an obvious means of maintaining American (and to some extent Anglo-American) supremacy over the alliance. From 1960 onward, he became determined to undermine gradually the integrated character of the organization and hoped, with German collaboration, to reduce it to a conventional alliance in which U.S. predominance would be markedly reduced.

The year 1962 was perhaps the best year of Gaullist policy, the year in which it seemed that, however dubious the foundations, the system might be about to succeed. With the end of the Algerian war, the French president would at last be free of "trivial" colonial preoccupations and the French army could be devoted entirely to being the prestigious arm of a grand diplomacy. Franco-German collaboration was at its highest point and the official visit of the French president to Germany seemed to manifest the European (as distinct from merely French) stature of the general. As the German magazine *Der Spiegel* said after the occasion, "De Gaulle came to Germany as French president and left as European emperor." A treaty was to be negotiated between the two countries (it was indeed to be signed early in the following year) which would formalize the special relationship existing between them and would in particular lead to the development of regular exchanges and conferences at all levels of foreign policy-making. But 1962 was also the year in which the British, at last, did recognize that EFTA was only a limited success, while the Common Market was an unqualified one. At Brussels, for several months, British ministers gradually made concessions on various aspects of economic policy, though perhaps not enough in the agricultural field. De Gaulle seemed on the verge of achieving what the "Europeans" had not been able to do; the old British independence was being brought to an end and was being replaced by full participation. Though such a change might mean more policy-sharing on the part of the French president, British entry into the Common Market would mean the creation of the kind of powerful unit which Gaullist policies needed if autonomy from the United States was ever to be achieved.

THE MOVES TOWARD THE THIRD WORLD

De Gaulle did fear, however, the consequences of British entry. Clear independence from the United States was going to be more difficult. The two-person game with the German chancellor would be replaced by a more difficult three-person relationship, with the last entrant in the team having long been expert at diplomacy and having practiced the balance of power for several generations. For once, de Gaulle clearly overplayed his hand, though he was quite possibly cornered into doing so; by vetoing British entry into the Common Market, he stopped any intrusion from complicating the elaborate system which he had so cleverly built, but he also was quickly to find that the system itself was about to crumble. With the end of the Adenauer era, in the summer of 1963, he was presented with a new German opposite number, Ludwig Erhard, who had less admiration for his talents, was less interested in maintaining at all costs a real Franco-German friendship, and was generally more convinced of German economic leadership in continental Europe. As a result during the following years, France was to pursue a more bitter and less successful foreign policy than during most of the postwar period.

The second phase of the foreign policy of the Fifth Republic thus opened in 1963. It seemed to be based on gradual withdrawal from all classic alliances with the hope of gaining a compensation in the Communist world and in the Third World, for the losses suffered in the Western world. Negotiations became increasingly difficult inside the Common Market; the toughness of French negotiators was not merely a reply to German efforts aimed at maintaining some special advantages for German agriculture.

Though no desire to break was overtly expressed, at least in the first instance, warnings were more frequent and the French foreign minister, Maurice Couve de Murville, became increasingly less amenable to the idea of compromise. Yet there was surprise when, in June 1965, the French delegation walked out of a Brussels meeting and when France subsequently decided unilaterally to put the Common Market in cold storage. But the evolution followed logically from the events of the previous two years; the technical difficulties of the Common Market were no greater at the time than they had been in the past and particularly during the early period when, thanks to the personal alliance between de Gaulle and Adenauer, the French president seemed to reap many benefits in the field of foreign policy. By 1965, de Gaulle had turned his back on a European Economic Community which he could not use for his own aims, since the other five had shown little or no interest in the confederal and strictly governmental plans which the French government had launched.

Thus de Gaulle abandoned Western Europe; he moved toward a policy of collaboration with the Communist countries and attempted a new leadership of the developing world. The difficulties between Russia and China and the increased independence shown by Eastern European countries seemed to help the new line of the French president. The recognition of China, which took place in 1964, was presented as a piece of realism, which indeed it was; but hopes were also raised at the time, not merely of trade arrangements, but of a broader collaboration. These were quickly to prove groundless, but as the views long expressed by de Gaulle about a Europe stretching "to the Urals" seemed more realistic in view of the unfreezing of the Communist Bloc, the French president saw in various Eastern countries, in particular Rumania, a possible outlet for his new "global" policy. Yet it was in the Third World, and particularly in Latin America, that de Gaulle seemed to look for the real basis for his alternative policy. The 1964 Latin-American trip, organized with great pomp, appeared to be a clear success. While, during the Algerian war, France had had to use all her skill to keep the friendship of a section of the Third World (and while, indeed, as we saw, only the independence of West Africa enabled France to maintain her position in parts of the developing world), the new anti-American and apparently neutralist postures of the French government seemed to lead, almost overnight, to a complete reversal. Admittedly, French aid, particularly in West Africa, did help to modify some of the attitudes. But de Gaulle's apparent determination to produce a middle way by capitalizing on the anti-American feelings of much of the Third World seemed to increase the prestige of a country which had always longed for status; it also injected attitudes of superiority among many diplomats who had been forced, through the 1950s, to endure rebuffs and remain humble.

THE BREAKUP OF THE GRAND STRATEGY

By the end of 1965, however, this policy had had little concrete effect. French morale might have been boosted; French diplomats might have felt life more bearable among their foreign colleagues. But the collapse of de Gaulle's European master plan in the early 1960s had not been replaced by an effective leadership of the Third World or an arbitrating position in East-West conflicts. In fact, even the French, more concerned with the future of the Common Market than with the potential of a *politique de grandeur*, came to signify to the president, when the presidential election took place in 1965, that Europe (an *integrated* Europe) was important to them; de Gaulle was elected on the second ballot only, the Center candidate having capitalized on the pro-European feelings of the population. While the people as a whole remained largely unperturbed when foreign policy was concerned mainly with world questions—though perhaps secretly pleased sometimes, the majority of the French simply did not take very seriously the global vision of Gaullist policy—there were considerable rumblings over the Common Market breakdown. De Gaulle seemed to have realized that he might have gone too far. Drawing the lesson from his failure to be elected at the first ballot, he decided, slowly but unmistakably, to come back to Brussels and to start negotiations where they had been left. By mid-1966, all difficulties had been fairly easily solved and the European Economic Community had gone through the last phase of the negotiations of the transitional period.

Yet de Gaulle soft-pedaled only on European economic integration. On defense matters, his determination to replace the North Atlantic Treaty by bilateral arrangements went even further: he requested and obtained the departure from French soil of American forces and of the headquarters of the organization. But the move, however irritating and unwelcome to the other members, was not of great moment. By and large, NATO had accomplished its mission long before de Gaulle came back to power, and few of the countries had taken their duties seriously in the course of the 1960s. But this move was also accompanied by increasing attempts made at carrying the battle with the United States on the monetary field, by stressing the need to return to gold (of which France had acquired much) as the basis for international commercial operations, and to obtain in this way the devaluation of the dollar and a reduced role for the U.S. currency. Opposition to this move was almost universal among Western nations, and Germany in particular (as well as Britain) proved unwilling to remain even neutral in what was clearly an impossible battle for the French president, even though the Vietnam war had reduced American support all over Europe and was becoming a source of serious international economic difficulties. The strikes of 1968, the loss of production, and the decreased French external earnings were to solve temporarily the problem; the drain on French reserves was such that the devaluation of the franc became inevitable, though, by one last gesture of nationalistic fervor in which little skillful realism was shown, de Gaulle asserted that he would refuse to devalue and left his successor with the need to solve the problem through devaluation in the following year.

Meanwhile, de Gaulle's foreign policy had grown increasingly bitter and was showing little real success. Britain's entry into the Common Market was vetoed a second time; a serious rift occurred with Canada when de Gaulle cried *"Vive le Québec libre"* and seemed to support openly and officially the cause of separatism; relations with Israel came to a near breaking point when, after the Six Day War of 1967, the French government decided to stop selling even those weapons which had been already ordered and paid for by the Israeli government. Yet these various postures had little effect on the flow of world affairs. They were markedly criticized at home; they displayed a lack of realism, even of diplomatic *savoir-vivre* which reduced the credibility abroad of the French president. Thus it seemed ironic—indeed amusing to some—that de Gaulle should have been in Rumania when troubles broke out in May 1968. He had to return hurriedly to deal with chaos in the country—a chaos which the Fifth Republic had been created to avoid, and his foreign policy ended in the process. For many in Europe and outside, this was clearly a relief; for many in France itself, the time had surely come to look at home affairs and cease using the country for plans which were beyond her means and thus were probably impairing her economic progress. But de Gaulle's foreign policy left a greater legacy than had seemed at the time. It had found an echo in all groups of Frenchmen and in part contributed to giving to many greater pride in the country while bridging some of the gap between the Communist-inclined (who wished to be neutralist) and the majority who looked toward the West. It had created a style and given some habits which were to be kept alive, more than had been expected, in the post-de Gaulle phase of the Fifth Republic.

FOREIGN POLICY SINCE 1969

In all their basic moves, Georges Pompidou and his governments have followed the main tenets of Gaullist policy. In the first year, of course, much was made of changes which were more in manner and approach than in ultimate goals. Unlike de Gaulle, Pompidou always had more the characteristics of the fox than those of the lion; not being de Gaulle, he was not credible and accepted at home and abroad in the way de Gaulle had been. While de Gaulle's high-sounding pretensions were already difficult to tolerate, but were expected, similar manners by the newly elected successor of the founder of the Fifth Republic would have scarcely been received with equanimity. Moreover, the country was temporarily in economic difficulty, its currency being in question; it seemed in more profound social trouble, agitation among students and workers being seemingly rampant and likely to flare again. For a period at least, Pompidou had to keep alive the main tenets of Gaullist policy while being unassertive and reassuring to partners in the Six and elsewhere. Yet the new president had to conduct affairs in the shadow of de Gaulle, with the old leader seemingly leaking comments, often disparaging, on changes in policy, and with part of the Gaullist party (and in particular de Gaulle's last prime minister and long-standing minister of foreign affairs, Couve de Murville) being apparently anxious to seize on Pompidou's mistakes to create serious problems to the new incumbent. The first move, the devaluation of the franc, which was reminiscent of de Gaulle's own decision of eleven years earlier, but which was of course in part a judgment on the previous era, was bold, needed, but not wholly appreciated by the loyal Gaullists; nor were seemingly warmer relations with the United States (which the president visited officially) and even Britain. Thus Pompidou had succeeded in asserting his independence of manners, within the same framework of goals, during the first year of the presidency, by the time of de Gaulle's death at the end of 1970.

The broad terms of this foreign policy remained the desire to maintain France's and Europe's independence vis-à-vis the United States, to appear to the Third World as an alternative pole of attraction to all existing blocs, and, within Europe, to proceed with greater cooperation and unity among nations, but on the basis of nations and with France in a position to exercise leadership. Though of course Pompidou would not have succeeded in moving in the direction of these goals had not de Gaulle, during the previous decade, asserted France's "rights" and fought numerous battles, often of prestige, with all developed nations, Pompidou has been seemingly much more successful than de Gaulle, though in a quieter and less aggressive fashion, in furthering the main goals. Admittedly, he benefited from the increasing economic difficulties which beset the United States as a result of the war in Indochina (as he probably benefited also from Britain's economic difficulties); admittedly, too, he was able to find, in the Conservative government elected in Britain in 1970 and in Edward Heath leaders much more prepared to come close to Europe and to sever special ties with the United States and the

Commonwealth than previous British leaders. But Pompidou's skill in using these opportunities and in showing understanding for allies and partners, in avoiding being isolated on a number of issues, and in appearing to try to explain, rather than assert, has surely played a large part in the changing climate of relations among European nations and Western nations in general, while France's standpoint has been taken into account and even prevailed more often. The dollar was devalued; moves toward economic, social, and political unity in Europe have taken place on the basis of French or near-French standpoints—Britain's entry into the Common Market being one of the main consequences of the new "manners," in which fewer vetoes are made, and the general climate is better (though, on this, too, de Gaulle's previous vetoes clearly helped to bring Britain nearer to a more "independent European" vision than in the past).

Because of the apparent change in the tone of speeches and the "rounder" way in which Pompidou conducted affairs—and also because de Gaulle's behavior appears even more flamboyant as he retreats into history—it is easy to underestimate the extent to which France's policy in the post-de Gaulle era has been both worldwide and independent, perhaps even still more independent than its means can afford. While courting nations of the Third World, Pompidou did not desist from the atomic policy of his predecessor, even if this meant alienating some Latin American countries with which France presumably wants to remain friendly. Meanwhile, the stress has been placed on attempting to maintain a special position in the Middle East, by striking bargains with Arab countries over oil, and by providing weapons while maintaining a posture of "neutrality" between Arabs and Israel. Difficulties with Algeria were settled amicably; visits made by the president to ex-French Black Africa suggested that the leadership of France was still unquestioned in her former territories. The result may not have given Pompidou the possibility of playing a major part in such major conflicts as the Arab-Israeli dispute, the Bangla Desh war of independence, let alone the Indochina war, but neither did de Gaulle play a major part in the same or similar conflicts.

It is of course in the complex game of intra-European and

European-American affairs that the role of the French president
was to be largest and is likely to have most impact on the shape of
foreign policy. On the surface, French views on the future of the
European communities are being constantly challenged, while the
entry of Britain into the game of Brussels politics complicated
appreciably the conditions of the "power equation." But, as long
as it remains accepted that decisions are to be by governments
rather than by the "technicians"—a basic Gaullist tenet—the
standpoint of the French president can be made to prevail, at
least in the long run. France's economic position is strong in the
early 1970s, seemingly stronger than that of all other European
countries save West Germany, while the financial strength of the
Deutschemark creates such unease that it contributes, paradoxically, to increasing France's leeway.

From the very start, Pompidou conceived of foreign affairs as a
nonending process in which one of the cardinal rules is to wait,
patiently, until others slowly come to adopt one's position. He
benefited from the one major strength which he inherited from de
Gaulle—a sense that his office was markedly above the daily
contingencies of a prime minister; thus he could devote, more
than his counterparts, most of his attention to foreign policy.
Whatever tribulations and setbacks summit conferences of European leaders (and that of October 1972 turned rather more to
Pompidou's advantage than had been forecast), ministerial exchanges in Brussels, or indeed talks with other leaders brought in
the short-term, the French president could always hope for
further meetings, for a gradual change, for new opportunities. His
moves were always cautious; his sentences—this time like de
Gaulle's—were always sufficiently elliptic and cryptic to allow for
escapes if the position appeared too dangerous. Perhaps his major
ally turned out to be, somewhat surprisingly, his finance minister,
Giscard d'Estaing, who played cunningly and toughly the game of
currencies in the best interests of a foreign policy which was
dominated by the periodic recurrence of the dollar crisis, more
profound and more urgent than de Gaulle himself had ever
predicted.

The examination of foreign affairs thus brings us back to the
president, who, both in de Gaulle's time and after him, is the key

actor. Foreign ministers and prime ministers have accepted a secondary role and the other ministers, as well as the whole "political class," have scarcely questioned the president's position. As long as this remains the rule in the Fifth Republic, France is likely to have an assertive foreign policy; de Gaulle had seemingly predicted such a development. The office gives independence to the holder; the holder needs to give meaning to the position. From the combination of these two factors stems the nature of the policy. If, in a somewhat Gaullist fashion, one adds the latent longing of the French for great power status—or at least for an active foreign policy—and the ability of the foreign service to exercise a mixture of cunning and idealism (which the French would label hypocrisy if exercised by other nations), one can understand why, having been set on its rails by de Gaulle, French foreign policy did not alter markedly in the early 1970s from what it had come to be in the 1960s and was indeed rescued from some of its more bizarre moves by the change of president.

This foreign policy depends therefore more on the presidency than on the president. The presidency depends of course in turn on the climate of internal peace which cannot be predicted with assurance from the difficulties experienced in the late 1960s and from the problems which the administrative structure, particularly at the local and regional levels, leaves to the Fifth Republic. Were these problems to become more serious, the French president might no longer claim the leadership of the country in a credible fashion, and European partners would no longer be prepared to tolerate the pretensions of guidance and direction which have typically created a mixture of bad temper and eventual resignation, in part in order to save the "communities" from disintegration and in part because of the technical strength and the bargaining skills of the French negotiators. Meanwhile, economic integration must neither come too quickly nor too slowly if France is to keep, through her president, a leadership role. After the almost total collapse of 1965, the dangers of a break-up have wholly disappeared, thus leaving the French leader without ultimate sanction. The pace of integration may quicken, and French presidents may therefore be left with even less room for maneuver, both among Europeans and in the world context. Both internally and abroad, the scope for policies of "greatness" is likely to shrink in the coming decades. But, as long as the scope exists, de Gaulle and the post-Gaullists can be said to have made maximum use of the opportunities.

12

Problems of the Future

In the 1950s and 1960s, the French economy was transformed dramatically; the colonial problems which destroyed one regime and brought another at times near the precipice have been solved and are forgotten; the international status of the country is high. Yet social tensions, which seemed to diminish for a while in the 1960s, reemerged dramatically in 1968. This reinforced the feeling, among many Frenchmen, that the regime remained provisional. Admittedly, the disappearance of de Gaulle did not shake the foundations of the State; quite the contrary, the transition was smooth, almost uneventful. But the institutions are not fully accepted. Even the most forceful of the Gaullist supporters seem to praise the regime more loudly than their innermost convictions warrant. Indeed, changes made by de Gaulle himself, whether through constitutional amendment (as in relation to the election of the president) or through customary practice (as in relation to the powers of the president) seem to reinforce the feeling of transition. We noted that, from a strict interpretation of the constitution, the system was not really made to fit de Gaulle; but we also noted that the twist given to the institutions gave the president the room for maneuver which he intensely desired. Yet this change has increased the fragility of the new system. Instead of providing France with institutions which he could support and help to grow by protecting them with his authority, de Gaulle had, to some extent, been concerned with his own scope for action; by contributing so much to shaping the present political arrangements, he mortgaged his influence of the future of the country.

CONSTITUTIONAL PROBLEMS

Thus the problems are, as usual, still, in the first instance and quite ostensibly, political and constitutional. During its early years, the Fifth Republic hesitated at the crossroads. Disregarding the advice given him by numerous political scientists, leaders of political clubs (and in particular the *Club Jean Moulin*), the head of the new regime decided not to take a firm line in the direction of presidential government. Various reasons have been given. Cynics said that de Gaulle wanted to have it both ways, namely to be able to run the executive and yet have considerable control over the legislature, to have the elbow room of a U.S. president but the hold over the chamber of a British premier, or, in practical terms, to be immovable for seven years but to be able to dissolve Parliament and to appeal to the people. Others claimed that de Gaulle was incapable of understanding and appreciating the importance of constitutional structures. There is, indeed, some truth to this view, though the attitudes of the president on this matter were complex. He seemed at the same time to consider that constitutional arrangements were matters for lawyers who can always find solutions if they are firmly led, and yet he had a simple, naïve, almost religious belief in the virtues of constitutional reform to redress the imperfections of a political system. His approach to political analysis was more "institutional" than "behavioral," to use the common expression of modern political scientists. Still other students of the French scene have claimed that the country was not ripe for a presidential system (and that de Gaulle knew it, whether consciously or not); the memories of 1851 were said to die hard and only if the move were made by stages, consisting of first an election by universal suffrage, combined with a *de facto* increase in powers, then a formalization of the system by the disappearance of the prime minister, would the country accept the transition. If de Gaulle did indeed make this calculation, he showed himself to be both more far-sighted and more mysterious in his ways than even his most fervent admirers claimed. But none of his pronouncements seemed to suggest that he visualized a step-by-step transformation of the constitution; the temporary and precariously balanced character of the system of government which he created did not appear to cause him great concern.

If de Gaulle had not wanted to establish a presidential system, he could have moved in the direction of a more "responsible" and more streamlined party system, as Adenauer aimed at doing and indeed succeeded in doing in West Germany. There are clear signs that this is slowly happening, though the evolution took place almost against de Gaulle's will and clearly without the president realizing the importance of the change for the political future of the country. To be a true parliamentary leader, de Gaulle would have had to abandon many prejudices and reconsider many standpoints; he would have had to condescend to remaining prime minister, rather than becoming president; he would have had to be prepared to go and discuss matters in the Assembly (he tried in 1945, and was thoroughly miserable and pained); he would, most importantly, have had to recover from his hurt pride at being betrayed by his political friends, first of the MRP, who continued the Fourth Republic without him, later of the RPF, many of whom broke away at the first sign of a new conservative policy. De Gaulle's attacks on parties (much more common at the beginning than at the end of his presidency, interestingly enough) prevented him from recognizing that a modern political system needs parties to operate at all and that a parliamentary system needs disciplined parties to work efficiently. Thus de Gaulle stumbled on the UDR because something had to be created (but he was too sore, this time, to organize the party himself); he used the new grouping in 1962 because his government had been overthrown by the Assembly and some means had to be found of separating the sheep from the goats. But de Gaulle never *willed* the development of the UDR; he was never anxious to generate and favor regroupings; he did not seem happy to see better arrangements taking place on the Left. It may be that, despite its curiously undesired birth, the UDR will survive as a solid party—but the leader of the country did little to reinforce its permanent structure.

THE STRENGTH OF THE COMMUNIST PARTY AND THE FUTURE OF THE LEFT

Of course, the main stumbling block against a real streamlining of the party system remains; whether de Gaulle strongly supported the UDR or not, the Communist party is responsible for the permanent division of the Left. Changes in the character of the CP are slow; changes in the leadership did not markedly affect the main line of approach, and indeed no move by the party, short of voluntary disbanding, could really be a new deal. A whole way of life has been created; prejudices and taboos have erected a wall isolating Communist leaders, activists, and electors from the rest of the political community. Even if the party wanted a change and was prepared to abandon its total and unconditional opposition to the "capitalist system," and even if, more importantly, it was to become committed to a liberal, democratic, form of government, it would find itself, perhaps for decades, intellectually entangled in the maze of the enormous edifice which it built to protect itself. French political circles look for signs of Communist "liberalization"; they try to measure the size of the changes, though these are often obscured by the almost hermetic jargon which the party produces in attempting to popularize Marxism. But these changes are small, and they cannot be other than small. Only a sizable decrease in the Communist vote which would clearly give the party second place among the forces of the Left would produce the real unfreezing. Socioeconomic changes may bring about this decline, but the signs are still weak, confused, and even contradictory.

Meanwhile, some strengthening of the forces of the Left may come about from the efforts toward greater collaboration between Communists and Socialists under François Mitterrand. Efforts made in the 1960s in the direction of a non-Communist Left alliance or merger did not have a long-lasting effect. The *Fédération de la Gauche Démocrate et Socialiste*, which seemed on the verge of constituting at one point a greater electoral force than the Communists, floundered because Socialist leaders did not agree among themselves, Radicals did not agree with Radicals, and the Gaullist victory of 1968 upset all the calculations of politicians. But Mitterand's determination to bring about more unity among the various elements on the Left did at least lend to some rejuvenation of the Socialist party and to the recognition by Communists and Socialists that some efforts should be made towards greater cooperation beyond a mere electoral alliance. Mitterrand himself is increasingly viewed by all Frenchmen as the leader of the Left; it will become more difficult for historians to deny him this leadership. Yet many more strides will have to be made before the Left becomes united and emerges as an alternative. The opposition of the tiny left-wing Maoist and Trotskyite groups may be small and uncoordinated, but it does detract voters from left-wing parties, as the fear of the Communist party remains strong. This contributes in turn to maintain the strength of the Center parties, and specifically of the Radicals, who may agree to fight electoral battles with Communists but are unlikely to come to support faithfully a coalition of the Left.

Thus the system has changed markedly during the Fifth Republic. But the prospects of further moves and the speed at which these moves might take place are difficult to ascertain. On balance, there is still a definite possibility that the Fifth Republic might return to a style of politics more akin to the Third and Fourth Republics, as long as the unity of the Left does not become a reality, accepted by all, and as long as the chances of a marked UDR decline in favor of the traditional parties cannot be ruled out. The system is not wholly accepted. What is indeed needed is a thorough renewal of the personnel and the arrival of new generations to the political limelight; what is also needed is enough time for the effect of the profound social changes to be felt in the political structure. Even in the best of circumstances, the streamlining of politics might still be only temporary, as the problems raised by the presidency in its relation to the Assembly and to the prime minister need to be solved in a way which makes changes of the party in power possible and indeed regular.

Beyond the "Guided Democracy" of the Civil Service?

Whatever happens to the political system, the role of the administration will remain profound in the economic field and perhaps decisive in many aspects of social development. The administration, as we saw, is also at the crossroads, though the question naturally receives less attention and the dangers arising from any mistakes in direction may be, at first sight at least, less worrisome. The administration is at the crossroads, but it is still only moving from "enlightened despotism" (or paternalism) toward a form of "guided democracy" (in the best literal meaning of the expression). The question of decentralization, particularly in the form of regionalism, is likely to test the ability of the administration to steer, advise, warn, and yet let representatives act. The larger the groupings, the less the officials of the central government are likely to be able to impose their views and directly influence people; one cannot treat representatives of regions in the way one used to deal with the mayors of small villages. Moreover, "guided democracy" is also being attempted on other planes. It goes further than consultation; it does not simply mean hearing the representatives of the various groups, trade unions, employers' associations, and professional bodies; it means trying to enlist the cooperation of these representatives in the operations by which, for instance, the plan is gradually prepared. The first experiments in this democratic form of corporatism led to numerous criticisms and met with only limited success. But French higher civil servants are obstinate. They have now been sold on the idea of a joint enterprise in social engineering, and they often have a personal stake in the success of the whole venture. Many more forms of participation and cooperation will have to be devised before a satisfactory formula can be found, but ingenuity and imagination are not lacking. Paradoxically, and unlike the more rigorous line adopted in economic planning, the French approach to social pluralism is even more empirical and less doctrinaire than the notions of Fabian socialism once devised by the British, and it is also accepted by more people in the top administrative circles. It has, thus, greater chances of success.

But, beyond the experiments made by the administration in involving groups rather more in the determination and implementation of policy, the key problem which remains unresolved is that of the genuine participation of a variety of bodies—principally local bodies—in decision-making. The onslaught of 1968 on the institutions, the State, the regime, was both temporary and uncoordinated: at one level it corresponded to a desire for "great holidays" rather than for a profound change in the society; at another, it corresponded to a deep-rooted opposition of the French to the centralized State, though this opposition does not translate itself easily into daily demands for reform. Both government and civil service have to recognize that a major move must be made to involve the population in decision-making at the local and regional levels. Such a move may be followed by a difficult period of adjustment, marred by much irresponsibility on the part of the new local leaders. But, if the move is not made, discontent will probably grow, not diminish, despite the economic rejuvenation of the country, and indeed perhaps because the economic transformation of the country has given to all more consumer goods, and thus a greater interest in the cultural and social life in the community in which they live.

Observers around the world admire the British form of government, but they are fascinated by the French political system. For a while, under the Fifth Republic, it was fashionable to say that a new French political system, streamlined and dull, was developing. This was scarcely true at a time when the Algerian war was giving rather too much virulence and unpleasantness to the political fights of the French; it has not become true with the end of the colonial wars. The long search for an equilibrium in the constitutional powers still goes on, as lively as ever, in a rejuvenated country. The players are somewhat different. While one great personality dominated the scene, individuals have ceased to play as prominent a part as they did in the past; groups and forces now have the major role in a country which is reexperiencing pluralism after a century and a half in which it was proscribed, legally or in fact. The growth and tactics of these groups are fascinating to study; they are also more relevant to a modern society than the personal battles conducted in the "house without windows" of the old Parliament. The moves made by the associations—as well as those of the administrative and semiadministrative bodies—are perhaps somewhat more difficult to perceive than those of deputies, but they have more impact on the whole community. Neither in the Fifth Republic nor in the Fourth or Third has France been able to create a political model, easy to export, or ready for imitation, but parts of the inside machinery are brilliantly put together and should, after a closer look, be followed and used elsewhere. The main trouble with the French political system does not lie in a lack of responsiveness or in an inability to forecast and meet new problems. It lies in the undue emphasis placed on constitutional or other formal elements of the political system at the expense of very lively and relevant structures which, often without being noticed, are slowly being created.

The French Constitution*

* Adopted by referendum on September 28, 1958, promulgated on Octob
1958, and amended in 1960, 1962, and 1963.

PREAMBLE

The French people hereby solemnly proclaims its attachment to the Rights of Man and the principles of national sovereignty as defined by the Declaration of 1789, reaffirmed and complemented by the Preamble of the Constitution of 1946.

By virtue of these principles and that of the free determination of peoples, the Republic hereby offers to the Overseas Territories that express the desire to adhere to them, new institutions based on the common ideal of liberty, equality and fraternity and conceived with a view to their democratic evolution.

Article 1

The Republic and the peoples of the Overseas Territories who, by an act of free determination, adopt the present Constitution thereby institute a Community.

The Community shall be based on the equality and the solidarity of the peoples composing it.

TITLE I: ON SOVEREIGNTY

Article 2

France is a Republic, indivisible, secular, democratic and social. It shall ensure the equality of all citizens before the law, without distinction of origin, race or religion. It shall respect all beliefs.

The national emblem is the tricolor flag, blue, white and red.

The national anthem is the "Marseillaise."

The mótto of the Republic is "Liberty, Equality, Fraternity."

Its principle is government of the people, by the people and for the people.

Article 3

National sovereignty belongs to the people, which shall exercise this sovereignty through its representatives and by means of referendums.

No section of the people, nor any individual, may attribute to themselves or himself the exercise thereof.

Suffrage may be direct or indirect under the conditions stipulated by the Constitution. It shall always be universal, equal and secret.

All French citizens of both sexes who have reached their majority and who enjoy civil and political rights may vote under the conditions to be determined by law.

Article 4

Political parties and groups shall be instrumental in the expression of the suffrage. They shall be formed freely and shall carry on their activities freely. They must respect the principles of national sovereignty and democracy.

TITLE II: THE PRESIDENT OF THE REPUBLIC

Article 5

The President of the Republic shall see that the Constitution is respected. He shall ensure, by his arbitration, the regular functioning of the governmental authorities, as well as the continuance of the State.

He shall be the guarantor of national independence, of the integrity of the territory, and of respect for Community agreements and treaties.

Article 6

The President of the Republic shall be elected for seven years by universal direct suffrage.

The modalities of implementation of the present Article shall be determined by an organic law.[1]

Article 7

The President of the Republic shall be elected by an absolute majority of the votes cast. If no such majority obtains at the first ballot, a second ballot shall take place on the second Sunday following the first ballot. May only stand at the second ballot the two candidates who received the greatest number of votes at the first ballot, if necessary after taking into account better placed candidates having withdrawn.

[1] New text adopted by referendum of October 28, 1962. The old Article 6 read as follows:

The President of the Republic shall be elected for seven years by an electoral college comprising the members of Parliament, of the General Councils and of the Assemblies of the Overseas Territories, as well as the elected representatives of the municipal councils.

These representatives shall be:

—the mayor for communes of fewer than 1,000 inhabitants;

—the mayor and the first deputy mayor for communes of from 1,000 to 2,000 inhabitants;

—the mayor, first deputy mayor and a municipal councillor chosen according to the order in which he appears on the council list for communes of from 2,001 to 2,500 inhabitants;

—the mayor and the first two deputy mayors for communes of from 2,501 to 3,000 inhabitants;

—the mayor, the first two deputy mayors and three municipal councillors chosen according to the order in which they appear on the council list for communes of from 3,001 to 6,000 inhabitants;

—the mayor, the first two deputy mayors and six municipal councillors chosen according to the order in which they appear on the council list for communes of from 6,001 to 9,000 inhabitants;

—all the municipal councillors for communes of more than 9,000 inhabitants;

—in addition, for communes of more than 30,000 inhabitants, delegates appointed by the municipal council in the ratio of one delegate for every 1,000 inhabitants above 30,000.

In the Overseas Territories of the Republic, the elected representatives of the councils of the administrative units shall also form part of the electoral college under the conditions to be determined by an organic law.

The participation of member States of the Community in the electoral college for the President of the Republic shall be determined by agreement between the Republic and the member States of the Community.

The procedures implementing the present article shall be determined by an organic law.

The Government shall be responsible for organizing the election.

The election of the new President of the Republic shall take place twenty days at the least and thirty-five days at the most before the end of the mandate of the current President.

In the case of vacancy of the office for any cause whatsoever or if the President is duly declared impeded from exercising his functions by the Constitutional Council, the matter being referred to the latter by the Government and the decision being taken by an absolute majority of the members of the Council, the functions of the President, except for those listed under Articles 11 and 12, shall be provisionally exercised by the President of the Senate, or, if the latter is in turn impeded, by the Government.

In case of vacancy or if the Constitutional Council declares the President permanently impeded from exercising his functions, the ballot for the election of the new President shall take place, except in case of *force majeure* officially noted by the Constitutional Council, twenty days at the least and thirty-five days at the most after the beginning of the vacancy or the declaration of the permanent character of the impediment.

In case of vacancy of the Presidency of the Republic or during the period between the declaration of the impediment of the President of the Republic and the election of his successor, the procedures of Articles 49, 50, and 89 may not be invoked.[2]

---

[2] New text adopted by referendum of October 28, 1962. The old Article 7 read as follows:

The President of the Republic shall be elected by an absolute majority on the first ballot. If this is not obtained, the President of the Republic shall be elected on a second ballot by a relative majority.

The voting shall begin at the summons of the Government.

The election of the new President shall take place twenty days at the least and fifty days at the most before the expiration of the powers of the President in office.

In the event that the Presidency of the Republic has been vacated, for any cause whatsoever, or impeded in its functioning as officially noted by the Constitutional Council, to which the matter has been referred by the Government, and which shall rule by an absolute majority of its members, the functions of the President of the Republic, with the exception of those provided for by Articles 11 and 12 below, shall be temporarily exercised by the President of the Senate. In the case of a vacancy, or when the impediment is declared definitive by the Constitutional Council, the voting for the election of a new President

Article 8

The President of the Republic shall appoint the Premier. He shall terminate the functions of the Premier when the latter presents the resignation of the Government.

On the proposal of the Premier, he shall appoint the other members of the Government and shall terminate their functions.

Article 9

The President of the Republic shall preside over the Council of Ministers.

Article 10

The President of the Republic shall promulgate the laws within fifteen days following the transmission to the Government of the finally adopted law.

He may, before the expiration of this time limit, ask Parliament for a reconsideration of the law or of certain of its articles. This reconsideration may not be refused.

Article 11

The President of the Republic, on the proposal of the Government during [Parliamentary] sessions, or on joint motion of the two assemblies, published in the *Journal Officiel,* may submit to a referendum any bill dealing with the organization of the governmental authorities, entailing approval of a Community agreement, or providing for authorization to ratify a treaty that, without being contrary to the Constitution, might affect the functioning of [existing] institutions.

When the referendum decides in favor of the bill, the President of the Republic shall promulgate it within the time limit stipulated in the preceding article.

Article 12

The President of the Republic may, after consultation with the Premier and the Presidents of the assemblies, declare the dissolution of the National Assembly.

---

shall take place, except in case of *force majeure* officially noted by the Constitutional Council, twenty days at the least and fifty days at the most after the beginning of the vacancy or the declaration of the definitive character of the impediment.

General elections shall take place twenty days at the least and forty days at the most after the dissolution.

The National Assembly shall convene by right on the second Thursday following its election. If this meeting takes place between the periods provided for ordinary sessions, a session shall, by right, be held for a fifteen-day period.

There may be no further dissolution within a year following these elections.

Article 13

The President of the Republic shall sign the ordinances and decrees decided upon in the Council of Ministers.

He shall make appointments to the civil and military posts of the State.

Councillors of State, the Grand Chancellor of the Legion of Honor, Ambassadors and envoys extraordinary, Master Councillors of the Court of Accounts, prefects, representatives of the Government in the Overseas Territories, general officers, rectors of academies [regional divisions of the public educational system] and directors of central administrations shall be appointed in meetings of the Council of Ministers.

An organic law shall determine the other posts to be filled in meetings of the Council of Ministers, as well as the conditions under which the power of the President of the Republic to make appointments to office may be delegated by him and exercised in his name.

Article 14

The President of the Republic shall accredit Ambassadors and envoys extraordinary to foreign powers; foreign Ambassadors and envoys extraordinary shall be accredited to him.

Article 15

The President of the Republic shall be commander of the armed forces. He shall preside over the higher councils and committees of national defense.

Article 16

When the institutions of the Republic, the independence of the nation, the integrity of its territory or the fulfillment of its international commitments are threatened in a grave and immediate manner and when the regular functioning of the constitutional governmental authorities is interrupted, the President of the Republic shall take the measures commanded by these circumstances, after official consultation with the Premier, the Presidents of the assemblies and the Constitutional Council.

He shall inform the nation of these measures in a message.

These measures must be prompted by the desire to ensure to the constitutional governmental authorities, in the shortest possible time, the means of fulfilling their assigned functions. The Constitutional Council shall be consulted with regard to such measures.

Parliament shall meet by right.

The National Assembly may not be dissolved during the exercise of emergency powers [by the President].

Article 17

The President of the Republic shall have the right of pardon.

Article 18

The President of the Republic shall communicate with the two assemblies of Parliament by means of messages, which he shall cause to be read, and which shall not be followed by any debate.

Between sessions, Parliament shall be convened especially for this purpose.

Article 19

The acts of the President of the Republic, other than those provided for under Articles 8 (first paragraph), 11, 12, 16, 18, 54, 56 and 61, shall be countersigned by the Premier and, should circumstances so require, by the appropriate ministers.

TITLE III: THE GOVERNMENT

Article 20

The Government shall determine and direct the policy of the nation.

It shall have at its disposal the administration and the armed forces.

It shall be responsible to Parliament under the conditions and according to the procedures stipulated in Articles 49 and 50.

Article 21

The Premier shall direct the operation of the Government. He shall be responsible for national defense. He shall ensure the execution of the laws. Subject to the provisions of Article 13, he shall have regulatory powers and shall make appointments to civil and military posts.

He may delegate certain of his powers to the ministers.

He shall replace, should the occasion arise, the President of the Republic as chairman of the councils and committees provided for under Article 15.

He may, in exceptional instances, replace him as chairman of a meeting of the Council of Ministers by virtue of an explicit delegation and for a specific agenda.

Article 22

The acts of the Premier shall be countersigned, when circumstances so require, by the ministers responsible for their execution.

Article 23

The office of member of the Government shall be incompatible with the exercise of any Parliamentary mandate, with the holding of any office at the national level in business, professional or labor organizations, and with any public employment or professional activity.

An organic law shall determine the conditions under which the holders of such mandates, functions or employments shall be replaced.

The replacement of members of Parliament shall take place in accordance with the provisions of Article 25.

TITLE IV: THE PARLIAMENT

Article 24

The Parliament shall comprise the National Assembly and the Senate.

The deputies to the National Assembly shall be elected by direct suffrage.

The Senate shall be elected by indirect suffrage. It shall ensure the representation of the territorial units of the Republic. Frenchmen living outside France shall be represented in the Senate.

Article 25

An organic law shall determine the term for which each

assembly is elected, the number of its members, their emoluments, the conditions of eligibility and ineligibility and the offices incompatible with membership in the assemblies.

It shall likewise determine the conditions under which, in the case of a vacancy in either assembly, persons shall be elected to replace the deputy or senator whose seat has been vacated until the holding of new complete or partial elections to the assembly concerned.

Article 26

No member of Parliament may be prosecuted, sought, arrested, detained or tried as a result of the opinions or votes expressed by him in the exercise of his functions.

No member of Parliament may, during Parliamentary sessions, be prosecuted or arrested for criminal or minor offenses without the authorization of the assembly of which he is a member except in the case of *flagrante delicto.*

When Parliament is not in session, no member of Parliament may be arrested without the authorization of the Secretariat of the assembly of which he is a member, except in the case of *flagrante delicto,* of authorized prosecution or of final conviction.

The detention or prosecution of a member of Parliament shall be suspended if the assembly of which he is a member so demands.

Article 27

All binding instructions [upon members of Parliament] shall be null and void.

The right to vote of the members of Parliament shall be personal.

An organic law may, under exceptional circumstances, authorize the delegation of a vote. In this case, no member may be delegated more than one vote.

Article 28

Parliament shall convene by right in two ordinary sessions a year. The first session shall begin on October 2nd and last eighty days.

The second session shall begin on April 2nd and may not last longer than ninety days.

If October 2nd or April 2nd is a public holiday, the opening of the session shall take place on the first weekday following.[3]

Article 29

Parliament shall convene in extraordinary session at the request of the Premier, or of the majority of the members comprising the National Assembly, to consider a specific agenda.

When an extraordinary session is held at the request of the members of the National Assembly, the closure decree shall take effect as soon as the Parliament has exhausted the agenda for which it was called, and at the latest twelve days from the date of its meeting.

Only the Premier may ask for a new session before the end of the month following the closure decree.

Article 30

Apart from cases in which Parliament meets by right, extraordinary sessions shall be opened and closed by decree of the President of the Republic.

Article 31

The members of the Government shall have access to the two assemblies. They shall be heard when they so request.

They may call for the assistance of commissioners of the government.

Article 32

The President of the National Assembly shall be elected for the duration of the legislature. The President of the Senate shall be elected after each partial reelection [of the Senate].

Article 33

The meetings of the two assemblies shall be public. An *in extenso* report of the debates shall be published in the *Journal Officiel*.

Each assembly may sit in secret committee at the request of the Premier or of one tenth of its members.

[3] As adopted by parliamentary amendment in 1963. The old Article 28 read as follows:

Parliament shall convene, by right, in two ordinary sessions a year.

The first session shall begin on the first Tuesday of October and shall end on the third Friday of December.

The second session shall open on the last Tuesday of April; it may not last longer than three months.

TITLE V: ON RELATIONS BETWEEN PARLIAMENT AND THE GOVERNMENT

Article 34

All laws shall be passed by Parliament.

Laws shall establish the rules concerning:

—civil rights and the fundamental guarantees granted to the citizens for the exercise of their public liberties; the obligations imposed by the national defense upon the persons and property of citizens;

—nationality, status and legal capacity of persons, marriage contracts, inheritance and gifts;

—determination of crimes and misdemeanors as well as the penalties imposed therefore; criminal procedure; amnesty; the creation of new juridical systems and the status of magistrates;

—the basis, the rate and the methods of collecting taxes of all types; the issuance of currency.

Laws shall likewise determine the rules concerning:

—the electoral system of the Parliamentary assemblies and the local assemblies;

—the establishment of categories of public institutions;

—the fundamental guarantees granted to civil and military personnel employed by the State;

—the nationalization of enterprises and the transfer of the property of enterprises from the public to the private sector.

Law shall determine the fundamental principles of:

—the general organization of national defense;

—the free administration of local communities, the extent of their jurisdiction and their resources;

—education;

—property rights, civil and commercial obligations;

—legislation pertaining to employment, unions and social security.

The financial laws shall determine the financial resources and obligations of the State under the conditions and with the reservations to be provided for by an organic law.

—Laws pertaining to national planning shall determine the objectives of the economic and social action of the State.

The provisions of the present article may be developed in detail and amplified by an organic law.

Article 35

Parliament shall authorize the declaration of war.

Article 36

Martial law shall be decreed in a meeting of the Council of Ministers.

Its prorogation beyond twelve days may be authorized only by Parliament.

Article 37

Matters other than those that fall within the domain of law shall be of a regulatory character.

Legislative texts concerning these matters may be modified by decrees issued after consultation with the Council of State. Those legislative texts which may be passed after the present Constitution has become operative shall be modified by decree, only if the Constitutional Council has stated that they have a regulatory character as defined in the preceding paragraph.

Article 38

The Government may, in order to carry out its program, ask Parliament to authorize it, for a limited period, to take through ordinances measures that are normally within the domain of law.

The ordinances shall be enacted in meetings of the Council of Ministers after consultation with the Council of State. They shall come into force upon their publication, but shall become null and void if the bill for their ratification is not submitted to Parliament before the date set by the enabling act.

At the expiration of the time limit referred to in the first paragraph of the present article, the ordinances may be modified only by law in those matters which are within the legislative domain.

Article 39

The Premier and the members of Parliament alike shall have the right to initiate legislation.

Government bills shall be discussed in the Council of Ministers after consultation with the Council of State and shall be filed with the Secretariat of one of the two assemblies. Finance bills shall be submitted first to the National Assembly.

Article 40

Bills and amendments introduced by members of Parliament shall not be considered when their adoption would have as a consequence either a diminution of public financial resources, or the creation or increase of public expenditures.

Article 41

If it appears in the course of the legislative procedure that a Private Member bill or an amendment is not within the domain of law or is contrary to a delegation [of authority] granted by virtue of Article 38, the Government may declare its inadmissibility.

In case of disagreement between the Government and the President of the assembly concerned, the Constitutional Council, upon the request of either party, shall rule within a time limit of eight days.

Article 42

The discussion of Government bills shall pertain, in the first assembly to which they have been referred, to the text presented by the Government.

An assembly, given a text passed by the other assembly, shall deliberate on the text that is transmitted to it.

Article 43

Government and Private Members bills shall, at the request of the Government or of the assembly concerned, be sent for study to committees especially designated for this purpose.

Government and Private Members bills for which such a request has not been made shall be sent to one of the permanent committees, the number of which shall be limited to six in each assembly.

Article 44

Members of Parliament and of the Government shall have the right of amendment.

After the opening of the debate, the Government may oppose the examination of any amendment which has not previously been submitted to committee.

If the Government so requests, the assembly concerned shall decide, by a single vote, on all or part of the text under discussion, retaining only the amendments proposed or accepted by the Government.

Article 45

Every Government or Private Members bill shall be examined successively in the two assemblies of Parliament with a view to the adoption of an identical text.

When, as a result of disagreement between the two assemblies, it has become impossible to adopt a Government or Private Members bill after two readings by each assembly, or, if the Government has declared the matter urgent, after a single reading by each of them, the Premier shall have the right to have a joint committee meet, composed of an equal number from both assemblies and instructed to offer for consideration a text on the matters still under discussion.

The text prepared by the joint committee may be submitted by the Government for approval of the two assemblies. No amendment shall be admissible except by agreement with the Government.

If the joint committee fails to approve a common text, or if this text is not adopted under the conditions set forth in the preceding paragraph, the Government may, after a new reading by the National Assembly and by the Senate, ask the National Assembly to rule definitively. In this case, the National Assembly may reconsider either the text prepared by the joint committee or the last text adopted [by the National Assembly], modified, when circumstances so require, by one or several of the amendments adopted by the Senate.

Article 46

The laws that the Constitution characterizes as organic shall be passed and amended under the following conditions:

A Government or Private Members bill shall be submitted to the deliberation and to the vote of the first assembly to which it is submitted only at the expiration of a period of fifteen days following its introduction.

The procedure of Article 45 shall be applicable. Nevertheless, lacking an agreement between the two assemblies, the text may be adopted by the National Assembly on final reading only by an absolute majority of its members.

The organic laws relative to the Senate must be passed in the same manner by the two assemblies.

Organic laws may be promulgated only after a declaration by the Constitutional Council on their constitutionality.

Article 47

Parliament shall pass finance bills under the conditions to be stipulated by an organic law.

Should the National Assembly fail to reach a decision on first reading within a time limit of forty days after a bill has been filed, the Government shall refer it to the Senate, which must rule within a time limit of fifteen days. The procedure set forth in Article 45 shall then be followed.

Should Parliament fail to reach a decision within a time limit of seventy days, the provisions of the bill may be enforced by ordinance.

Should the finance bill establishing the resources and expenditures of a fiscal year not be filed in time for it to be promulgated before the beginning of that fiscal year, the Government shall immediately request Parliament for the authorization to collect the taxes and shall make available by decree the funds needed to meet the Government commitments already voted.

The time limits stipulated in the present article shall be suspended when Parliament is not in session.

The Court of Accounts shall assist Parliament and the Government in supervising the implementation of the finance laws.

Article 48

The discussion of the bills filed or agreed upon by the Government shall have priority on the agenda of the assemblies in the order set by the Government.

One meeting a week shall be reserved, by priority, for questions asked by members of Parliament and for answers by the Government.

Article 49

The Premier, after deliberation by the Council of Ministers, may pledge the responsibility of the Government to the National Assembly with regard to the program of the Government, or with regard to a declaration of general policy, as the case may be.

The National Assembly may question the responsibility of

the Government by the vote of a motion of censure. Such a motion shall be admissible only if it is signed by at least one tenth of the members of the National Assembly. The vote may only take place forty-eight hours after the motion has been filed; the only votes counted shall be those favorable to the motion of censure, which may be adopted only by a majority of the members comprising the Assembly. Should the motion of censure be rejected, its signatories may not introduce another motion in the course of the same session, except in the case provided for in the paragraph below.

The Premier may, after deliberation by the Council of Ministers, pledge the Government's responsibility to the National Assembly on the vote of a text. In this case, the text shall be considered as adopted, unless a motion of censure, filed in the succeeding twenty-four hours, is voted under the conditions laid down in the previous paragraph.

The Premier shall be entitled to ask the Senate for approval of a general policy declaration.

Article 50

When the National Assembly adopts a motion of censure, or when it disapproves the program or a declaration of general policy of the Government, the Premier must submit the resignation of the Government to the President of the Republic.

Article 51

The closure of ordinary or extraordinary sessions shall by right be delayed, should the occasion rise, in order to permit the application of the provisions of Article 49.

TITLE VI: ON TREATIES AND INTERNATIONAL AGREEMENTS

Article 52

The President of the Republic shall negotiate and ratify treaties.

He shall be informed of all negotiations leading to the conclusion of an international agreement not subject to ratification.

Article 53

Peace treaties, commercial treaties, treaties or agreements relative to international organizations, those that imply a commitment for the finances of the State, those that modify provisions of a legislative nature, those relative to the status of persons, those that call for the cession, exchange or addition of territory may be ratified or approved only by a law.

They shall go into effect only after having been ratified or approved.

No cession, no exchange, no addition of territory shall be valid without the consent of the populations concerned.

Article 54

If the Constitutional Council, the matter having been referred to it by the President of the Republic, by the Premier, or by the President of one or the other assembly, shall declare that an international commitment contains a clause contrary to the Constitution, the authorization to ratify or approve this commitment may be given only after amendment of the Constitution.

Article 55

Treaties or agreements duly ratified or approved shall, upon their publication, have an authority superior to that of laws, subject, for each agreement or treaty, to its application by the other party.

TITLE VII: THE CONSTITUTIONAL COUNCIL

Article 56

The Constitutional Council shall consist of nine members, whose term of office shall last nine years and shall not be renewable. One third of the membership of the Constitutional Council shall be renewed every three years. Three of its members shall be appointed by the President of the Republic, three by the President of the National Assembly, three by the President of the Senate.

In addition to the nine members provided for above, former Presidents of the Republic shall be members ex officio for life of the Constitutional Council.

The President shall be appointed by the President of the Republic. He shall have the casting vote in case of a tie.

Article 57

The office of member of the Constitutional Council shall be incompatible with that of minister or member of Parliament. Other incompatibilities shall be determined by an organic law.

Article 58

The Constitutional Council shall ensure the regularity of the election of the President of the Republic.

It shall examine complaints and shall announce the results of the vote.

Article 59

The Constitutional Council shall rule, in the case of disagreement, on the regularity of the elections of deputies and senators.

Article 60

The Constitutional Council shall ensure the regularity of referendum procedures and shall announce the results thereof.

Article 61

Organic laws, before their promulgation, and standing orders of the Parliamentary assemblies, before they come into application, must be submitted to the Constitutional Council, which shall rule on their constitutionality.

To the same end, laws may be submitted to the Constitutional Council, before their promulgation, by the President of the Republic, the Premier or the President of one or the other assembly.

In the cases provided for by the two preceding paragraphs, the Constitutional Council must make its ruling within a time limit of one month. Nevertheless, at the request of the Government, in case of emergency, this period shall be reduced to eight days.

In these same cases, referral to the Constitutional Council shall suspend the time limit for promulgation.

Article 62

A provision declared unconstitutional may not be promulgated or implemented.

The decisions of the Constitutional Council may not be appealed to any jurisdiction whatsoever. They must be recognized by the governmental authorities and by all administrative and judicial authorities.

Article 63

An organic law shall determine the rules of organization and functioning of the Constitutional Council, the procedure to be followed before it, and in particular the periods of time allowed for having disputes before it.

TITLE VIII: ON JUDICIAL AUTHORITY

Article 64

The President of the Republic shall be the guarantor of the independence of the judicial authority.

He shall be assisted by the High Council of the Judiciary.

An organic law shall determine the status of magistrates.

Magistrates may not be removed from office.

Article 65

The High Council of the Judiciary shall be presided over by the President of the Republic. The Minister of Justice shall be its Vice President ex officio. He may preside in place of the President of the Republic.

The High Council shall, in addition, include nine members appointed by the President of the Republic in conformity with the conditions to be determined by an organic law.

The High Council of the Judiciary shall present nominations for judges of the Court of Cassation and for First Presidents of Courts of Appeal. It shall give its opinion, under the conditions to be determined by an organic law, on proposals of the Minister of Justice relative to the nomination of the other judges. It shall be consulted on questions of pardon under conditions to be determined by an organic law.

The High Council of the Judiciary shall act as a disciplinary council for judges. In such cases, it shall be presided over by the First President of the Court of Cassation.

Article 66

No one may be arbitrarily detained.

The judicial authority, guardian of individual liberty, shall ensure respect for this principle under the conditions stipulated by law.

TITLE IX: THE HIGH COURT
OF JUSTICE

Article 67

A High Court of Justice shall be instituted.

It shall be composed of members [of Parliament] elected, in equal number, by the National Assembly and the Senate after each general or partial election to these assemblies. It shall elect its President from among its members.

An organic law shall determine the composition of the High Court, its rules, and also the procedure to be followed before it.

Article 68

The President of the Republic shall not be held accountable for actions performed in the exercise of his office except in the case of high treason. He may be indicted only by the two assemblies ruling by identical vote in open balloting and by an absolute majority of the members of said assemblies. He shall be tried by the High Court of Justice.

The members of the Government shall be criminally liable for actions performed in the exercise of their office and deemed to be crimes or misdemeanors at the time they were committed. The procedure defined above shall be applied to them, as well as to their accomplices, in case of a conspiracy against the security of the State. In the cases provided for by the present paragraph, the High Court shall be bound by the definition of crimes and misdemeanors, as well as by the determination of penalties, as they are established by the criminal laws in force when the acts are committed.

TITLE X: THE ECONOMIC AND
SOCIAL COUNCIL

Article 69

The Economic and Social Council, whenever the Government calls upon it, shall give its opinion on the Government bills, ordinances and decrees, as well as on the Private Members bills submitted to it.

A member of the Economic and Social Council may be designated by the latter to present, before the Parliamentary assemblies, the opinion of the Council on the Government or Private Members bills that have been submitted to it.

Article 70

The Economic and Social Council may likewise be consulted by the Government on any problem of an economic or social character of interest to the Republic or to the Community. Any plan or any bill dealing with a plan of an economic or social character shall be submitted to it for its advice.

Article 71

The composition of the Economic and Social Council and its rules of procedure shall be determined by an organic law.

TITLE XI: ON TERRITORIAL UNITS

Article 72

The territorial units of the Republic are the communes, the departments, the Overseas Territories. Other territorial units may be created by law.

These units shall be free to govern themselves through elected councils and under the conditions stipulated by law.

In the departments and the territories, the Delegate of the Government shall be responsible for the national interests, for administrative supervision, and for seeing that the laws are respected.

Article 73

Measures of adjustment required by the particular situation of the Overseas Departments may be taken with regard to their legislative system and administrative organization.

Article 74

The Overseas Territories of the Republic shall have a special organization, which takes into account their own interests within the general interests of the Republic. This organization shall be defined and modified by law after consultation with the Territorial Assembly concerned.

Article 75

Citizens of the Republic who do not have ordinary civil status, the only status referred to in Article 34, may keep their personal status as long as they have not renounced it.

Article 76

The Overseas Territories may retain their status within the Republic.

If they express the desire to do so by a decision of their Territorial Assemblies taken within the time limit set in the first paragraph of Article 91 [which is omitted here], they shall become Overseas Departments of the Republic or member States of the Community, either in groups or as single units.

TITLE XII: ON THE COMMUNITY

Article 77

In the Community instituted by the present Constitution, the States shall enjoy autonomy; they shall administer themselves and manage their own affairs democratically and freely.

There shall be only one citizenship in the Community.

All citizens shall be equal before the law, whatever their origin, their race and their religion. They shall have the same duties.

Article 78

The Community's jurisdiction shall extend over foreign policy, defense, currency, common economic and financial policy, as well as over policy on strategic raw materials.

It shall include, in addition, except in the case of specific agreements, the supervision of the tribunals, higher education, the general organization of external transportation and transportation within the Community, as well as of telecommunications.

Special agreements may create other common jurisdictions or regulate any transfer of jurisdiction from the Community to one of its members.

Article 79

The member States shall benefit from the provisions of Article 77 as soon as they have exercised the choice provided for in Article 76.

Until the measures required for implementation of the present title go into force, matters within the common jurisdiction shall be regulated by the Republic.

Article 80

The President of the Republic shall preside over and represent the Community.

The institutional organs of the Community shall be an Executive Council, a Senate and a Court of Arbitration.

Article 81

The member States of the Community shall participate in the election of the President according to the conditions stipulated in Article 6.

The President of the Republic, in his capacity as President of the Community, shall be represented in each State of the Community.

Article 82

The Executive Council of the Community shall be presided over by the President of the Community. It shall consist of the Premier of the Republic, the heads of Government of each of the member States of the Community, and the ministers responsible for the common affairs of the Community.

The Executive Council shall organize the cooperation of members of the Community at Government and administrative levels.

The organization and procedure of the Executive Council shall be determined by an organic law.

Article 83

The Senate of the Community shall be composed of delegates whom the Parliament of the Republic and the legislative assemblies of the other members of the Community shall choose from among their own membership. The number of delegates of each State shall be determined according to its population and the responsibilities it assumes in the Community.

The Senate of the Community shall hold two sessions a year, which shall be opened and closed by the President of the Community and may not last longer than one month each.

The Senate of the Community, when called upon by the President of the Community, shall deliberate on the common economic and financial policy before laws on these matters are voted upon by the Parliament of the Republic and, should circumstances so require, by the legislative assemblies of the other members of the Community.

The Senate of the Community shall examine the acts and treaties or international agreements, which are specified in Articles 35 and 53, and which commit the Community.

The Senate of the Community shall take executive decisions in the domains in which it has received delegation of power from the legislative assemblies of the members of the Community. These decisions shall be promulgated in the same form as the law in the territory of each of the States concerned.

An organic law shall determine the composition of the Senate and its rule of procedure.

Article 84

A Court of Arbitration of the Community shall rule on litigations occurring among members of the Community.

Its composition and its jurisdiction shall be predetermined by an organic law.

Article 85

By derogation from the procedure provided for in Article 89, the provisions of the present title that concern the functioning of the common institutions shall be amendable by identical laws. passed by the Parliament of the Republic and by the Senate of the Community.

The provisions of the present title may also be amended by agreements concluded between all the States of the Community; the new provisions shall be put into force under the conditions required by the Constitution of each State.[4]

Article 86

A change of status of a member State of the Community may be requested, either by the Republic, or by a resolution of the legislative assembly of the State concerned confirmed by a local referendum, the organization and supervision of which shall be ensured by the institutions of the Community. The procedures governing this change shall be determined by an agreement approved by the Parliament of the Republic and the legislative assembly concerned.

Under the same conditions, a member State of the Commu-

---

[4] Added by parliamentary amendment of May 18, 1960.

nity may become independent. It shall thereby cease to belong to the Community.

A member State of the Community may also, by means of agreements, become independent without thereby ceasing to belong to the Community.

An independent State not a member of the Community may, by means of agreements, join the Community without ceasing to be independent.

The position of these States within the Community shall be determined by agreements concluded to this end, in particular the agreements mentioned in the preceding paragraphs as well as, should the occasion arise, the agreements provided for in the second paragraph of Article 85.[5]

Article 87

The special agreements made for the implementation of the present title shall be approved by the Parliament of the Republic and the legislative assembly concerned.

TITLE XIII: ON AGREEMENTS OF ASSOCIATION

Article 88

The Republic or the Community may make agreements with States that wish to associate themselves with the Community in order to develop their own civilizations.

TITLE XIV: ON AMENDMENT

Article 89

The initiative for amending the Constitution shall belong both to the President of the Republic on the proposal of the Premier and to the members of Parliament.

The Government or Private Members bill for amendment must be passed by the two assemblies in identical terms. The amendment shall become definitive after approval by a referendum.

However, the proposed amendment shall not be submitted to a referendum when the President of the Republic decides to

[5] Added by parliamentary amendment of May 18, 1960.

submit it to Parliament convened in Congress; in this case, the proposed amendment shall be deemed to be approved only if it is accepted by a three-fifths majority of the votes cast. The Secretariat of the Congress shall be that of the National Assembly.

No amendment procedure may be undertaken or followed when the integrity of the territory is in jeopardy.

The republican form of government shall not be subject to amendment.

Suggestions for Further Reading

There are now a number of texts dealing with the institutions and life of the Fifth Republic, but no "classic" has as yet been written, either in French or English, which compares with J.E. Bodley's *France*, 2 vols. (London, 1898), which analyzes the first part of the Third Republic, and with P.M. Williams's *Crisis and Compromise* (London, 1964), which covers in great detail the political life of the Fourth. As we saw that changes during the present regime often originated from problems which arose under the previous system, P.M. Williams's text should be consulted and indeed studied by all those who want to acquire a better understanding of French political life. Among the shorter works devoted to the Fifth Republic, the most valuable are perhaps P.M. Williams's and M. Harrison's *Politics and Society in de Gaulle's Republic* (London, 1971), P. Avril's *Politics in France* (London, 1969), and H. Ehrman's *France* (Boston, 1972). Readers should also consult some of the French texts on the subject, such as M. Duverger's *Institutions politiques et droit constitutionnel* (Paris, 1970), F. Goguel's and A. Grosser's *La vie politique en France* (Paris, 1964), and the three-volume study of the *Institutions politiques de la France* published by *La Documentation Française* (Paris, 1959).

Many studies provide readers with background information on French political and social life. Some of these are more specifically devoted to the French intellectual tradition, while others look at the problem of the slow decadence and rapid rejuvenation France experienced in the course of the twentieth century. The most authoritative English historical study of the Third Republic is that of D.W. Brogan, *The Development of Modern France* (London, 1940); the period of Vichy is analyzed in Robert Aron's *Histoire de Vichy* (Paris, 1954); and the Fourth Republic's life is described in J. Fauvet's *La Quatrième République* (Paris, 1959). The most brilliant study of French political traditions and ideologies is probably that of D. Thompson, *Democracy in France* (London, 1958). Traditional attitudes and modern recovery are examined perceptively in *France against Herself* by H. Luethy (New York, 1955), while both modern and old are studied at the local level with great incisiveness by L. Wylie in *Village in the Vaucluse* (Cambridge, Mass., 1964) and by S. Hoffman *et al.* in *In Search of France* (Cambridge, Mass., 1964). A collection of essays published by J. D. Reynaud under the title of *Tendances et volontés de la société française* (Paris, 1966) is perhaps the best introductory survey of the complex problems of modern French society. Finally, it is hardly necessary to observe that a reading of de Gaulle's *Memoirs* (New York, 1968–1972) is essential to an understanding of what remains after all "his" republic, while one of the best accounts of the life and actions of the great French leader can be found in A. Werth's *De Gaulle* (London, 1965).

One can mention only a few of the numerous works on elections and parties, a general account of which can also be found in most of the texts listed and in particular in P.M. Williams's and M. Harrison's *Politics and Society in de Gaulle's Republic* (New York, 1972). The best and most comprehensive account of electoral systems is to be found in P.W. Campbell's *French Electoral Systems and Elections since 1789* (London, 1965). Studies of voting patterns started very early in France, mostly on a geographical basis, the classic in the field being A. Siegfried's *Tableau politique de la France de l'Ouest* (Paris, 1913); this has been followed by many detailed monographs of elections in the provinces. Since 1956, the *Foundation Nationale des Sciences Politiques* has published studies of national elections and referendums, that of 1962 being still the most comprehensive (F. Goguel *et al, Le référendum d'octobre et les élections de novembre 1962* [Paris, 1965]). Electoral behavior based on surveys developed rapidly in the 1960s, one of the earliest and most perceptive being P. Fougeyrollas's *La conscience politique dans la France contemporaine* (Paris, 1963) and the most comprehensive being perhaps J. Charlot's *Les Français et De Gaulle* (Paris, 1971).

The best account of the earlier life of parties can be found in F. Goguel, *La politique des partis sous la Troisième République* (Paris, 1946) and of more recent developments in F. Goguel and A. Grosser, *La vie politique en France* (Paris, 1964). There are individual party studies, among which should be mentioned those of the Communist party by J. Fauvet, *Histoire du parti communiste français*, 2 vols. (Paris, 1965) and by A. Kriegel, *The French Communists* (Chicago, 1972); that of the Socialist party by D. Ligou, *Histoire du socialisme en France* (Paris, 1962); that of the Radical party by F. de Tarr, *The French Radical Party from Herriot to*

Mendès-France (London, 1961); and those of the UNR by J. Charlot, *L'UNR* (Paris, 1967) and *The Gaullist Phenomenon* (London, 1971). The behavior of deputies and of French politicians in general is analyzed, for the pre-1958 period, by N. Leites in *On the Game of Politics in France* (Stanford, 1959), and for the Fifth Republic, by P. Avril in *Les français et leur parlement* (Paris, 1972), as well as by P. Williams in *The French Parliament* (London, 1968).

Groups and their position in the political studies were first analyzed by J. Meynaud in *Les groupes de pression en France* (Paris, 1958); a number of works have been devoted to the developments of trade unions' agricultural interest groups, among which are A. Barjonet's *La CGT* (Paris, 1968) and *La CFDT* (Paris, 1968), S. Mallet's *La nouvelle classe ouvrière* (Paris, 1964), and M. Gervais *et al.*'s *Une France sans paysans* (Paris, 1965). Studies of business groups are still relatively rare, but the classic in the field, H. Ehrman's *Organized Business in France* (Princeton, 1957), gives a vivid account of both the characteristics of the traditional forms of pressure and the more modern forms of development.

A general study of French administration can be found in F. Ridley's and J. Blondel's, *Public Administration in France* (London, 1964), while the most systematic sociological analyses of attitudes of civil servants are those of M. Crozier, *The Bureaucratic Phenomenon* (London, 1964) and *La société bloquée* (Paris, 1970). There are also many monographs of a more detailed character on various aspects of administration, such as R. Grégoire's *French Civil Service* (Brussels, 1964), B. Chapman's *Introduction to French Local Government* (London, 1953), and P. Bauchet's *Economic Planning: the French Experience* (London, 1963).

Governmental policy before and since 1958 is naturally the subject of countless articles and books as are the trends and possible evolution of the new regime. The best short account can perhaps be found in the section of the *Revue Française de Science Politique* devoted to the analysis of current political events in each of its issues. Special mention should be made of the two studies by A. Grosser on foreign policy, *La politique extérieure de la Quatrième République* (Paris, 1961), and *La politique extérieure de la Cinquième République* (Paris, 1965). The events of May–June 1968 have led to the publication of numerous works, many of which seemed to have had only a passing influence; the essays published under the title of *Reflections on the Revolution in France: 1968* by C. Posner (London, 1970) are informative in giving an account (though perhaps one-sided) of the aims of the promoters and actors in the movement. Also informative is J. Ardagh, *The New French Revolution* (London, 1968). No single work can be expected to explain the many currents and countercurrents of this complex society; readers have always to remember how France and the French are constantly in search of themselves and how the politics of tomorrow are slowly emerging from the mixture of old and new which still typifies the politics of today.

INDEX